Parapsychology

Parapsychology

The science of unusual experience

RON ROBERTS
Social, Genetic and Developmental Psychiatry Research Centre, Institute of
Psychiatry, London

and

DAVID GROOME
Department of Psychology, University of Westminster, London

A member of the Hodder Headline Group
LONDON

Co-published in the United States of America by
Oxford University Press Inc., New York

First published in Great Britain in 2001 by
Arnold, a member of the Hodder Headline Group,
338 Euston Road, London NW1 3BH

http://www.arnoldpublishers.com

Co-published in the United States of America by
Oxford University Press Inc.,
198 Madison Avenue, New York, NY 10016

The advice and information in this book are believed to be true and
accurate at the date of going to press, but neither the author[s] nor the publisher
can accept any legal responsibility or liability for any errors or omissions.

British Library Cataloguing in Publication Data
A catalogue record for this book is available from the British Library

Library of Congress Cataloging-in-Publication Data
A catalog record for this book is available from the Library of Congress

ISBN 0 340 76169 5 (hb)
ISBN 0 340 76168 7 (pb)

1 2 3 4 5 6 7 8 9 10

Production Editor: Wendy Rooke
Production Controller: Martin Kerans
Cover Design: Mouse Mat

Typeset in 11pt Times by Saxon Graphics Ltd, Derby
Printed and bound in Great Britain by MPG Books, Bodmin, Cornwall

What do you think about this book? Or any other Arnold title?
Please send your comments to feedback.arnold@hodder.co.uk

For Antje and Merry (RR)
For Glenys, Alexander, Robin and Jenny (DG)

It is not the spoon that bends,
only yourself.

(quoted from *The Matrix*)

Contents

Tables, figures and boxes

Contributors

Steve Benton BSc PhD Department of Psychology, University of Westminster, London

Anthony Esgate BSc MSc PhD Department of Psychology, University of Westminster, London

Chris French BSc PhD Department of Psychology, Goldsmiths College, University of London, London

David Groome BSc PhD Department of Psychology, University of Westminster, London

Antje Mueller BSc Methodology Institute, London School of Economics, London

Ron Roberts BSc MSc PhD Social, Genetic and Developmental Psychiatry Research Centre, Institute of Psychiatry, London

Chris Roe BSc PhD Department of Psychology, University College, Northampton

Tony Towell BSc PhD Department of Psychology, University of Westminster, London

Caroline Watt MA PhD Koestler Parapsychology Unit, Department of Psychology, University of Edinburgh, Edinburgh

Richard Wiseman BSc PhD Division of Psychology, University of Hertfordshire, Hatfield

Preface

Over the years our students have repeatedly requested more information about popular concepts in psychology about which they have read and heard in the media. Currently there are few resources available which present a rational approach to evaluating these on the basis of research evidence. This book grew out of this demand. It is intended to bridge the gap between traditional psychology and its so-called fringe areas, providing accessible accounts of how science works on the border of its last frontier – the human mind. The emphasis throughout is on evaluating evidence in order to develop informed opinions. We have organized the book into three sections. The first of these addresses aspects of scientific method and scientific reasoning. The opening chapter in this section discusses the nature of the scientific method and the particular problems which the study of human experience poses. This chapter sets out the 'rules of the game' for interpreting the evidence which follows in the rest of the book, and it serves to place science within a social context. This will familiarize readers with the perspective which scientists bring to the study of such a difficult subject. Anthony Esgate and David Groome then consider some pitfalls of human reasoning when faced with events whose occurrence is explicable on the basis of the laws of large numbers (i.e. statistics), but which appear so meaningful that additional explanations are routinely sought. Careful reading of this chapter is particularly recommended. Chris French completes this section with a review of the puzzling nature of the placebo effect – what it is and what it is not. This should prove illuminating to professional and lay readers alike as many popular misconceptions are laid to rest. The second section explores issues of belief and deception in chapters which address belief in the predictive power of astrology and the techniques employed by psychic fraudsters to foster audience belief in the paranormal nature of decidedly non-paranormal phenomena. Richard Wiseman, himself a well-known magician turned psychologist, gives the inside story.

The final section – and by far the largest – deals with an array of unusual and intriguing experiential phenomena. There is something here (we hope) to delight everyone, including up-to-date summaries of unconscious awareness, dreams, ESP research, reports of alien abductions and near-death experiences, among other things. The various contributors to this section have attempted to convey not only what is known about these phenomena but also what has yet to be established. We believe that raising questions is just as important as answering them, and we therefore hope that these chapters are revealing in terms of both the successes and the struggles of the scientific method to come to terms with consciousness in its many forms. We conclude the book with a few thoughts about why the paranormal is so important in our society, what lessons can be learned from studying it, and how it may (or may not) help us to form a vision of humanity that is compatible with the knowledge which has been accrued in the human sciences. Here we pose questions about the relationships between religious and paranormal belief with the intention of fostering some serious debate about a side of the discipline of parapsychology which has too often been neglected.

As an added extra, and in keeping with our philosophy that it is the evidence which counts, we have included within the text opportunities for readers to participate in ongoing research projects. We sincerely hope that you will feel challenged by the material we have collected together in the pages which follow and that you will be roused to debate and argument well into the wee small hours of the night. For sceptics and believers alike there is material here to challenge and unsettle established opinion. Sit back and enjoy the trip.

Ron Roberts
David Groome
London, 2000

Acknowledgements

We would like to thank everyone who has contributed to the book, as well as anyone and everyone who has contributed ideas and suggestions on what to include. The preparation of this book has been influenced over the years by many people – too numerous to mention, but their input to the finished product is gratefully acknowledged. We would also like to thank the many students who have appreciated our endeavours to teach both parapsychology and critical thinking in an informative and entertaining manner. Thanks are due to our editor Christina Wipf Perry, whose light touch and relaxed manner has made the process of completing this project more enjoyable than it might otherwise have been. Additional thanks to Antje, Merry, Wandia, Subira and anyone else who has managed to make us laugh and to support us.

Preamble

Unusual and paranormal experiences

We live in an age of science. However, there are many types of human experience which continue to defy any scientific explanation, at least in terms of the scientific knowledge that we have at the present time. In some cases we may have a partial explanation, but in other cases the underlying mechanism is completely unknown. These cases which completely defy any normal scientific explanation are referred to as 'paranormal' phenomena. In practice there is considerable overlap between what is regarded as 'paranormal' and what is considered to be merely 'unusual', so this book will review both categories without necessarily making a distinction between them. The purpose of this book is to review the scientific evidence that is available about unusual and paranormal experiences. The main categories of unusual and paranormal experience are listed below, and they will all be examined in detail later in the book.

- Extra-sensory perception (ESP) refers to the perception of input through some channel other than the five known senses. It is also referred to as 'paranormal cognition', 'telepathy' or the use of a 'sixth sense'. All of these terms basically denote a capacity of the brain to receive information from other sources by some unknown mechanism of transmission.
- Astrology is based on the assumption that the stars have an influence over people's lives, character and destiny. Again the mechanism by which this might occur is still unknown.
- Sightings of aliens and UFOs (unidentified flying objects) refer to extra-terrestrial visitors and their spacecraft. Some people believe that they have been the victims of alien abduction. These experiences (and claimed UFO sightings) are generally classified as paranormal because as yet there is no objective evidence of the occurrence of visits to this planet by aliens.

- Many people who are close to death (or who are resuscitated after being clinically dead) describe experiences for which it is difficult to provide a straightforward scientific explanation. These near-death experiences may include visions of the afterlife and out-of-body experiences.
- Meditation involves techniques which apparently achieve unusual states of consciousness such as trances. Hypnotism is generally considered to be related to these techniques.
- Dreams are the images that we experience during sleep, and although they are well established as real phenomena, as yet there is no agreement about their underlying mechanism or purpose.
- Unconscious awareness and subliminal perception refer to the brain's ability to take in information without being conscious of perceiving it.
- The placebo effect is the tendency for a therapy to have a beneficial effect which exceeds its known therapeutic mechanisms, sometimes as a result of mere suggestion and expectation on the part of the patient. The placebo effect is a well established phenomenon, but its mechanism of action is not well understood.

These are some of the more commonly reported forms of unusual experience which continue to puzzle the scientific world. They are all linked by one common factor, namely that in each case the mechanism underlying the phenomenon is still unknown. However, these phenomena have all been subjected to scientific investigation, and the findings of this research will be considered in this book. Each of the phenomena listed above will be dealt with in a separate chapter. There is an additional chapter on probability and coincidence, because these concepts are fundamental to any evaluation of research into claims of unusual and paranormal experiences.

Belief in the paranormal

Although we live in an age of science, belief in the paranormal remains surprisingly widespread. For example, a survey of 1236 adult Americans conducted by Gallup and Newport (1991) yielded the following findings.

- Three people out of every four admitted to reading their horoscope in the newspaper.
- One in four expressed a firm belief in astrology.
- One in four claimed to have experienced telepathy.
- One in four believed in ghosts.
- One in six claimed to have seen a UFO.

There is evidence that belief in the paranormal is fairly widespread in other countries, too. For example, Blackmore (1997) reported that 59% of a UK sample expressed some belief in paranormal phenomena, although these individuals were not a true cross-section of the population, as study subjects were obtained by a newspaper appeal (in the *Daily Telegraph*). With such widespread belief in the paranormal, it is obviously important for scientists to establish the validity of these phenomena. For some people an interest in the paranormal is little more than harmless fun, but for many others it plays a major part in helping them to make decisions about important events in their lives. Some people decide to get married or change their job on the advice of an astrologer. Others move house to get away from a ghost or poltergeist. Some take significant actions on the basis of information which they believe they have obtained by telepathy or from a clairvoyant. Beliefs about paranormal phenomena may also create fears and anxieties. Some people live in constant fear of alien abduction, or even believe that they have already been victims of alien abduction, while others live in fear of ghosts, demons or even the devil. There are other more subtle consequences of beliefs about the paranormal – for example, when people blame their own failures and misjudgements on paranormal phenomena. After an accident or catastrophe has occurred, it is sometimes tempting to blame the intervention of some unknown force. The disaster was fated, in the stars, or brought about by demons or the vengeful dead. This type of attribution can provide a convenient excuse for those who are actually responsible, and in failing to face up to reality they may also fail to learn from their mistakes.

Many people maintain beliefs in the paranormal which have a very real influence on their lives. If these beliefs are based on valid phenomena, then they might possibly add useful knowledge and insights to the decision-making process, which should be made available to as many people as possible. Telepathy, clairvoyance and astrology might all have the potential to enrich and improve our lives, provided that they are valid and genuine. However, if it turns out that these paranormal phenomena are not genuine, then they represent a source of considerable confusion, misjudgement and bad decision-making. A person who bases their major life decisions on false beliefs will probably not be very effective in dealing with the demands of their life and their relationships. This is why it is so important that paranormal phenomena should be subjected to scientific investigation, so that we can judge whether or not they are valid. Such investigations are essentially the subject matter of the rest of this book.

Part I

Myth and method

Who could suppose that angels move the stars, or be so superstitious as to suppose that because one cannot see one's soul at the end of a microscope it does not exist?

(R.D. Laing)

1 Science and experience

Ron Roberts

> *'How many fingers am I holding up, Winston?'*
> *'I don't know, I don't know. You will kill me if you do that again.*
> *Four, five, six – in all honesty I don't know.'*
> *'Better,' said O'Brien.*
>
> (George Orwell, *Nineteen Eighty-Four*)

How we propose to understand reality is central to the pursuit of scientific activity. Many lay people would be surprised to discover that, as a topic, the question of what specific characteristics distinguish the theory and practice of science from other human activities has provoked fierce debate among scientists. In this chapter we shall consider some of the main points to emerge from these debates and their relevance to confronting the unusual and mysterious aspects of human experience which form the subject matter of this book.

First of all, however, let us be clear with regard to what is fundamental to the nature of scientific enquiry, about which few scientists would argue. Simply put, this is that the nature of scientific knowledge does not and ought not to rely on authority. In this respect it is different from almost all other forms of knowledge. According to Karl Marx, what we think of as history merely consists of the tales told by the victorious. The alternative renderings which the vanquished may have bequeathed are lost. What makes for good art is increasingly decided by the whims of art critics and collectors whose assessments are tainted by the influence of the potential economic value of works. The postmodern society which we all inhabit would propose that of all the values, morals and judgements which muster expression, none may lay claim to any special status compared to others. In the totalitarian nightmare which was Orwell's *Nineteen Eight-Four*, this principle was elevated to encompass our very definitions of reality. What was real and true consisted of whatever was decreed in the name of Big Brother to be real and true. However, the assault on the notion of objective truth is far from fictitious. Orwell's own story was rooted in the chilling reality of Stalinist Russia, since which time there have been other appalling variations on the same theme.

Science stands fundamentally opposed to such a philosophy. This challenge which science throws down does not claim that scientists have access to any absolute knowledge or ultimate truth. Rather, what is asserted is that the relationships between events which science describes in some way mirror or approximate to events that are assumed to occur in a world which is real and exists in some way independently of any human sensory contact with it. This doctrine is known as scientific realism. For example, a knowledge of the mathematical relationships which describe motion enables spacecraft to be placed in orbit. These mathematical descriptions are not arbitrary in any post-modern sense – they do not depend upon a social or public consensus that they are correct. They must fit with reality in some deep sense – otherwise the spacecraft could not remain in orbit, and the practical possibilities of satellite communications and human space travel could not be brought into being.

Science, belief and truth?

Science is not without its critics – some from within its own camp. Like Kuhn (1962), Feyerabend (1975) took the view that shifts in scientific paradigms owe more to the dominating influence of powerful interest groups and particular belief systems within the scientific community than to any logically and empirically derived truths. Indeed, the physicist Max Planck famously remarked:

> a new scientific truth does not triumph by convincing its opponents and making them see the light, but rather because its opponents eventually die, and a new generation grows up that is familiar with it.
>
> (cited by Kuhn, 1962: 151)

Because of this, many worthy and interesting hypotheses simply do not get to see the light of day, or find that their emergence into a wider public consciousness is seriously delayed. Silvers (1997) provides an interesting collection of such ideas and the fates that befell them. What can we learn about the nature of science from these stories? Certainly they lead us to ask exactly what science is or is not. One of the recurring themes in the quest to pin down its nature, has been whether to conceptualize it in terms of what scientists actually do (which is at times illogical, beset by personal and social bias, subject to cultural and ideological whims and swayed by power politics), or instead to describe it in the ideal abstract terms of what scientists ought to do. In a nutshell, the question is whether to depict it in a descriptive or a prescriptive language. Those who lean towards the latter position may cite the views of Karl Popper (Popper, 1972), who argued that science progresses through cycles of hypothesis generation and refutation. However, he was acutely aware that the first half of this cycle – the business of generating hypotheses – could not be captured by any formal system of (hypothetico-deductive) rules. It is in essence a creative act. He was also cognizant that theories have frequently stood their ground and prevailed despite apparent falsifications and their inability to account for well-known observed phenomena. For example, during his own lifetime Newton's laws of motion were known to be incapable of explaining the observed motion of the planet Mercury through the heavens.

Such difficulties, among others, led Feyerabend to contend that no coherent account of a universal unchanging scientific method would suffice (in short, that there is not nor could not be such a thing as scientific method). Furthermore, it is true that science also embodies an article of faith – a fundamental principle, if you like, that the 'laws of nature' are in principle comprehensible and consistent throughout the universe. Without such a guiding belief it is difficult if not impossible to contemplate how science could be 'done' at all. Beyond that one article of faith, however, no ideas are to be considered sacrosanct. Yet if science is so difficult to pin down, how is it possible that ideas come to fruition which in their structure and functioning seem to correspond so closely to that which is observable in the world? Consider our example of the laws of motion as set forth initially by Newton and later by Einstein. We do need to understand this if we are maintain that the scientific path offers the best prospect of coming to terms with human behaviour and the wealth of reported human experience which is on offer.

Although workable and testable hypotheses cannot be produced by following a recipe, there are certain aspects of scientific activity which, if viewed from a broad enough perspective, do permit it to be distinguished from other activities which might also lay claim to truth. At the beginning of this chapter we mentioned what is perhaps the most important of these, namely the disjunction between truth and authority. The proclamations of Nobel-prizewinning scientists and other eminent authorities are not true by virtue of who they are or the position which they hold in the scientific community. Certainly over short periods of time this fact can sometimes be obscured and the art of political persuasion may triumph over reality. For example, Boyle (1990) provides a convincing case for the abandonment of schizophrenia as a scientific concept because, after almost 100 years, there is no empirical evidence to support its validity. Perhaps we should be thankful that the work of Machiavelli does not form part of the scientific curriculum! However, because science is fundamentally pursued in order to solve intellectual and practical problems, the flaws in any proposed solutions which rely more on power and persuasion than on reason tend more often than not to be rooted out eventually. It is less than certain but more than a hope that this will happen.

The self-correcting tendency which science (in any field worthy of the name) tends to exhibit over time is therefore another hallmark which distinguishes science from other subjects. And what is being corrected is the mismatch (or potential mismatch) between what is predicted from theory and what may be suggested by observation. For example, there are elements in the presentation of astrology or psychoanalysis which superficially resemble those found in scientific work, such as data collection, its representation in graphical form, and a grand theory to 'explain' what is 'in the data'. However, theories in truly scientific domains do not simply consist of *ad-hoc* ideas (however interesting they may be) and nice pictures. To qualify for the status of a theory, an idea must organize already existing data within a coherent explanatory framework, that allows new propositions to be derived logically – propositions which necessitate making new observations which in principle can either support the theory or fail to do so. If more and more observations are built up which challenge a particular theoretical stance, then pressure is generated to reject that stance and come up with an alternative. The alternative should be equally adept at explaining the old observations, be able to accommodate the new ones, and also permit further empirical testing of itself. As such, inconsistency or apparent inconsistency as expressed through people's ideas and theories is the fertile ground on which scientific theories are constructed. Neither astrology nor psychoanalysis has an enviable track record for dealing with predictive failures. The same could also be said for religion and politics.

This reiterative cycle of generating ideas and testing them has been likened to a form of artificial selection whereby 'unfit' frameworks, theories and conjectures are progressively weeded out, leaving in the long term only those which tend to fit the facts well and thereby accord with reality. Viewed from this perspective science is a form of cultural evolution. Its environment is the world of competing theories and explanations. This allows us to understand those instances where theories persist even though they fail certain tests. What is crucial is the context within which they operate. Failure to account for known facts may not be fatal if the competition is no better either, and if in addition it fares worse in other respects. A flawed state of order is deemed to be preferable to unbridled intellectual chaos.

A science of experience: questions of method

All psychological science begins with real-world experience – from introspection of our own mental processes to our experience of our own interactions with others. In this respect investigators in pursuit of a science of persons function as instruments of both data collection and data interpretation. In recent years a vehement argument has been unfolding about what methods are most appropriate for studying human beings. In close proximity to this debate has been another, namely whether the concept of truth in (psychological) science can be protected. Some advocates of qualitative research methods have questioned the very notion of objectivity. They contend that in psychological research it is inextricably bound up with the normative beliefs of groups (chiefly western, economically powerful, white males) who have for so long occupied pivotal roles at the heart of political, economic, cultural and social life. These notions chiefly pertain to maintaining emotional and physical distance between the investigator and the investigated, and the perpetuation of this as a standard through the reproduction of existing power structures in each new generation. Under such conditions, our ideas of truth (which, for example, stress universality, emotional neutrality and freedom from moral values) mirror the means by which those in power have conducted themselves in the pursuit of both personal and public profit. Because of this, it is argued that the use of impersonal methods – most notably those which describe aspects of human relationships in a quantitative fashion – contributes further to our alienation and can tell us nothing useful about what it means to be human. Therefore they should be rejected outright. The dismissal of quantitative methods of working has also frequently been accompanied by calls to reject repeatability as a necessary criterion for scientific truth. It is held that human meanings and actions conjoin at unique moments and may never be repeated.

There is undoubted force (both polemical and logical) behind this argument. Paradoxically, however, the rejection of ideas of truth and objectivity would mean that the very categories critics have used to locate the origins of the manufacture and distortion of 'objectivity' and 'truth' (e.g. social class and gender) cannot be regarded as belonging within the realm of the real, for the very idea of the real has been discarded. They are instead merely socially constructed entities, discredited because of their class/gender origins. As such it is problematic to consider from such a perspective what the aims of knowledge are or could be. If they are merely linked to some competing ideological project, then the more extreme dangers of the political manufacture of scientific truth loom on the horizon – and what would it mean to make assertions if the evidential basis for them was not replicable? Shorn of realism and replicability, what goals can inform research? History already bears witness to the costs of this approach. The rejection of Mendelian genetics in the Soviet Union during the Stalinist era led to mass famine, and the promotion of racial science in the Nazi era led to genocide and world war. When concepts of truth are rejected throughout a society, then tyranny appears a willing beneficiary. What starts as intellectual tyranny is usually a sign of physical tyranny to come.

A more considered criticism of scientific practice in both the quantitative and qualitative realms accepts the presence of bias emanating from certain interest groups, and indeed regards the study of this as important in its own right. Furthermore, the addition of qualitative research to extend the role of human meaning in scientific discourse is welcome. Proponents of 'critical realism' as it has come to be called accept the basic tenets of scientific realism (i.e. that the world exists independently of our attempts to describe it, and that successful scientific theories describe relationships between theoretical constructs which approximate to those which exist between real entities or processes in the world). Against this backdrop they seek simultaneously to reveal the distorting influences of specific social and historical processes as they bear upon the institutional organization of science and the actual reasoning of practising scientists. Because historical analyses reveal that numerous changes in the fundamental tenets of scientific reasoning have occurred (see Chalmers, 1999), a universal conception of scientific method that is true for all time is rejected. However, at any one time the process of asking questions and interpreting evidence is broadly similar in all scientific disciplines, although each favours the use of methods and techniques that are particularly well suited to handling the problems which arise in that domain. The more common elements that comprise scientific method in the modern age do not comprise the use of mathematical or statistical computations *per se*. As we have said, what is crucial is the gathering of data for the purpose of generating and testing ideas about what is or can be observed. The reiterative use of this process, informing and in turn influenced by the cultural milieu, is what leads over time to a more accurate and useful account of things (see Figure 1.1).

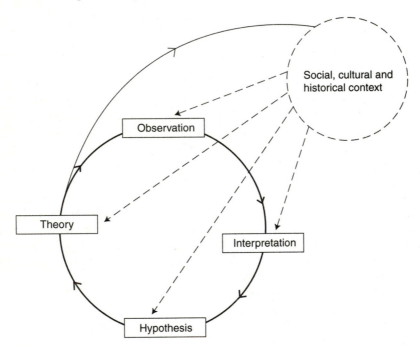

Figure 1.1 Science as an iterative cycle

Experience and science: the moral landscape

We have argued thus far that science does not follow perfectly prescribed rules, and that although subject to a number of different sources of bias, its organization and practice tend over time to favour the survival of well-ordered theoretical schemes that are able coherently to account for large bodies of data, whilst at the same time possessing sufficient flexibility to make novel testable predictions. In order to address the issue of whether science is a suitable vehicle for undertaking the study of experience, we need first to look at the wider question of its moral fitness to do this. One of the fiercest objections to a scientific study of experience contends that science objectifies human beings, ignores our fundamental status as sentient, reasoning, feeling, self-conscious creatures, and thus threatens our dignity. It must be admitted that, in the name of science, many acts have been carried out which provide ammunition for this argument. The twentieth century witnessed the forging of ever closer links between the global military industrial complex and the scientific community. The means to wage mass campaigns of technological and psychological war against civilian populations (Glover, 1999) has only been made available because science increasingly serves the interests of big business – and the manufacture of the means to kill and terrorize people with ever greater 'efficiency' is big business. To many this is a source of dismay and a grotesque parody of the beauty and elegance which are more fitting testaments to scientific enterprise.

One of the problems is that science was originally invented, constructed and elaborated for the study of natural objects. However, unlike inanimate objects, the behaviour of people in objective three-dimensional space is a function of their experience of themselves, their experience of others and their experience of the world around them, as well as the behaviour of other people and material objects. This poses unique challenges for the study of experience. The task of constructing an appropriate science of people has for some been the holy grail of psychology. As an explicit goal it has been addressed by engineer-turned-psychologist George Kelly (Kelly, 1955) and psychiatrist R.D. Laing (Laing and Cooper, 1964; Laing, 1967). Through his theory of personal constructs, Kelly sought to develop an idea of the 'person as scientist' actively constructing and reconstructing the building blocks of their mental life as they negotiated their way through the successive experiments which constituted their unfolding life. Highly influential as this notion has been at times, its radical premise of reconstructing psychology as an entire discipline has floundered. Meanwhile, the emerging metadisciplines of neuroscience, cognitive science, health science and social science threaten to pick off the various constituents of what appears increasingly to be a fragmented discipline. Laing's efforts embodied a synthesis of Marxism, psychoanalysis and existentialism in which normality was depicted as an estranged and appalling state of alienation, and set out a radical agenda for a science of people to support and discover pathways back to reality. As psychiatry became entrenched in biological reductionism and the optimism of the 1960s faded, Laing's critique was left on the sidelines. The current dominance of global free-market capitalism and its invasion of the private domain (through, for example, the twin channels of pornography and the 'talk show', whereby people bare their bodies and their souls for mass-market entertainment) only makes the need for us to reassess our position all the more urgent. The problem thus remains. How can we study experience in a way that does not do psychological violence to us?

Experience and method

A consistent difficulty for practitioners of the scientific method has been what status to accord the self-reported experiences of humans. Dreams, near-death experiences, apparent instances of telepathy and alien abductions are just some of the reported experiences that scientists must contend with, yet the private unobservable nature of human experience seems to render it unsuitable for scientific scrutiny. Can systematic methods of enquiry be applied both to the empirical data of self-reports and within the experiential realm? If so, how are these to be approached?

Anchored in the philosophy of realism, one strategy is to seek correlations between such reports and other more easily observable phenomena, and to attempt to establish the conditions (e.g. biological, social or cognitive) under which such reports are made. This might tell us something about the nature of the reports, but by itself it is insufficient to establish the veracity of the putative experiences to which the reports allude. For example, evidence for the existence of both sleep and dreaming (see Chapter 7) relies on the self-reports of human subjects (Malcolm, 1959). In the case of sleep, these reports are validated by the appearance of particular behavioural and physiological indicators linked to levels of arousal which occur immediately prior to a report. Where dreams are concerned, it is more the cognitive correlates of reporting, in combination with the temporal correlate of reporting them immediately subsequent to waking, that points to the existence of a different mental state – which is unobservable to others – occurring under the conditions of sleep. This inference is further aided by the fact that an over-whelming majority of people report these experiences. I would stress that what is being validated here is the notion that dreaming as a different mental state occurs – not the contents of any one particular dream. Despite earlier misapprehensions, dreams are reported from all stages of sleep, not simply during the stage where rapid eye movements occur (REM sleep) (Foulkes, 1960). If applied to experiential reports, systematic investigations of their properties, correlates and implications are likely to yield valuable insights into what these mean, not just in framing causal explanations for these reports (i.e. what the reports can tell us about the internal and external realities in which people live), but in what they also tell us about human life and the struggles which being human entail.

Similar rationales have been employed in the study of meditation. However, it is important to note that once scientific practitioners are satisfied that a particular phenomenon is real, if they wish to explore further the nature of a particular type of conscious experience, then they must orientate themselves with respect to the actual contents of the experience and systematically explore ways in which the experiences can be modified or transformed. Such means may be externally induced (e.g. through drugs or sensory deprivation), but may also be induced through intended acts of will or cognition, which are themselves repeatable and which others may learn through instruction. Accordingly, it can be argued that a certain type of systematic questioning and evaluation of the nature of some kinds of experience and its attendant possibilities is only possible through having the experience. Later chapters will consider the merits and potential of applying such an approach to states of consciousness induced by meditation and lucid dreaming. It is important to note here that this is only made possible through the replicable nature of the phenomenon. However, the initial stages of scientific exploration must begin with establishing the veracity of experience – determining its boundary conditions, if you like – moving through exploring its content and structure and proceeding to ascertain the means to mould and transform the experience (see Figure 1.2 for a summary of this process). Although experiences such as dreaming, remembering and consciously experiencing the world are private, we assume their veracity in others, partly through our mutual identification with them as beings like us who have the same kind of conscious experiences that we do. When it comes to claims of more esoteric experiences (e.g. alien abductions), this type of common ground simply does not exist.

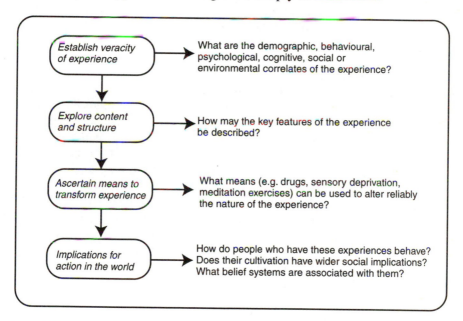

Figure 1.2 The science of experience

In addition to exploring the veracity, content, form and malleability of experience, all psychologies of experience also invariably address some aspect of how experiential knowledge contributes to and transforms one's actions in the world. Such study can involve taking an anthropological stance towards the culture where certain experiences are cultivated or are held to occur. This may involve asking how belief in particular experiences shapes the actions of those who adhere to it.

In the terms we have just described, then, science is not opposed in any fundamental way to the study of experience. Where science differs is in the interpretative stance towards reported experience. 'Seeing is believing', so the saying goes. And although Aristotle considered reliance on the senses to be critical for establishing scientific truth, this criterion has long since been abandoned (Chalmers, 1999). By itself experience cannot be and is not regarded as sufficient evidence for the independent reality of what people observe. The difficulties of interpreting reports of certain experiences, particularly the kind addressed by the contributors to this book, are compounded by virtue of their frequently being presented in terms of an interpretation – an explanation of their origins – rather than an account of only the contents (the phenomenology) of the experience. For example, reports of alien abductions, out of the body experiences (OBEs) or apparent telepathy are usually described in terms which already presuppose the causes behind them (i.e. people report experiences of being abducted by aliens because they have been so abducted, OBEs are caused by the mind leaving the body, and people share common thoughts, feelings or impressions because telepathy, or thought transmission, occurred between two or more people). When faced with this, it is important to disentangle the process by which people arrive at an interpretation of their experience from what it was that they originally experienced. For example, in discussions with people who claim to have sensed the presence of departed spirits in haunted houses, closer questioning frequently reveals a distinction between perceived physical sensations (e.g. coldness) or psychological sensations (e.g. anxiety, fear) experienced at the location, and the subsequent attribution that these are causally linked to someone having died there. This attribution may be made immediately after the experience if information about a death was already known, or it may occur some time later as information comes into someone's possession. The psychology of how and why people make attributions about the world in which they live has much to offer here. It can help us to shed light not just on the wild and wonderful experiences which people report that they have, but also on their beliefs about the very way in which the world is structured. One of the critical features which distinguishes scientific from lay accounts of events concerns not just the methods adopted to arrive at an answer, but also what is being accounted for. Pletcher (1987: 136) expressed this succinctly: 'an important part of our understanding of the world lies in knowing what *not* to explain'. Thus science begins with the report as the prime data, not the assumed reality of what is reported as experienced. Similarly, it may be more instructive to investigate people's understanding of coincidence rather than to begin by assuming that some acausal connecting principle (e.g. synchronicity, telepathy, etc.) underlies the temporal juxtaposition of two events which to one person are highly meaningful.

We repeat that this does not mean that science is antagonistic to experience, but merely that something more is required before one moves from a person's expressed belief in a phenomenon to believing wholeheartedly in the reality of the phenomenon as described. The correct attitude of the scientist faced with reports of unusual experiences is to seek further evidence for or against the existence of such experiences. It does not mean that such accounts must *necessarily* be dismissed. Absence of evidence is not of course the same as evidence of absence. However, when very large numbers of people make persistent extraordinary claims (e.g. the presence of alien beings on Earth) in the absence of any supporting evidence (which one would logically expect to exist were the claims actually to be true), and where *ad-hoc* untestable explanations are continually proposed to account for the failure to produce evidence, one is entitled to remain sceptical until such evidence emerges (Sagan, 1997).

We need to exercise considerable caution where beliefs are concerned, particularly those which are firmly held despite contradictory evidence, and which appear to be unfalsifiable by any criterion. One stance that investigators into unusual (or indeed controversial) beliefs can take is to contemplate the kind of contradictory evidence which might lead a rational person to give them up. Of course, to varying degrees we have all been guilty at one time or another of holding on to beliefs which have passed their 'sell-by date', and methods suited to investigating unusual beliefs and experiences, if they belong to the general corpus of scientific knowledge, will also very probably be fruitful in the study of more familiar aspects of human behaviour. However, it must be remembered that beliefs cannot be validated in the same way that the existence of different states of consciousness can. No amount of neurophysiological reductionism will ever be able to point to the neurophysiological location of our everyday beliefs (Dennett, 1995a). Beliefs are unavoidably grounded in our shared social realities. On the basis of their beliefs people may be deemed criminal, eccentric, worthy of psychiatric treatment or may even be murdered. But is there a paradox here? On the one hand we are saying that science is concerned with discovering what is real and true, and on the other we are faced with a social reality which is grounded on consensus – a consensus which numerous studies of human history have shown to be malleable. Under such conditions we are brought back to the question of how science can lay claim to any kind of objective truth about the world. We have seen that such claims can only be made provided that the social consensus which exists is not one brought about by coercion, and is not a collection of simple personal opinions (shared common sense), but rather which depends on adherence to broadly agreed conventions for collecting and reporting data, formulating conjectures or hypotheses to explain the data, and providing logical and empirical argument to support them. The nature and limitations of science need to be well understood. At the end of the day no theories can lay claim to a final or ultimate truth. Scientific truths, unlike dogmatic assertion, must of necessity be temporal in their nature and open to revision. They are fallible, but therein lies one of their major strengths. Science is of course not the only way to understand human experience but if we are to use our experiences as a basis for understanding the world in which we live – and not merely a source of recreation or wonder – then an alliance with a systematic critical outlook should yield useful rewards. Some of the claims made by people with regard to their experiences present fundamental challenges to views of the world which are dominant in the scientific community. They must not be rejected simply on the basis of this discordance. However, in a fair and critical hearing matters of evidence and logic must be paramount.

Suggested further reading

Chalmers, A.F. (1999) *What is this thing called science?*, 3rd edn. Buckingham: Open University Press.
Popper, K. (1972) *Conjectures and refutations*. London: Routledge and Kegan Paul.
Sagan, C. (1997) *The demon-haunted world*. London: Headline Books.

2 Probability and coincidence

Anthony E. Esgate and David Groome

> *God does not play dice.*
>
> (Albert Einstein)

Chance and coincidence

Unexpected events and coincidences happen from time to time, and when they do, it is a matter of personal judgement whether we attribute them to chance or to some other factor such as paranormal influences. Consider the following three examples, and try to decide whether they offer support for the occurrence of paranormal phenomena, or whether they can be dismissed as merely chance events.

1. In an experiment on extra-sensory perception (ESP), the experimenter turns over playing cards one at a time and tries to convey to a partner whether she is looking at a red card or a black one. Although the partner cannot see the cards, he begins the experiment by guessing the correct colour three times in a row. Is this just luck or was it due to ESP?
2. A student looking through a list of his classmates discovers that one of the other students has the same birthday as him. There are only 23 people in the class, so would you regard this as a fairly amazing coincidence?
3. A man dreams about a plane crash, and then wakes the next day to read in the newspaper that there actually has been a real plane crash. Was the dream a premonition or just a coincidence?

   In all of these examples we are faced with the same basic dilemma. Can the events be dismissed as mere chance, or were they just too improbable for such a mundane explanation? This question really is quite fundamental to every claim of a 'psychic' or 'paranormal' experience, and in order to answer it we need to be able to judge how probable it was that such an event could have occurred by chance alone.

Probability

All of these examples require a judgement of how probable it was that the event would occur by chance. In some cases this level of probability can be precisely measured, and is usually expressed as either a percentage or a fraction. For example, the probability (P) of a coin falling down 'heads' is one chance in two, which can be expressed either as a percentage (50%) or as a fraction ($P = 0.5$). We can now return to the three examples given above, this time making an estimate of probability.

1. In the ESP experiment (example 1), the probability of guessing the colour (red or black) of each card correctly is 0.5 (50%), so the chances of guessing a whole series of cards correctly will be halved with each card selected. This means that there is a 50% chance of guessing the first card correctly, a 25% chance of guessing two in succession correctly, and a 12.5% chance of guessing three cards in a row correctly. From this we can conclude that there is actually a fairly high probability of making three correct guesses in a row by sheer chance ($P = 0.125$ or 12.5%), so there is no reason to look for any other explanation.
2. With the classmates' birthdays (example 2) we can calculate the probability of two people sharing the same birthday from a group of a given size, although it is a little complicated because we need to consider every possible comparison between each member of the group and every one of the other 23 members. This produces a surprisingly large number of pair comparisons, and consequently the probability of a shared birthday is higher than most people think. In fact, the chance of finding a shared birthday in a group of 23 people is 50% ($P = 0.5$), so such a coincidence is far from remarkable and can be expected to occur as often as not. This rather high probability illustrates how people tend to underestimate the chances of an event happening when there are a large number of possibilities or combinations to take into account. (Note that a fuller account of the method of calculating this probability is given later in this chapter).
3. With the plane crash premonition (example 3) we are dealing with events which cannot be readily quantified or measured. How likely are we to dream of a plane crash? And what are the chances of a real plane crash occurring on the same day? A precise probability cannot be calculated, so we need to accept a fairly rough estimate. What we do know is that air crashes are reported on the TV news fairly regularly, and dreams of disasters and accidents are also fairly common. Given that both events have a high probability of occurring, the likelihood of their coinciding by

sheer chance will also be reasonably high. One must therefore conclude that the dream/air crash coincidence can be adequately explained by chance, without any need to assume any psychic or paranormal explanation such as a premonition.

These examples highlight the basic question we must ask when investigating claims of 'paranormal' experiences. We need to estimate the probability of the particular event occurring by chance alone. If the event was reasonably likely, then we need look no further than chance to provide an explanation. We should only consider the possibility of a non-chance explanation (e.g. the intervention of psychic forces) when the probability of a chance occurrence is extremely low. Even then, of course, we should not automatically accept a paranormal explanation, as there may be other possible causes which need to be ruled out. For example, in the ESP example above there could be subliminal cues passing between the two partners in the experiment, or one of them could have been cheating. So-called 'paranormal' experiences often turn out to have a normal and straightforward explanation, so it is necessary to look carefully for these before we consider paranormal explanations.

In sciences such as psychology, experimenters test their findings against probabilities, in this case the probability of their finding being just a 'chance' event. By convention, if the probability of obtaining a result by chance is less than 1 in 20 (also expressed as $P = 5\%$ or $P = 0.05$), then it is deemed to be a 'significant' finding – one which is unlikely to have occurred by chance. Alternatively, a probability of less than 1 in 100 ($P = 1\%$ or $P = 0.01$) represents a higher level of significance, where we can have far greater confidence that our findings would not have occurred by chance.

Probability judgements and belief in the paranormal

There is some evidence that people who believe in the paranormal may be less accurate in making judgements of probability than non-believers (Blackmore and Troscianko, 1985). Specifically, the believers are more likely to underestimate the probability of a chance event. This might explain why they are more likely to accept a paranormal explanation of their experiences, since they are more likely to consider an unusual event to be so improbable as to be beyond coincidence. Those with a more accurate grasp of probability, on the other hand, would judge the same event to fall within the bounds of chance. Believers may thus tend to misperceive chance events as being beyond coincidence. A number of experiments have provided support for the hypothesis that believers in the paranormal have a tendency to underestimate probabilities. These studies have used a variety of tasks, including estimates of probability in computer-controlled coin-tossing (Blackmore and Troscianko, 1985), random number generation (Brugger *et al.*, 1990) and estimations of the probability of shared birthdays (Matthews and Blackmore, 1995). However, although these experiments provided some support for the 'probability misjudgement' theory of paranormal belief, not all studies have found this (Blackmore, 1997), so it appears that believers in the paranormal may be prone to probability misjudgements in some situations but not in others.

Probability judgements in everyday life

The notion of probability is fundamental to many forms of human endeavour, and actually underpins most forms of human reasoning. Among the more obvious examples are gambling and games of chance such as the UK National Lottery. However, most other types of judgement involve estimation of a probability, even though it may not be obvious. In a court of law, a defendant is usually found guilty or innocent on the basis of a balance of probability. The jury must decide whether the defendant is likely to be innocent or guilty. Absolute certainty is rarely possible, so instead the jury only has to decide the defendant's guilt or innocence 'beyond reasonable doubt'. That is, they must decide in which direction the balance of probability lies. Similarly, in scientific work just about everything we know about the world is based on observation of patterns and regularities. We then take those patterns to imply certain things about the probability of such events occurring again in the future. For example, the sun has risen on every morning of the authors' life, so it will probably do so tomorrow. However, we can never be absolutely certain that this will be the case, since on some morning in the distant future when the sun has burnt itself out there will be no sunrise. This type of inference, in which we base future predictions upon regularities in the past, is referred to as inductive reasoning and is characteristic of much scientific thought. On a more mundane level probability pervades our daily activities, since whenever we make a decision we implicitly make some assessments of probability. For example, in deciding to do a university degree, all kinds of assumptions are made concerning the probabilities of various costs and benefits, but most students are betting on the probability that the rigours and deprivations of university study will pay off in the long run (e.g. in terms of increased salary).

Definitions and measures of probability

For a concept that is so pervasive, probability is remarkably poorly understood. Much of the blame for this may lie in the way that mathematics is taught (since a proper treatment of probability requires some mathematics), but at least some blame may be attached to the fact that human intuition seems to be ill equipped to handle probability. Probability may be defined in a number of ways. Manktelow (1999) suggests three ways of defining it. The first of these is in terms of observed frequencies. For example, if I stand at a street corner and count both the number of passing cars and the number of passing cars that happen to be red, then it may be possible for me to arrive at an estimate of the probability of the next car being red. Defined in this way, in terms of observed frequencies, the probability of an event A, written $P(A)$, is the frequency of event A divided by the frequency of all types of events in which A could have occurred. That is:

$$P(\text{next car red}) = \frac{\text{number of red cars counted}}{\text{total number of cars counted.}}$$

Of course it is not always possible to carry out a frequency count of the kind described above. Under such circumstances we may instead use the second definition, which is based on the total number of possibilities available. The probability of an event A is now the total number of ways that A can occur divided by the total number of possible outcomes. We can apply this definition readily to the probability of winning the UK National Lottery. It would take many human lifetimes to assess the probability of a particular combination of numbers coming up if we did this by frequency counting. However, if we work out the probability of a particular sequence by enumerating possibilities, it is quite simple to assess the probability. There is only one way in which a particular sequence can come up, and that is by all of the six numbers being chosen (provided that we ignore the actual order in which they occur). Again ignoring the order in which individual numbers are called, the total number of sequences that can possibly come up is approximately 14 million (14,000,000). Hence:

$$P(\text{winning lottery}) = \frac{1}{14,000,000 \text{ (approximately).}}$$

This ratio illustrates one of the problems that people have in handling probabilities, namely the difficulty in comprehending very large numbers. What does a probability of 1 in 14 million actually mean? In fact it means that in order to have a reasonable expectation of winning the lottery once, you would need to compete every week for 250,000 years, during which time you would have spent £14 million and lived for twice as long as modern humans are thought to have been in existence. In other words, your chances are so low as to be almost negligible. What is the relationship between frequency-based and possibility-based definitions of probability? Fortunately, the law of large numbers can be invoked (of which more later) to show that both definitions are equivalent. Given a large enough number of observations from which to estimate frequency, the probability value that is obtained comes closer and closer to the 'true' value based on possibility. However, just as it is not always feasible to conduct a long enough study of frequencies (as with the lottery), so it may not be possible actually to enumerate all of the possibilities available. Consider the probability of being knocked down in the London traffic. It is simply not possible to enumerate all of the combinations of events that may bring this about. Our estimates in the latter case would therefore have to be based on observed frequencies (e.g. the frequency of accidents per pedestrian mile).

The third and final way of estimating probability is by using subjective estimates, where we essentially make an informed guess. This is what book-makers do when they offer odds on a horse winning a race (although in this case matters are complicated by the fact that the odds offered actually represent something more like the amount that the bookie can afford to pay you if their probability estimate is wrong, whilst still making a profit!). Subjective estimates of this type underlie much intuitive decision-making. Although subjective probability estimation may be the greyest area of proba-bility, there do exist ways of making the estimates more reliable by modi-fying them in the light of the available data. The statistician Bayes called the subjective estimate the 'prior' odds, and showed how this could be modified to give the 'posterior' odds by reference to observed frequencies. Unfortunately, research indicates that humans are fairly poor Bayesian esti-mators, (i.e. they are not skilled in making these types of modifications to subjective probabilities) (Kahnemann *et al.*, 1982).

Whichever definition of probability we apply, one thing is clear – the events we are interested in can never be more frequent than the possible events, since they will only occur on some occasions and not on others. Thus the lowest value that a probability can be is zero. This value indicates that the event has not occurred (frequency count) or cannot occur (possibility). Again, if the event of interest happens all of the time, then the ratio of the number of times that this happens to the number of total events is 1, since those numbers are equal. Therefore probability, when expressed mathematically, is a simple matter of a number between 0 and 1. A probability of 0 means that one can be certain that an event will not happen. A value of 1 indicates that it certainly will happen. More often we have a number between 0 and 1, indicating that the event happens some of the time. The nearer this number is to 1, the more often we can expect the event to occur. We can also express probabilities as percentages by multiplying them by 100. Thus a probability of 0.41 is equivalent to a 41% chance of a particular outcome happening.

Independent events and the gambler's fallacy

An important aspect of probability is the notion of independent events. These are events that have no bearing upon each other. For example, when tossing a coin several times, each spin of the coin is an independent event, and its outcome is unaffected by any previous outcomes. Each time we spin the coin, it is equally likely to come down 'heads' (H) or 'tails' (T), so there is a probability of 0.5 in either case. The concept of independent events is not always well understood. Roulette players sometimes make the assumption that if 'red' has come up several times in a row, then the next spin of the wheel is more likely to come up 'black'. This is an example of the 'gambler's fallacy'. In reality, the outcome of the next spin is unaffected by the outcome of the preceding ones, and the probability of 'red' or 'black' remains 50:50 (assuming, of course, that the wheel has not been tampered with). The gambler's fallacy is typical of the type of errors that people commonly make when estimating probabilities. The reasons why people are prone to such flawed thinking are probably quite complex. It seems that they either fail to understand the nature of independent events, or else they actually prefer to believe that one event can somehow affect another. Perhaps some people like to believe that events are in some way controlled, either by themselves (e.g. by blowing on the dice or 'willing' red to come up) or by some influence which they believe they can predict. Such beliefs may allow the gambler to attribute their success to their own efforts rather than to pure luck, which may increase their self-esteem. This situation is compounded by people's proneness to 'confirmation bias', which is the tendency to focus on events which confirm their beliefs and to ignore events which contradict them (Wason, 1968). For example, a roulette wheel which has come up red twice in succession is still only 50% likely to come up black on the next spin, but this means that it will do so about half the time, and the gambler's tendency to overestimate this frequency may lead to a false confirmation of their belief. The gambler's fallacy is only one example of the systematic flaws in thinking to which people are prone when estimating probability. There are other similar fallacies, including those relating to conjunctions of events.

Conjunctions

If we spin two coins in the air, what are the chances of both coming down 'heads'? This is an example of a 'conjunction' of two events, and we shall now consider the possibilities. If we spin a coin once, there are two possible outcomes, heads (H) or tails (T), each of which has the same probability of 0.5. However, if we spin a coin twice, there are four possible outcomes, namely HH, TT, HT or TH. Each of the four outcomes is equally likely, so each has a probability of 0.25. This illustrates the basic rule for combining the probabilities of independent events, which is that the probabilities multiply. For example, the probability of obtaining the outcome HH is 0.25 (0.5 × 0.5). This is known as the probability of a conjunction of the two events (in this case HH). The probability of a conjunction of two events A and B can be expressed as follows:

$P(A \text{ and } B) = P(A) \times P(B)$.

This basic formula describes the conjunction of any two independent chance events. For example, the probability of dreaming of an air crash on the same day as an actual air crash would be calculated by multiplying the two probabilities in this way. However, first we would need to have an estimate of those probabilities, for which purpose we would need to know the frequency of air-crash reports in the newspaper and the frequency of air-crash dreams for that particular individual. One consequence of the way in which probabilities of independent events combine is that the probability of a conjunction can never be greater than the probability of the events comprising it. This is because both of the latter probabilities are numbers less than 1, and when they are multiplied together the answer must be less than each (for example $\frac{1}{4} \times \frac{1}{2} = \frac{1}{8}$).

People often fall victim to a type of conjunction fallacy that was illustrated by Tversky and Kahneman (1983). They used the following example.

Problem 2.1

Imagine someone called Linda who is '31 years old, single, outspoken and very bright. As a student, she was deeply involved with issues of discrimination and social justice, and also participated in anti-nuclear demonstrations'. What do you think is her most likely current situation. Is she:
(a) a bank clerk
(b) a feminist
(c) a bank clerk who is a feminist?

When asked to rank the options (a), (b) or (c) in order of likelihood, 89% of subjects thought (c) was more likely than (a). However, since (c) is a conjunction, we know that this has to be the least likely alternative. It seems that subjects use some other (and less accurate) basis for judgement than probability, and Kahneman and Tversky (1983) argue that subjects actually make use of certain heuristics or rules of thumb in probability estimation, and that these in turn give rise to biases. One significance of such biases is that they may underlie many examples of social judgement. These would include prejudiced judgements in which, for example, members of one group would be seen as more likely than members of another group to have committed certain crimes.

Unremarkable coincidences

What are the chances of two or more people in a group having the same star sign? When it happens to you it may seem an unlikely coincidence, but in fact the number of people required for such coincidences to occur is quite low. If instead of looking for absolute certainty that such a coincidence will occur (which will require a group of 13 people), one can instead content oneself with it having a likelihood of 50% (i.e. as likely to happen as not), then the numbers required are quite easy to calculate. The probability of someone not having the same star sign as someone else is 11/12. If the group has a third member, then the probability of him or her not sharing a star sign with either of the other two is 10/12. The probability of a fourth member not sharing a star sign with the other three is 9/12. Since these are independent events, the probability of none of them having a common star sign is the product of multiplying all of those probabilities together. This value is 0.573, which means that there is a probability of 0.427 that two of the four people will share a star sign, since conjunctive probabilities add (and $1 - 0.573 = 0.427$). Thus it is almost as likely as not that in a group of four people, two of them will share a star sign.

If we consider birthdays, we obtain an even more surprising result. We need only 23 people in a group in order for there to be a 50% likelihood that two of those people will share a birthday. The reason for this low figure is that 23 people can actually be paired off for comparison in no less than 253 different ways. With 30 people, as may be found on the average rugby pitch, the likelihood is in fact 70% that two people will share a birthday. Note, however, that this does not specify which people or which day, but just that such a pairing is likely. As Dawkins (1998) points out, someone could make a good living going around rugby pitches on Sunday mornings offering to take bets on exactly this outcome. Most people will underestimate the probability of such a coincidence occurring, and the bookmaker could expect statistically to win on 7 out of 10 occasions. Exactly the same basis can be found for many other games of chance, which all give the bookmaker much greater chances of winning than they give the punters.

Quacks often peddle fraudulent medical treatments with remarkable success, at least as measured by the willingness of people to pay for their services. Paulos (1988) describes why so many people may be easily taken in. The knowingly fraudulent operator takes advantage of the natural ups and downs of the disease cycle, preferably becoming involved while the patient is getting worse. There are only three possible outcomes – the patient gets better, stays the same or gets worse. In two of those cases the quack may take credit for a desirable outcome – either he stabilized the patient's condition or he caused them to improve. Thus there is a 2/3 probability that the quack will appear to be successful. Moreover, these two out of every three cases will be the ones remembered as 'miracles'. In line with confirmation bias, the others will be discounted as 'he did his best, but it was too late'. Thus simply taking advantage of the laws of chance and an ability to enumerate outcomes enables a fraudster to make a good living.

Randomness and chance

Many examples of erroneous use of probability information derive from the difficulties that humans have in dealing with concepts of randomness and chance. Randomness is an article of faith in statistical science, and it forms the basis of many of our most important scientific theories. For example, both modern physics and evolutionary theory explicitly acknowledge the role of random or chance factors. However, it is not merely lay people who have difficulty in dealing with these ideas. Albert Einstein, one of the founders of modern physics, famously remarked that he could not believe that 'God plays dice with the universe'.

Given a set of events that are equally likely, such as a coin falling 'heads' or 'tails', then what happens is a matter of chance. In a lump of radioactive uranium the atom which emits its radioactive particle at a particular moment is decided entirely by chance. All of the atoms are equally likely to decay, and it is therefore impossible in principle to determine which will do so at any given time – it just happens by chance. It is difficult even to program a computer to simulate the random selection processes at work here. Any computer algorithm that is used to generate random numbers must operate in a mechanical and deterministic way, since the computer is a machine in which any event must be caused by a predictable process. Any number that is generated must therefore be determined by the previous state of the machine (the last number produced). However, since the number is determined, by definition it cannot be random. For this reason, computer-generated random numbers are often referred to as 'pseudo-random' numbers. Truly random numbers can only be obtained by some analogue process such as picking numbered balls from a bag.

Although there is good evidence for random processes, humans have a poor appreciation of randomness and have difficulty in simulating it. Strategies that people employ when filling in lottery sheets are informative in this regard. Thus if asked to generate randomly numbers between 1 and 49, most naive lottery players choose one number between 1 and 9, one between 10 and 19, and so on, somehow believing this to be a likely sequence. However, as players become more sophisticated and experienced at playing the lottery they note that numbers often come up in clusters – for example, three numbers between 1 and 9 and none in some of the other intervals. Players may then start to try to simulate the behaviour of the random selection device that chooses the winning numbers by similarly clustering numbers. Of course, the actual numbers chosen are of little consequence, since all combinations are equally likely to come up, with a probability of 1 in 14,000,000. The motive behind number selection for the truly sophisticated player then becomes one of estimating a conditional probability (of which more later). Basically they are saying to themselves 'If I win I want to share my winnings with as few people as possible, so I need to choose a very unusual sequence of numbers'. In order to do this many people started to choose sequences such as 1, 2, 3, 4, 5, 6. The authors are reliably informed that some 10,000 people competing in the UK National Lottery each week actually choose that very sequence, thereby completely defeating their objective of not having to share their winnings with anyone in the unlikely event of a win!

Conditional probabilities

Conditional probability may be expressed as the probability that something will occur given that something else has occurred. By definition, such events are not independent. Consider the case of someone being able to speak English. If they live in England this probability is high, say 0.95. If, on the other hand, they are merely living somewhere on the planet, then the probability that they can speak English is much lower, say 0.4. In these cases we can express the conditional probabilities as:

1. the probability that the person speaks English, given that they live in England; and
2. the probability that they speak English, given that they are human.

Conditional probabilities are written as $P(A|B)$, which is read 'the probability of A given B'. Thus:

$P(X$ speaks English$|X$ is English$) = 0.95$.

Base rates

When considering conditional probabilities it is important to take base rates into account. The base rate is essentially the background frequency of some occurrence in the general population. Consider the following illustration.

For most people having pains in the chest is a worrying experience. This is because they know that most people who have heart disease suffer pains in the chest, so they worry that they, too, may have a serious heart condition or an impending heart attack. However, what they may not realize is that chest pains are extremely common in people who do *NOT* have heart disease (usually being caused by something innocuous such as indigestion), and there are far more people in this group. This means that the vast majority of chest pains actually occur in people who have no heart problems, or any other serious health problems for that matter. However, in order to understand this, you need to know the frequency of chest pains among the general public, which is the base rate in this particular example.

The following is another example from Tversky and Kahneman (1983):

Problem 2.2

A taxi is involved in an accident at night. In the city there are two taxi-cab firms. One has green taxis and the other has blue taxis. In total, 85% of the taxis in the city are green. A witness identifies the taxi involved as blue. In tests involving the witness in identifying cab colours at night, she correctly identified the colour of the cab 80% of the time. Should we believe her testimony?

This question actually concerns conditional probability. In order to believe the witness we need to estimate the probability that the cab was blue, given that the witness says that it was blue. There is a way of working out this probability mathematically using Bayes' rule, but it is somewhat complex. Instead, a simpler version is presented here which involves enumerating possibilities.

Imagine that there are 100 cabs in the city. We shall consider what happens when the witness sees each one of these. We know that 85 cabs are green and 15 cabs are blue. The witness says that the taxi was blue, but is only right 80% of the time. Enumerating all of the possibilities, if she sees each of the 15 blue cabs then she will be correct in identifying their colour on 12 occasions (80% of 15). On the other hand, if she sees all 85 green cabs, then she will misjudge their colour and identify them as blue on 17 occasions (20% of 85).

Thus there are 29 (12+17) ways in which she can identify a cab as blue. Of these, only 12 are correct (i.e. those which actually are blue). The conditional probability that the cab is blue when she says that it is blue is therefore:

P(cab is blue|witness says it is blue) =

number of times she says 'blue' correctly

number of times she says 'blue'

$$= \frac{12}{29} = 0.41.$$

Thus the witness was probably wrong, since the probability that the cab was blue given that she says it was blue is less than 0.5. In their studies, Kahneman and Tversky presented problems such as the above to subjects. A robust finding was that subjects ignored the base rate. In the above example the base rate reflects the overwhelming probability of a cab being green, given that 85% of the cabs in the city are that colour. Neglect of base rates is also evident in the lottery player who tries to evaluate the conditional probability of having to share his winnings with others when choosing a sequence of numbers, but who completely ignores the absolutely dismal probability of ever actually winning!

Base rates, prejudice and medical diagnosis

One of the more disturbing implications of Kahneman and Tversky's research is that the processes underlying neglect of base rates may resemble those involved in prejudice. In an ingenious experiment, Hewstone *et al.* (1988) presented an exact analogue of the cabs problem to subjects, this time phrased in terms of crime and the colour of residents. They made the alarming discovery that white subjects were more inclined to take account of base rate data if the witness reported that the assailant was white, thereby producing a lower probability estimate of that suspect's guilt. Thus base rate data may be used selectively to justify judgements based on existing prejudices. Medical diagnosis provides another example where base rates are frequently ignored. Most diagnostic tests produce both misses (i.e. do not detect people who are ill) and false alarms (i.e. produce a positive test result for people who are well). In addition, the actual base rate of disease prevalence is often very low. Kahneman and Tversky presented problems similar to the following example to their subjects.

> **Problem 2.3**
>
> Fred has a test for prostate cancer. The test is positive in 90% of people who have the disease. It also produces false-positives in 20% of well people. People of Fred's age with symptoms like his have the disease 1% of the time. His test comes back positive. Should he be worried?

Perhaps the majority of readers would be very worried if they were in Fred's shoes. However, applying reasoning analogous to that applied to the taxis problem above yields a conditional probability that Fred has the disease – given that he has a positive test result – of only 0.043. This is because in a population of, say, 10,000 the test correctly identifies the disease in 90 people but incorrectly identifies it in 1980 healthy people. Thus:

P(person has disease|test identifies disease) =

$$\frac{\text{number of times test identifies disease correctly}}{\text{number of times it identifies disease}}$$

$$= \frac{90}{2070} = 0.043.$$

That is, Fred almost certainly does not have the disease. This is a statistical consequence of the prevalence rate of the disease and the false-positive rate of the test. Unfortunately, doctors tend to be extremely poor at communicating this kind of information to patients, who consequently experience much avoidable anxiety.

The law of large numbers and the law of small numbers

Most psychology students are aware of the law of large numbers. They use it intuitively every time they write at the end of one of their laboratory reports 'more subjects are needed'. By this they mean that the effect under investigation is rather weak and requires a larger sample in order for it to be demonstrated. More generally, the law of large numbers states that a sample will only be representative of a population if the former is sufficiently large. A small sample may well have similar characteristics (mean and standard deviation) to the whole population, but in most cases it will not. Fortunately, small samples are not a complete dead loss, as the central limit theorem of statistics tells us something about the distribution of means of samples and this forms the basis of much of statistical testing. Kahneman *et al.* (1982) identified a number of heuristics or rules of thumb that people apply when handling probabilities that serve to introduce errors and biases into their thinking. One of these is representativeness. This is a 'law of small numbers' that leads people to believe that a very limited finding has some ability to represent a wider population. In many cases the item that is chosen to be representative just happens to be one that the individual has to hand. This is the so-called 'availability heuristic'. In effect this works on the basis of 'If I know about it then it must be important'. Thus someone may in all seriousness claim that cigarette smoking is not harmful because their Uncle Sid smoked 500 cigarettes a day and lived to be 93. Unusual, yes – but it tells us absolutely nothing about smoking and health, as Uncle Sid is unlikely to be representative of much. Perhaps he just had genetic resilience to lung cancer (lucky him!). The true picture can only be obtained by examining a large sample that is representative of the population as a whole. The 'Linda' example (the case of our anti-nuclear demonstrator above) may also be an application of representativeness. Her description causes subjects to think in terms of a very small group of women with particular likely characteristics, and judgements are then made by reference to this stereotype, rather than by reference to considerations of probability.

Risk perception

What is the most risky activity in which you can legally engage in most countries? Having unprotected casual sex? Eating British beef? Flying in a plane? Rock-climbing? Bungee-jumping? Going to university? No doubt the reasonably sophisticated reader knows the answer to this. By far the most risky activity you can legally engage in is cigarette-smoking. This is followed (some considerable way behind, as the risks of smoking are so high) by involvement with motor transport. Of course it depends on the type of risk outcome we are talking about. Risk theorists such as Adams (1998) provide a measure of risk that combines the probability of an outcome with the importance of that outcome. Thus a game like the UK National Lottery which carries an almost 100% chance of losing £1 would not be seen as very risky because £1 is not a serious loss. Even though the probability of winning is so low, losing a pound is not a great concern to most people, especially if they enjoy the game. The greatest risk is when the odds are against you and the potential loss is high. This is why smoking is such a poor risk. The outcomes that the smoker risks are extremely unattractive. They include death and disabling illnesses, many of which eventually result in a long and lingering death. These illnesses include heart disease, bronchitis, emphysema and a range of cancers (lung, bronchus, throat, mouth, etc.). Moreover, the probability of these outcomes is extremely high. The following are true statements:

1. Most smokers (i.e. more than 50%) die as a result of smoking-related diseases.
2. Smoking kills more people than all other drugs, legal and illegal, including alcohol, put together.

Individuals employ a range of psychological ruses to defend themselves against these facts. Some use an availability heuristic. Others are ignorant of the diseases and therefore do not worry about them. Yet more are fatalistic and think that something else will get them first, since the time-course of smoking-related effects is so long (perhaps they think that they will give up smoking in time). Some employ other heuristics, such as the better-than-average effect (Klar and Giladi, 1997), which leads them to believe that their chances of not acquiring diseases are somehow better than those of most other people.

There can be few better illustrations of the irrational nature of anxiety and obsessive-compulsive disorders than in the difference in attitudes to various types of risk. The authors have never encountered a cigarette phobic, even though this would seem to be an entirely rational fear to hold. In contrast, many people experience terrible anxiety about air travel, a mode of transport that is extremely safe. The chances of dying as a result of air travel are approximately the same as those of winning the UK National Lottery. It has been calculated that someone could fly every day for more than 8000 years before expecting to be involved in a plane crash. Perhaps the fear of flying derives from its unnaturalness and, for most people, its rarity, as well as the lack of control experienced by the passenger, who hands over all responsibility for his or her safety to the crew. However, many of these considerations (with the exception of rarity) also apply to travel in motor cars. Car phobia is rare, but car crashes are much more common than air crashes, and the consequences can be little better. Bizarrely, many drivers, despite those statistics, think that car-driving is a suitable arena for risk-taking behaviour. Media exposure is probably a major factor here, since air crashes, despite their relative rarity, tend to be sensationalized by television and the newspapers, whereas car accidents occur every day on a huge scale but go largely unrecorded.

Whilst many individuals experience irrational phobias, many others make their lives a misery with obsessive-compulsive attention to dietary and exercise regimes that at best have only a marginal effect on health. One of the authors has had personal experience of being provided with unsolicited dietary and exercise advice by someone who was both smoking a cigarette and driving a car at the time. The following example, from Paulos (1988), illustrates just how poor individuals' risk assessments can be. This example concerns unprotected sex with an AIDS victim. Although no one in their right mind would advocate unnecessary risk-taking, the example illustrates the extent to which risks may be overestimated. This example concerns the risk of acquiring AIDS heterosexually. It should be noted that the example is simplified, since a single figure is given for infectability (the probability of becoming infected from a sexual encounter), but this is actually thought to be different in males and females. It should also be noted that the figure applies only to heterosexual sex and are based on UK data. In other parts of the world a variety of factors may increase the risk of transmission of the HIV virus and the subsequent progression to AIDS.

Problem 2.4

It has been independently estimated that the probability of getting infected by a single unprotected heterosexual episode with an infected partner is about 1 in 500. Thus the probability of not getting infected is 499/500. If these risks are independent, then, since

499/500 multiplied by itself 346 times is approximately 0.5, there is an even chance of acquiring HIV infection by having unprotected heterosexual intercourse every day for nearly a year with someone who has the disease. However, with a condom the chance of being infected falls to 1 in 5000 per episode. One could then have safe sex every day with an infected partner for 10 years (assuming their survival) before one's chances of being infected reached 50%. If the partner's disease status is not known but he or she is not a member of an at-risk group, the chance per episode of being infected is estimated to be 1 in 5,000,000 if unprotected and 1 in 50,000,000 with a condom. One is much more likely to die in a car crash on the way home from such an encounter. Similar considerations may well apply to other 'risky' activities, such as taking recreational drugs. These activities can in fact be substantially less risky than other, socially condoned risks such as smoking or driving in a car.

Summary

A number of sources of error that arise when assessing probabilities have been outlined. A failure to understand independent events or the probability of conjunctions makes people prey to a number of systematic errors in handling probabilities intuitively. Individuals typically have great difficulty in appreciating randomness, even when trying to generate random sequences of numbers when competing in a lottery. Conditional probabilities are particularly difficult to handle as a result of the tendency to disregard base-rate information. This can lead to prejudiced judgements and to a chronic overestimation of the likelihood of certain desired events, such as winning lotteries and other competitions. In addition, people have a tendency to base their judgements on a small sample of information and to be unduly impressed by the occurrence of unremarkable coincidences. Finally, individuals have a very distorted notion of risk, often being terribly worried about safe activities but unconcerned about very unsafe ones, such as smoking. For all of these reasons the average person tends to make highly inaccurate estimations of probability, and in most cases this takes the form of a considerable underestimation of the probability of an event occurring by chance. This systematic error may in some cases lead people to attribute chance events to other factors, which may sometimes include paranormal phenomena.

Suggested further reading

Hewstone, M., Benn, W. and Wilson, A. (1988) Bias in the base rates: racial prejudice in decision-making. *Cognition* **18**, 161–76.
Kahneman, D., Slovic, P. and Tversky, A. (eds) (1982) *Judgement under uncertainty: heuristics and biases.* Cambridge: Cambridge University Press.

3   The placebo effect

Christopher C. French

> *Use new drugs quickly, while they still work.*
> (Nineteenth-century medical dictum,
> sometimes attributed to Trousseau)

> *If you can believe fervently in your treatment, even though controlled*
> *studies show that it is quite useless, then your results are much better,*
> *your patients are much better, and your income is much better, too.*
> (Richard Asher, 1972, quoted in Skrabanek and McCormick, 1989: 7)

Introduction

Evelyn White was a patient with advanced recurrent breast cancer. The tumour had recurred in the left armpit and above the left clavicle, and had blocked the lymphatic channels of her arm so that it had become swollen. There had been a temporary response to the first chemotherapy we had tried, but a few months later the disease became progressive again, and we suggested a second type of chemotherapy.

Mrs White was unenthusiastic about the second-line chemotherapy and wanted to try a complementary medication called Cancell. I agreed to let her try it and asked her to keep seeing me regularly so that I could assess her progress and perhaps offer symptomatic therapy if required. She visited every two weeks. Over a period of two months or so, she told me that her left arm was definitely less swollen and felt more comfortable and less tight. At each visit I measured the girth of the arm (at exactly the same place, to avoid errors) and found that it was actually becoming more swollen. She asked me not to tell her what the measurements were, and I honoured her request. She gradually became iller as the disease progressed, but even at the end of her life she was convinced that the Cancell had done something for her. None of us argued with her – simply the subjective feeling that her arm was improving had given her a psychological boost which it would have been heartless (and pointless) to destroy.

(Buckman and Sabbagh, 1993: 172–3)

Until fairly recently, it was common to assert that a placebo was any form of medicine or treatment which was given to patients more to please than to cure them. The word 'placebo' is in fact Latin for 'I will please'. However, many aspects of the concept of placebos are controversial. Indeed, Shapiro and Shapiro (1997a) devote an entire chapter to the different definitions of placebo and placebo effect which have been employed in the medical literature. These authors define a placebo as 'any therapy prescribed...for its therapeutic effect on a symptom or disease, but which is actually ineffective or not specifically effective for the symptom or disorder being treated'. They define the placebo effect as 'the nonspecific, psychological or psychophysiologic therapeutic effect produced by a placebo, or the effect of spontaneous improvement attributed to the placebo' (Shapiro and Shapiro, 1997b: 12).

Before discussing the nature of placebo effects in more detail, the reader's attention should be drawn to the existence of the placebo's wicked alter ego, the so-called nocebo (which translates as 'I will harm'). Whereas placebos lead to positive effects, nocebos lead to negative effects. Thus if sugar pills are administered to a group of people and they are told that, say, headaches or drowsiness may result, a sizeable proportion of the group may well report such effects. Even less research has been directed towards understanding the nocebo effect than towards the placebo effect, but it seems likely that similar explanations may apply to both phenomena (Benson, 1997; Hahn, 1997a, b; Spiegel, 1997; Wynder, 1997). It is claimed that, as with placebos, effects can vary from slight to extremely strong. Indeed, in the most extreme case, claims that voodoo curses can actually lead to death have been explained in terms of extreme nocebo reactions!

The nature of placebo effects

From the vantage point of modern Western medical knowledge, from antiquity until the last few decades virtually all treatments were therapeutically worthless over and above their value as placebos. This view is reinforced by the extensive lists of drug treatments in pharmacopoeias from previous centuries, which included such useless but exotic items as usnea (moss from the skull of victims of violent death), Vigo's plaster (viper's flesh, live frogs and worms), parts of the skulls of executed criminals, oil of brick, ants, spiders' webs, saliva of a fasting man, sexual organs, and excreta of all kinds, to name but a few! Patients were also subjected to such extreme but therapeutically worthless procedures as 'purging, puking, poisoning, cutting, cupping, blistering, bleeding, freezing, heating, sweating, leeching and shocking' (Shapiro and Shapiro, 1997b: 15).

Although the development of truly effective and specific therapies is a very recent phenomenon, throughout recorded history all societies have revered those special individuals who have responsibility for healing, whether they be physicians or witch-doctors. The fact that such healers have always had this special status is an indication that they are widely perceived as having the ability to treat and cure ailments, and this in itself provides an illustration of the power of the placebo. The truth is, of course, that the placebo effect is still a major part of modern medicine, although typically it is not exploited in any systematic way. Whether it should be poses a tricky ethical dilemma which is explored further in Box 3.1.

Box 3.1: Should conventional medicine make more use of the placebo effect?

Assuming that placebo effects are real, opinions are sharply divided as to whether or not conventional medicine should exploit them more than it does at present. Alternative (or complementary) therapists would appear to maximize the placebo effect in their approach. Even though their treatments have rarely received strong support from (or even been tested with) double-blind RCTs, alternative therapists are invariably convinced of the effectiveness of their treatment. This is based on their clinical experience of hundreds of satisfied clients and their lack of knowledge of alternative explanations for improvements in health, such as those discussed in this chapter. As a result, they are supremely confident about their diagnostic ability, their explanation of the illness in question, and the effectiveness of their treatment. This confidence is likely to rub off on the client, raising his or her expectations of recovery. Furthermore, the practitioner is likely to spend a long time listening sympathetically to the client, taking all of their symptoms, however vague, very seriously.

In contrast, the average GP or hospital doctor is under great time pressure and will probably not be able to spend a long time listening to each patient. They will feel morally obliged to inform the patient of any uncertainties regarding diagnosis, and about the possibility that a particular form of treatment may not work and that it may have unpleasant side-effects. Most conventional doctors feel that it would be unethical not to provide full information to their patients. However, the very act of informing the patient of these doubts and uncertainties is likely to undermine the placebo effect.

Even worse than providing incomplete information would be the prospect of actually providing patients with false information. Even though a clinician may suspect that prescribing an inert sugar pill might help some patients to feel better, he or she may feel that to do so is a betrayal of the basic trust which should exist between doctor and patient. Asher's paradox was quoted at the beginning of this chapter. As Asher went on to say, 'It is better to believe in therapeutic nonsense than openly to admit therapeutic bankruptcy. Better in the sense that a little credulity makes us better doctors, though worse research workers ... if you admit to yourself that the treatment you are giving is frankly inactive, you will inspire little confidence in your patients, unless you happen to be a remarkably gifted actor, and the results of your treatment will be negligible' (quoted in Skrabanek and McCormick, 1989: 8).

Not surprisingly, many practitioners are incapable of the double-think that Asher, with tongue firmly in cheek, was recommending. However, there is more to the placebo effect than simply giving patients inert treatments such as sugar pills, as this chapter makes clear, and Brown (1998a, b) offers a great deal of sensible advice to doctors to allow them to maximize placebo effects in an ethically acceptable manner. He advises that the doctor should always give a thorough examination, even if they are certain of the correct diagnosis as soon as the patient enters the clinic. If, as is often the case, no specific diagnosis is possible, it is better to give a positive consultation ('I've examined you thoroughly and no serious illness has been found. You will almost certainly feel much better within a week or two') than simply to admit that you do not know what the problem is. Thomas (1987) found improvement rates of 64% for patients who were given such positive consultations, compared to 39% for those who received a negative consultation. Furthermore, the doctor should discuss various treatment options with the patient, allowing them to be involved in decisions about therapy. Finally, Brown recommends that by adopting a different conception of placebos, doctors could even ethically prescribe them: 'If physicians can see placebos – like many conventional drugs – as broadly effective therapies, whose mechanisms of action are not broadly understood and which tend to be more effective for some conditions than for others, they can then offer placebos both honestly and as plausible treatment' (Brown, 1998b: 73).

Given the ubiquity of the placebo effect within medicine, it is perhaps surprising that relatively little research has been directed towards attempts to understand it. As Wall (1999) points out, this is a reflection of traditional negative attitudes towards placebos within modern Western medicine. Placebos are often perceived as being somehow disreputable through their association with charlatans and quacks. While it is true that all manner of worthless remedies have been successfully promoted thanks to the placebo effect, this attitude fails to recognize that the placebo effect is an essential ingredient of all therapeutic interventions. What is more, the US Office of Technology Assessment estimates that only one-fifth of modern medical treatments in common use have been proven to be effective. Indeed, even the benefits produced by truly effective treatments will also include a contribution from the placebo effect. It is a conceptual mistake to assume that placebo effects only arise when inactive treatments are applied. Some researchers recognize this, but consequently view the placebo as an irritating artefact which they would like to eliminate in order to study the 'true' therapeutic effect of an active treatment. This attitude again probably reflects a misconception, but it has contributed further to the typically negative view of placebos within modern medicine.

It would appear that placebo effects can be found in all areas of medicine. For example, they have been reported for depression, anxiety, insomnia, headaches, nausea, asthma, diabetes and multiple sclerosis, to name but a few. One area which has received particular attention is that of pain control. If a group of patients suffering from pain are given a sugar pill but told that it is a powerful analgesic, a sizeable proportion of them will report a significant reduction in the level of pain. This will occur even if the pain is a consequence of a severe illness such as cancer. In recognition of such effects, all new drugs, whether for pain relief or any other application, now have to be tested in controlled clinical trials before they can be used on the general public.

Although the actual mechanisms underlying placebo effects are not yet fully understood, it is generally accepted that the expectations of the patient are an important factor. The patient must believe that there is a real chance of some improvement in their symptoms as a consequence of the administered treatment. The patient's expectations are to a large extent determined by the behaviour of those administering the treatment, especially their verbal communications about what the patient can expect to happen. The attitudes and expectations of the healers, be they doctors, nurses or alternative therapists, would therefore be expected to play a crucial role in determining the strength of any placebo effect.

In view of the above comments, we might predict different levels of placebo response if we compared a group of patients with great faith in modern Western medicine with one with great faith in alternative medicine, depending on the particular form of treatment employed. The former group might be expected to show the largest placebo effects in response to highly technological interventions. Indeed, clinicians often provide anecdotes of patients reporting great improvements in their illness following some technological intervention which, unbeknown to the patient, was actually not part of the treatment at all but part of the process of diagnosis. For example, Edzard Ernst reports that, following an electrocardiogram diagnostic procedure, one of his elderly patients said 'That was great, I feel much better, my chest pain has completely gone' (Ernst and Abbot, 1999) (see Brown, 1998a, for experimental evidence that diagnostic procedures alone can improve patient outcome). In contrast, the New Age believer may well show a stronger placebo response to a homeopathic remedy which conventional medicine would not recognize as having a single molecule of active ingredient. Although the attitudes of patients towards specific treatments are rarely considered when evaluating medical outcomes, the limited evidence available (e.g. Shapiro and Shapiro, 1997a: 222–6) appears to support such a relationship.

The double-blind randomized clinical trial (RCT) is now generally accepted as the best way to assess the effectiveness of any new form of treatment. This research design is based on the assumption that one cannot assess therapeutic effectiveness by simply comparing the outcomes for one group of patients who receive the new treatment with another group who receive no treatment at all. This is because the former group would be expected to show some improvement as a result of the placebo effect, even if the new treatment had no specific therapeutic effect on the disease. The basic idea is that the appropriate comparison group does not consist of patients who know that they are not receiving any treatment at all, but of a group of patients who are receiving placebo treatment. Ideally, the placebo treatment should appear to be as similar to the active treatment as possible, although in practice this may be impossible to achieve. The term 'double-blind' refers to the fact that neither the patient nor the person administering the treatment knows whether the patient is receiving the active treatment or the placebo treatment until the experiment is over. In fact, some studies even go one better by adopting a triple-blind methodology, whereby the person assessing the outcome also does not know which group the patient is in until all of the data have been analysed. The requirement for random allocation to groups is another means by which bias (either intentional or unintentional) on the part of researchers can be prevented.

However, some forms of treatment are not legally required to undergo such tests. Surgery is one such exception. Nowadays, it would generally be regarded as unethical to compare results from a group of patients who had undergone some new surgical procedure with those from a placebo control group of patients who had been anaesthetized and opened up, but not actually operated upon. The risks involved in undergoing such sham operations are considerable. However, such sham operations were performed in the past when ethical standards were different to those adopted today. In the 1950s, for example, the standard treatment for angina, a painful condition thought to be due to inadequate blood flow to the muscles in the wall of the heart, was to ligate (i.e. tie off) the internal mammary arteries. The idea was that the operation would force the blood to flow through new channels, thus improving circulation to the heart. Patients who had the operation reported great improvements, with a considerable reduction in pain, improvements in the ability to exercise and a reduced need for vasodilating drugs post-operatively. However, two studies in which surgeons did compare the outcomes for groups of patients who underwent either the full operation or a sham operation demonstrated conclusively that the majority of patients in both groups showed the same improvements (Cobb *et al.*, 1959; Dimond *et al.*, 1960).

Finally, the field of alternative (or complementary) medicine is full of therapies which have never been tested using proper clinical trials. Typically, however, both clients and practitioners are convinced of the effectiveness of these techniques. Which alternative therapies, if any, have a therapeutic effect over and above the placebo effect is a question that we cannot begin to answer until these therapies are subjected to proper clinical testing using double-blind RCTs (French, 1996). However, it seems likely, for the reasons outlined in Box 3.1, that alternative practitioners are in a much better position than conventional therapists to gain maximum benefit from the placebo effect.

Myths and methodology

As we enter the twenty-first century, placebo effects are still more likely to be controlled for than studied in their own right, but during the past 50 years this situation has begun to change. In 1955, Beecher published a paper entitled *The Powerful Placebo* which did much to focus interest on the topic. Ironically, as the placebo effect has gained acceptance, a number of myths about it have become widespread – and unfortunately some of them can be traced back to Beecher's seminal paper. Many of these myths reflect conclusions drawn from methodologically inadequate studies.

Myth 1: the placebo differentiates between organic and mental disease

According to Wall (1999: 1424), many 'old-school clinicians drilled in classic theory' still subscribe to this 'cruellest and most dangerous myth'. The claim that placebo effects only apply to mental disorders is only a short step away from the assertion that while such effects might be found for disorders that are 'all in the mind' (and therefore, perhaps, imagined?), they most certainly could not apply to 'real', physical, organic disorders. This is palpable nonsense in view of the many thousands of patients who have reported relief from pain caused by a wide range of properly diagnosed physical disorders.

Myth 2: the placebo is the equivalent of no therapy

The fact that patients who are receiving a placebo treatment reliably report improvements compared to a no-treatment control group clearly undermines this assertion. In fact, one can only be sure that placebo effects have been demonstrated if a no-treatment condition has been included in a study – and such studies are remarkably rare. It is far more common for a placebo condition to be compared only with the active treatment condition – not surprisingly, given that the main aim of most researchers is to evaluate the effectiveness of new forms of treatment, not to demonstrate the placebo effect *per se*. This leads to confusion between what Ernst and Resch (1995) call 'true' and 'perceived' placebo effects. The perceived placebo effect is the response observed in the placebo group of an RCT. However, this does not take into account the fact that some change may well have been seen even in a no-treatment group for a variety of reasons, including the following.

- *The natural history of the disease.* Some diseases get worse without treatment, but most minor ailments get better thanks to the body's natural recuperative abilities. As Kienle and Kiene (1996) point out, Beecher (1955) interpreted a 30% improvement rate over 6 days in patients with mild common colds as a placebo effect, completely ignoring the fact that colds usually show spontaneous improvement over a period of a few days without any form of treatment. (Note that even the Shapiros' definition of the placebo effect, given earlier in this chapter, confuses the true and perceived effect by including spontaneous improvement within the definition.)

- *Regression towards the mean*. This expression refers to certain situations in the social and biological sciences where measurements of some naturally fluctuating variable are taken at two points in time. If the participants in a study have been selected because they have extreme scores on a variable at time 1 (T1), then the average score at time 2 (T2) will tend to be nearer to the mean value. For example, if the participants were selected because of their high blood pressure at the start of a clinical trial, they will tend to have a lower average blood pressure at the end of the trial, even without any form of treatment. Given the natural variability of blood pressure, people who already have very high blood pressure are more likely to show a reduction in blood pressure than a further increase. Obviously it often makes sense for researchers to select patients for an RCT on the basis of extreme scores. After all, if you want to evaluate the effectiveness of a treatment for high blood pressure, it is sensible to select patients with that very condition. Regression towards the mean also has a role to play in convincing practitioners that particular therapies are effective on the basis of clinical experience. No disease – not even terminal disease – manifests itself as a relentless decline into death. Major fluctuations in well-being occur, with periods of decline being followed by periods of improvement, even if the overall trend is downwards.
- *Other time-related effects*. A whole range of other effects could influence the measurements taken from a placebo group at T2 compared to T1, including changes in the skill level of the investigator (perhaps as a result of increased familiarity with a new measurement technique), various changes in the patients (e.g. reduced anxiety as they get used to interacting with the research team, and alterations in behaviour and diet as a consequence of focusing more attention on their medical problem), seasonal effects, and so on (Ernst and Resch, 1995).

All of these factors show that one cannot be sure that a placebo effect has occurred at all unless one has a no-treatment comparison group. In the vast majority of cases such data are not available, and many assertions about the placebo effect in the medical literature are therefore unfounded. This would include the claim that 70% of patients who are treated with ineffective therapies show improvements as a result of placebo effects (Roberts *et al.*, 1993).

Myth 3: a fixed fraction of patients respond to placebos

It is often stated that around one-third of patients will respond to placebos, and an appeal to Beecher's (1955) paper is often made to support this assertion. However, it is clear that Beecher's figure of 35.2% was an overall average from 11 studies with widely varying response rates. Moreover, Kienle and Kiene (1996) assert that Beecher misreported the data in the majority of the studies he reviewed! Wall (1999) maintains that placebo response rates can vary from around 0% to 100%, depending on specific circumstances.

Myth 4: placebo responders have a special mentality

Linked to myths 1 and 3 above is the idea that a certain 'placebo-prone personality' exists. Underlying this suggestion may be the assumption that 'normal' people suffering from 'real' (i.e. organic) diseases only respond to 'real' treatments. Furthermore, only weak-minded folk who were only suffering from psychological (i.e. 'imaginary') illnesses in the first place would report positive responses to placebos. Such ideas, although attractive to certain old-school practitioners with a somewhat mechanistic approach to medicine, are completely without foundation. Most studies have shown no correlations between placebo response and personality measures, and the rest have yielded contradictory findings (Wall, 1999).

Myth 5: placebos only affect subjective aspects of illness, not objective measures of disease

Strictly speaking, although the terms are often used interchangeably, illness is not the same thing as disease. The former refers to how people feel about their health, whereas the latter refers to the existence of a pathological process. It is possible either to feel ill without having a disease or to have a disease without feeling ill. According to Skrabanek and McCormick (1989: 6), 'Placebos have no effect on the progress or outcome of disease, but they may exert a powerful effect upon the subjective phenomena of illness, pain, discomfort and distress. Their success is based upon this fact.' The case study presented at the beginning of this chapter was an example of a situation where objective measures showed a worsening of the condition whereas subjectively the patient felt better. However, Skrabanek and McCormick's view appears to represent a minority opinion. The majority opinion is expressed by Ernst and Abbot (1999: 211): 'Objective variables such as the results of blood tests, post-operative tissue swelling, body temperature or the healing of wounds are also placebo-prone.' However, as they go on to point out, 'there can be no doubt that certain conditions tend to respond better than others – premenstrual tension, depression, sleeplessness, migraine and other types of pain are complaints that usually respond well.'

Myth 6: patients in double-blind trials do not know which condition they are in

It follows from the rationale of double-blind RCTs that it is essential that neither the researcher nor the patient is aware of whether they are in the placebo or the active treatment condition. However, Shapiro and Shapiro (1997a, b) found that, in a review of 27 studies with a total of 13,082 patients, the condition was correctly guessed by 67% of clinicians, 65% of patients and 71% of relatives and other staff (compared to 50% expected by guessing). Patients can often tell that they are in the active treatment condition because of the side-effects of the drug (e.g. a dry mouth or drowsiness). Attempts are sometimes made to administer active placebos which mimic the side-effects of the treatment being evaluated, but are thought not to have a specific effect on the disease in question. However, this raises other complications relating to equivalence of conditions. There are no easy solutions to this methodological problem, which will certainly undermine many RCTs. At the very least, awareness of allocation to condition should be monitored and reported.

It is worth noting that although the first four myths listed above (but not the discussion following them) are taken from Wall's (1999) review, it was not Wall's intention to question the actual existence of placebo effects. He merely wanted to dispel various misconceptions surrounding them. However, Kienle and Kiene (1996) feel that the conceptual confusion and methodological errors associated with placebo research are such as to raise the question of whether placebo effects actually exist at all. In addition to some of the issues discussed above, they also refer to other problems, including the following.

Myth 7: in controlled trials, the placebo never has a specific therapeutic effect on the condition being treated

Once again, while the rationale of the double-blind RCT requires that this assumption is met, in practice it may sometimes not be true. Kienle and Kiene (1996) give the example of a much cited study by Ho *et al.*, (1988) which compared the effectiveness of ultrasound treatment for post-operative pain and swelling following tooth extraction. The active treatment, namely ultrasound, was compared with both a placebo control (in which the ultra-sound machine was switched off) and a no-treatment control. Compared to the no-treatment group, both the ultrasound group and the placebo group showed reductions in reports of pain and, more importantly, in objective measures of swelling. However, as Kienle and Kiene point out, both the active and placebo treatments involved the application of a moist, cooling cream, as is usual in ultrasound treatment, and it may have been this which reduced the swelling. They also refer to the classic studies of sham vs. placebo operations to treat angina, described earlier.

Myth 8: patients will always give an honest and accurate account of their subjective well-being

Patients often hold their doctors in great respect, and are very grateful when they expend considerable time and effort in treating their medical condi-tions. It seems likely, therefore, that on occasion patients would feel inclined to exaggerate the benefits of treatment if their doctor asked them, following treatment, whether they were feeling better. Such 'obliging reports' are seen by many patients as no more than simple good manners. The same type of bias is likely to manifest itself in RCTs. Kienle and Kiene (1996: 47) refer to experimental subordination: 'This term means that the subjects of an investigation say what they believe is expected from them without being careful to ensure that their statements are based on actual experiences or perceptions'. Many experimental studies of placebo effects do not rule out the possibility that the results could be accounted for in terms of obliging reports and experimental subordination. A true placebo effect would be one in which patients genuinely felt better and were not simply saying that they did in order to please their doctor or a researcher.

Attempts to explain the placebo effect

One approach to explaining the placebo effect is in terms of classical conditioning. In Pavlov's classic experiment, whenever food was presented to a dog, a bell was rung. The dog salivated in response to the food, but after repeated pairings the sound of the bell alone was enough to elicit the salivation response. Using the terminology of classical conditioning, initially the unconditioned stimulus (US) of food produced the unconditional response (UR) of salivation. As a result of repeated pairings, the conditioned stimulus (CS) of the bell eventually evoked salivation as a conditioned response (CR), even when it was presented alone.

Applying this reasoning to placebo effects, human beings experience the UR of physiological effects associated with the US of, say, drug treatments repeatedly in their lives. However, the context in which the treatments are given – the pills, syringes or creams, and even the clinics, white coats and stethoscopes – constitutes a CS which eventually, as a consequence of repeated pairings, becomes able to evoke an approximation of the physiological responses as a CR (Ader, 1997). The results of animal studies appear to offer some support for the role of conditioning in at least some examples of placebo responses. However, the picture is rather complicated. Sometimes animals that have been injected with an active drug on one or more occasions show a similar behavioural or physiological response when injected with an inert saline solution on a subsequent occasion, yet for other drugs, animals show a compensatory response to the saline injection. In other words, the behavioural and physiological reactions are such as to neutralize the effects of the previously administered active drug. In both cases there is a measurable response to an inert substance, but it may either be in the same direction as that produced by the previously administered active drug, or in the opposite direction.

As one might expect, the situation becomes even more complex when placebo responses in humans are considered. Voudouris and colleagues reported a series of ingenious experiments which appeared to demonstrate the role of conditioning in placebo analgesia (e.g. Voudouris et al., 1989, 1990). These researchers first trained participants to report reliably the intensity of a painful electrical shock, and to indicate the points at which shock became painful and then intolerable. The settings on the apparatus that was giving the shock were in full view. One group of participants was then given a bland cream and told that it would reduce the level of pain experienced. As expected, a few subjects demonstrated a placebo effect by reporting higher pain detection and tolerance thresholds than they experienced without the cream. So far, so predictable. However, with a different group the researchers surreptitiously turned down the shock level on the first trial when the cream was used. These participants were therefore under the impression that the cream had had a powerful analgesic effect. When they were subsequently tested with the shock levels returned to their original higher levels, a large proportion reported higher thresholds with the 'analgesic' cream. It appeared that the association of reduced pain with the inert cream had produced a conditioned placebo response.

Unfortunately, however, other interpretations of these results are possible. Montgomery and Kirsch (1997) repeated the study by Voudouris et al. (1990) and found the same pattern of results. However, they also included a group who received the same treatment as described for the second group above, but who were verbally informed that the intensity of the shock was being lowered and that the cream had no analgesic properties. If the placebo effect worked simply on the basis of conditioning, the association between the cream and pain reduction should lead to an effect for this group, too. However, it did not, suggesting to the researchers that expectancy is more important than conditioning. Kirsch (1997) has reviewed a range of evidence for the importance of the role of expectancy in determining placebo effects. Finally, as pointed out by Kienle and Kiene (1996), the results of Voudouris et al. (and, by implication, those of Montgomery and Kirsch) could, in fact, all be explained in terms of experimental subordination. They present convincing evidence that this is probably the best explanation, and that a true placebo effect may well not have occurred in these much cited studies.

There is one approach in particular which seems to offer most promise in accounting for placebo analgesia, and it also seems to provide the strongest evidence that the placebo effect is real. Levine and colleagues (1978) presented evidence that placebo analgesia was caused by the release of endorphins – opiate-like substances that are naturally produced by the brain at times of stress. They claimed that placebo analgesia could be eliminated by the administration of naloxone, which blocks the effects of these endogenous opioids. Unfortunately, their study was open to methodological criticism. However, a review of the few more recent studies that have employed improved methodology strongly suggests that the basic hypothesis was correct (ter Riet et al., 1998). The improved methodology that was used in these studies involved the technique of so-called hidden intravenous infusions of either naloxone or proglumide (a drug with the opposite effect to naloxone). The actual placebo treatment is an injection of saline in full view, and a no-treatment condition is included. Overall, the results support the notion that endorphins mediate the analgesic placebo response, and they cannot be explained in terms of experimental subordination.

Conclusions

Although a neurochemical explanation for placebo-related pain reduction is now supported by a growing amount of convincing experimental evidence, it is fair to point out that this by no means represents the end of the story. As Anne Harrington (1997: 5) points out, 'Endorphin release, rather, became just one more placebo-generated phenomenon to be explained – and we still did not understand the processes whereby a person's belief in a sham treatment could send a message to his or her pituitary gland to release its own endogenous pharmaceutics.' This chapter has demonstrated the urgent need for further studies, employing improved methodology and clearer conceptualizations of the placebo effect itself. It will almost certainly turn out to be the case that we should speak of placebo effects, rather than of a single effect, and each effect may have a different explanation. In the future, we can hope that further research will unravel the mysteries of these effects and perhaps even render the term 'placebo effect' redundant. In the mean time, clinicians could do worse than to find ways of ethically exploiting the effect in the interests of their patients.

Suggested further reading

Brown, W. A. (1998) The placebo effect. *Scientific American* **278**, 68–73.

Harrington, A. (ed.) (1997) *The placebo effect: an interdisciplinary exploration.* Cambridge, MA: Harvard University Press.

Kienle, G. S. and Kiene, H. (1996) Placebo effect and placebo concept: a critical methodological and conceptual analysis of reports on the magnitude of the placebo effect. *Alternative Therapies in Health and Medicine* **2**, 39–54.

Wall, P. D. (1999) The placebo and the placebo response. In Wall, P. D. and Melzack, R. (eds), *Textbook of pain*, 4th edn. Edinburgh: Churchill Livingstone, 1419–30.

Beliefs

*All argument is against it; but
all belief is for it.*

(Samuel Johnson)

4 The psychology of psychic fraud

Richard Wiseman

*A miracle, my friend, is an event which creates faith. That is the
purpose and nature of miracles...frauds deceive.*
(George Bernard Shaw, *Saint Joan*)

The sensuous curtain is a deception.
(F.H. Bradley, *Principles of Logic*)

Introduction

Many individuals claim to possess psychic ability. For example, faith healers
and psychic surgeons state that they are able to cure illness. Psychic readers
claim to be able accurately to divine the past and predict the future, and
mediums often seem to be able to contact the dead. Moreover, law
enforcement agencies are approached by individuals offering 'psychic tips'
that they feel might help to solve a crime, and alleged psychics have also been
used within industry and business. Investigations into these claims have often
revealed evidence of trickery (Hansen, 1990), and recently academics have
started to explore the psychology behind this rather unusual form of
deception (Hansen, 1990; Wiseman and Morris, 1995a; Lamont and
Wiseman, 1999).

Developing an understanding of 'psychic fraud' is important for several
reasons. First, both the lay public and professionals sometimes turn to alleged
psychics in times of need, and failure to detect trickery could result in serious
negative consequences. For example, in the 1970s the 'Reverend' Jim Jones
attracted several hundred followers to his US cult, often maintaining their
faith by faking biblical miracles such as healing and 'walking on water'

(Mills, 1979). Unfortunately, the personal power that Jones possessed is reflected in the fact that he was able to instigate the mass suicide of nearly all of his followers.

Second, some scientists wish to investigate psychics and need to be able to identify whether their alleged abilities are genuine or fake. The importance of detecting fakery during such work was illustrated when James Randi (an American magician and sceptic of the paranormal) sent two young magicians to be assessed at the McDonnell Parapsychology Laboratory in the USA. While they were at the laboratory, both magicians used conjuring techniques to fake various 'psychic' feats, including metal bending and extra-sensory perception. Although the researchers at the laboratory made no formal statements with regard to the validity of the claimants' psychic ability, neither did they manage to detect the trickery used by the two young men. Randi's revelation of the hoax contributed to the loss of funding and eventual closure of the McDonnell Laboratory (Randi, 1986).

Finally, an understanding of the techniques used to fake psychic ability may yield insight into the types of cognitive and social biases that disrupt perception, reasoning and memory. Cognitive psychologists attempt to understand how observers attend to, perceive, comprehend and store information from the environment. In addition, they are concerned with the way in which this information is recalled and utilized during thinking and problem-solving. Research into psychic fraud may reveal novel types of bias and, like the study of optical illusions, it can provide important new insights into the weaknesses of human information-processing. Moreover, the further analysis of psychic fraud may allow cognitive psychologists to undertake research into novel areas of enquiry which are recognized as important but which, up to this point in time, have proved problematic to investigate.

One aspect of research into the psychology of psychic fraud has involved identifying the stratagems used by fake psychics. This has involved collecting and collating information from several sources, including magazines, books and videos outlining methods for faking psychic ability (e.g. Fuller, 1975, 1980), investigations of fake psychics (e.g. Delanoy, 1987) and literature relating to the 'folk' psychology of magic and psychic fraud (e.g. Lamont and Wiseman, 1999). Additional research has involved experiments designed to help to evaluate the efficacy of some of these stratagems. This chapter will briefly outline some of the key findings from both strands of research.

Misframing

Sociologists use the term 'frame' to refer to abstract structures which observers use to define situations in a certain way (Goffman, 1974). Many situations can be framed in different ways. For example, before observing an alleged medium, sceptics might be expecting to see some kind of trickery, whereas believers might expect a display of genuine mediumistic ability.

Such expectations can play a large role in determining the way in which the observer approaches the situation:

> ...the frame of mind in which a person goes to see magic and to a medium cannot be compared. In one case he goes either purely for amusement or possibly with the idea of discovering 'how it was done', whilst in the other he usually goes with the thought that it is possible that he will come into direct contact with the other world.
>
> (Dingwall, 1921: 211)

Recent research has supported this notion, suggesting that expectation does indeed influence the observer's perception and memory of a 'psychic' demonstration. Jones and Russell (1980) asked both believers in the paranormal (termed 'Sheep') and disbelievers ('Goats') to observe a staged demonstration of extra-sensory perception (ESP). In one condition the demonstration was successful (i.e. ESP appeared to take place), whilst in the other it was not. All of the observers were then asked to recall the demonstration. Sheep who saw the unsuccessful demonstration distorted their memories of it and often stated that ESP had occurred. However, goats tended to recall the demonstration correctly, even if it appeared to support the existence of ESP.

Wiseman and Morris (1995b) also conducted two studies to investigate the effect that belief in the paranormal has on the observation of conjuring tricks. In both experiments observers were first shown a film containing fake psychic demonstrations. They were then asked to rate the 'paranormal' content of the film and to complete a set of recall questions. Observers were subsequently told that the film contained magic tricks, and they were asked to complete a second set of recall questions. The recall questions contained information that was both 'important' and 'unimportant' to the method of the tricks. Overall, the results suggested that sheep rated the demonstrations as more 'paranormal' than did goats, and goats recalled significantly more 'important' information than did sheep. Perhaps most interesting of all, even when they were told that the film contained trickery, goats still recalled more 'important' information than did sheep.

In a similar study, Smith (1993) investigated the effect that instructions given prior to watching a film which contained a demonstration of apparent psychic ability had on the recall of the film. Observers were divided into two groups. One group was told that the film contained trickery, whilst the other group was told that it contained genuine paranormal phenomena. The former group recalled significantly more information about the film than did the latter group. Given that this was the case, it is perhaps not surprising that fake psychics are eager to encourage observers to view their supposed abilities as genuine. Several stratagems have been developed for this purpose. For example, a fake faith healer may assure an observer that he never accepts payment for his services, insinuating that he has no motive to deceive. However, Morris (1986) has noted how fake psychics can be motivated by many other factors, including personal fame, raised self-esteem, a desire to be socially helpful and increased personal power. Various authors have also suggested that some observers deceive simply for enjoyment (e.g. Ekman, 1985). Randi (1982) has suggested that this may in part account for the success enjoyed by the two girls who fabricated the 'Cottingley' fairies (see Box 4.1).

Box 4.1: The Cottingley fairies

The story of the Cottingley fairies dates from 1917, when two young girls, Frances Griffiths and Elsie Wright, living in Cottingley, a small village in Yorkshire, produced a number of photographs of fairies. The girls had been teased about their claims of seeing fairies near Cottingley Beck, so Elsie borrowed a camera from her father and went off with Frances into the area near the family home. They returned soon afterwards. When the pictures were developed later that evening in Elsie's father's dark-room they showed the girls with fairies. Finally, in 1983, Elsie confessed that the pictures had been faked, stating that the girls had drawn the fairies, cut them out and fastened them to the ground with hatpins.

The two girls had no stake in the deception that could have brought them money....The assumption made is that only money and notoriety are plausible motives. Ego and just plain fun are not thought to be sufficient.

(Randi, 1982:37)

The fake psychic may also deliberately produce the type of psychic phenomena that the observer finds believable. For example, an observer may believe that psychokinesis (PK) can rarely be used to produce really large physical effects, and the fake psychic may therefore cause an object simply to move a small distance along a table top, as opposed to making it levitate above the table. The fake psychic may also exploit an observer's physical and emotional needs. If the observer has a serious illness, a fake psychic may claim to possess psychic healing powers. If the observer has recently experienced a bereavement, the fake psychic may promise some form of communication with deceased friends and relatives. Scientists may not be immune to such manipulation. One parapsychologist, after working with a fake psychic, noted:

We are all familiar with the difficulties arising from the so-called 'elusive nature of psi'. In short, we cannot study a phenomenon unless we can first produce it. Thus Tim's [the fake psychic's] claims, that he could produce macro PK at will, suggested exciting possibilities. *I wanted his claims to be true and this desire may have influenced my evaluation of his performance.* [my emphasis]

(Delanoy, 1987: 256)

Attention and distraction

During a demonstration it is often vital to the fake psychic that observers do not attend to the parts of their performance that might give some insight into the use of trickery. Fake psychics have developed several strategems to achieve this. For example, some fake psychics may say that they have little control over their ability and therefore cannot predict the phenomena that will occur. This strategy also helps the psychic if a performance does not go according to plan – a point that was recognized as long ago as 1878 by magician Robert-Houdin:

> However skilful the performer may be, and however complete his preparations for a given trick, it is still possible that some unforeseen accident may cause a failure. The only way to get out of such a difficulty is to finish the trick in another manner. But to be able to do this, the performer must have strictly complied with this important rule: *never announce beforehand the nature of the effect which you intend to produce*. [my emphasis]
>
> (Robert-Houdin, 1878:33)

Furthermore, most observers only start to concentrate their attention fully when they believe that paranormal phenomena are about to take place. A fake psychic may take advantage of this by making secret preparations long before the beginning of the demonstration. This technique is especially effective if the performer is able to anticipate the phenomena which might be requested by observers. A well-known Scottish conjurer called John Ramsey often used this technique to fool fellow magicians:

> Another John Ramsey saying was 'Hold and Hide'. It simply meant, be prepared well in advance. Before John went into company, he always palmed a coin or a thimble so that if anyone asked him to do a trick, he was ready....At one of the conventions he was having tea with some of his 'disciples'....They asked him if he would perform his cups and balls routine....John took out the cups and wand and went straight into the routine. This puzzled the onlookers because they knew that, according to John's book, at the start of the effect the performer must have four balls palmed in the right hand and they had not seen him make any steal. The explanation was simple. John had them palmed long before his friends asked him to do the trick. In fact he had eaten a meal with the balls concealed in his hand.
>
> (Galloway, 1969: 2–3)

Competent fake psychics can also manipulate the focal point of observers' attention. Fitzkee (1945) has outlined how the carefully planned introduction of movement, colour, sound and body language (including the positioning of the feet and hands, and eye contact) can be used to attract observers' attention to a desired location. Moreover, Fuller (1975) has described in his manual of psychic fraud how confusion can be generated to prevent attention being focused on any one location:

> When you're working for a group, keep talking and moving fast. Create maximum chaos. Flit from one task to another. Fail on one thing, put it aside, try something else, then go back and try again, and so on.
>
> (Fuller, 1975: 15)

Switching methods

A fake psychic may develop several ways of fabricating a certain type of psychic ability, thus enabling him or her to switch methods during a performance. For example, many texts on magic and psychic trickery contain several different methods for achieving just one effect. Tamariz (1988) has described 18 methods for performing one particular card effect, whilst Harris (1985) describes a whole range of methods that may be employed to fabricate PK metal-bending. The fake psychic may then switch methods to create what Diaconis (1985) has referred to as the 'bundle-of-sticks phenomena':

> An effect is produced several times under different circumstances with the use of a different technique each time...the weak points of one performance are ruled out because they were clearly not present during other performances. The bundle of sticks is stronger than any single stick.
>
> (Diaconis, 1985: 572)

Controlling performing conditions

Psychics often state that their ability only manifests itself under certain conditions. A fake psychic can exploit this concept by insisting upon working under conditions which are favourable to fraud. For example, Randi (1986) describes how, in Project Alpha, the two fake psychics complained about electronic equipment putting out 'bad vibes', with the result that the researchers were unable to videotape the demonstrations. In addition, Eugene Burger (1986) has outlined how fake mediums insist that all of the sitters must link hands during a seance (see Box 4.2). The fake medium may state that this is necessary in order to bring forth spirit communication. In reality it is designed to prevent curious sitters from reaching out into the seance room, and possibly discovering various forms of trickery (such as reaching rods and accomplices).

Box 4.2: The psychology of the seance

Many individuals have reported experiencing extraordinary phenomena during dark-room seances. Eyewitnesses claim that objects have mysteriously moved, strange sounds have been produced or ghostly forms have appeared, and that these phenomena have occurred under conditions which render normal explanations practically impossible. Believers argue that conditions commonly associated with a seance (such as darkness, anticipation and fear) may act as a catalyst to produce these phenomena. Sceptics suggest that reports of seances are unreliable, and that eyewitnesses are either fooling themselves or being fooled by fraudulent mediums.

The author conducted an experiment to assess the reliability of testimony relating to seance phenomena. A total of 25 people attended three seances. They were first asked to complete a short questionnaire, noting whether they believed that genuine paranormal phenomena might sometimes occur during seances.

A seance room had been prepared. All of the windows and doors in the room had been sealed and blacked out, and 25 chairs had been arranged in a large circle. Various objects – a book, a slate and a bell – had been treated with luminous paint and placed on a small table situated in the middle of the circle.

Everyone was led into the darkened seance room and shown to a chair. An actor played the part of the medium. He first pointed out the presence of a small luminous ball, approximately 5 cm in diameter, that was suspended on a piece of rope from the ceiling. Next, he extinguished the lights and asked everyone to join hands. The medium first asked the participants to concentrate on trying to move the luminous ball, and then to try in the same way to move the objects on the table.

After leaving the seance room, the participants completed a short questionnaire which asked them about their experience of the seance. During the seances, the slate, bell, book and table remained stationary. Despite this, 27% of participants reported movement of at least one of these. An interesting pattern emerges if the results are analysed by categorizing the participants according to belief. The ball suspended from the ceiling did not move at any time. In total, 76% of disbelievers were certain that it had not moved. In contrast, the same certainty among believers was only 54%. In addition, 40% of believers thought that at least one other object had moved, compared to just 14% of disbelievers. The answers to the question 'Do you believe that you have witnessed any genuine paranormal phenomena?' perhaps provide the most conclusive result with regard to the believer/disbeliever division. One in five believers stated that they thought they had seen genuine phenomena, whereas none of the disbelievers thought so.

The results suggest that although we are all vulnerable to trickery, a belief or expectation of paranormal phenomena during seances may add to that vulnerability.

Further details about the experiment can be found in Wiseman, R., Smith, M. and Wiseman, J. (1995) Eyewitness testimony and the paranormal. *Skeptical Inquirer* **19**, 29–32.

Have 'outs' ready in case something goes wrong

Fake psychics have developed many types of 'outs' to enable them to escape or minimize the damage caused by something not going according to plan during their performance. If the planned method of trickery proves problematic, the skilled fake psychic may be compelled to switch methods during a demonstration. For this reason, fake psychics often consider the ways in which a trick may go wrong, and develop various strategies to switch the method of that trick in order to salvage the demonstration. These are referred to as 'outs'. During a demonstration a fake psychic may find that the controls which are imposed prevent the type of trickery that he intended to employ. If this is the case, the fake psychic may explain away such failure by stating that the conditions of the demonstration were not psi conducive. For example, Burger (1986) notes that if a fake medium is unable to fabricate phenomena, he can state the following:

'Well, my friends, conditions sometimes are just not right for this sort of thing'. You see...there's always an 'out' – a non-humiliating, non-embarrassing, perfectly reasonable (given the folk-accepted

assumptions about seances and how they 'work'), perfectly acceptable out for a failure.

(Burger, 1986: 107)

Alternatively, the observer may have discovered evidence of possible
fraud. The competent fake psychic may have anticipated such a problem, and
created excuses to 'explain away' such evidence. For example, Baggally and
colleagues (1906) report how, during a seance given by the fake medium
Christopher Chambers, a false moustache (used to fabricate materializations
of spirits) was discovered in the seance room. Chambers attempted to explain
away such evidence by telling the sitters that it was difficult to materialize
whiskers and moustaches, so the 'guide' had made a false moustache, and left
it as a souvenir!

The fake psychic may make such excuses part of the 'lore' which govern
his or her psychic ability. For example, Randi (1982) has reported that one
researcher, Dr Lincoln (a specialist in blood group serology and forensic
medicine at London Hospital Medical College), investigated the claims being
made by Filipino psychic surgeons. Lincoln surreptitiously obtained some of
the apparently 'bad tissue' removed from a patient by an alleged psychic
surgeon, and analysed it. Lincoln discovered that the blood sample was from
a cow, and that the 'tumour' was a piece of chicken intestine. However, the
surgeons attempted to explain away this evidence, stating that it was a well-
known fact that 'supernatural forces' convert the tumours into innocuous
substances once they have left the patient's body.

Conclusion

This chapter has presented a brief outline of some of the main psychological
strategems that are used to fake psychic ability. It has discussed how fake
psychics encourage observers to misframe a demonstration, focus their
attention away from trickery and reject normal explanations. In addition, the
chapter has described how good fake psychics will control their performing
conditions and be prepared to explain away potential evidence of fraud.

A full and thorough understanding of psychic fraud would be of benefit for
the public and academics alike. As was noted in the introduction, the public
are often impressed by the performances staged by alleged psychics.
Unfortunately, some fake psychics can use the status and power they derive
from such performances to exert a negative influence over others, and thus
the public would benefit from ways of identifying trickery.

Parapsychologists are also aware that many individuals who claim to be
psychic use magic tricks to fabricate paranormal phenomena. Failure to
detect such fraud can lead to serious consequences, including loss of funding
and negative publicity. For this reason, parapsychologists need to understand
the psychology used by fake psychics in order to avoid being fooled during
their investigations. Unfortunately, most of the previous literature on psychic

fraud has tended to concentrate on the specific tactics of such trickery, usually taking the form of case studies or 'cook books' of methods for fabricating psychic ability. This emphasis is unfortunate, because observers interested in countering psychic fraud may find it more helpful to know about the stratagems of psychic fraud, as opposed to the specific means to achieve it. This is in part because, although there are only a limited number of stratagems involved in the fabrication of psychic abilities, there are an enormous number of methods used to implement those stratagems. Trying to detect these specific tactics may be problematic. First, the literature of magic and psychic fraud is not well organized, and consequently it may be difficult for an observer to discover all of the ways in which an ostensible psychic phenomenon can be fabricated. Second, both magicians and fake psychics are continually inventing new methods by which to fabricate psi. It would be problematic to discover the nature of these innovations, especially as some of this information is not widely disseminated, even within certain sections of the magical and fake psychic communities. It is hoped that the current emphasis on broad strategies rather than distinct techniques will help those scientists who wish to investigate strong psychic claims (see also Wiseman and Morris, 1995a).

Suggested further reading

Lamont, P. and Wiseman, R. (1999) *Magic in theory: an introduction to the theoretical and psychological elements in conjuring.* Hatfield: University of Hertfordshire Press.

Randi, J. (1986) The Project Alpha experiment. Part 1. The first two years. In Frazier, K. (ed.), *Science confronts the paranormal.* Buffalo, NY: Prometheus Books, 158–65.

Smith, M. D. (1993) The effect of belief in the paranormal and prior set upon the observation of a 'psychic' demonstration. *European Journal of Parapsychology* **9**, 24–34.

5 Astrology

David Groome

> *Men at some time are masters of their fates:*
> *The fault, dear Brutus, is not in our stars,*
> *But in ourselves that we are underlings.*
> (William Shakespeare, *The Tragedy of Julius Caesar,* Act I)

Astrology and its significance in modern life

Did you read your horoscope in the newspaper this morning? A survey by
Gallup and Newport (1991) found that 75% of Americans read their horoscope
regularly, and about 25% of the sample were convinced of the truth and accuracy
of astrology. These people would be likely to make real decisions about their
lives, such as whether to get married or when to make a journey, on the basis of
astrological advice. Thus for many people astrology is a serious matter which
has a very real impact on their lives. Even if you are not one of those people, you
could still find your life being affected by it, since other people may make decisions about you on the basis of your birth date. Some employers make use of
astrologers to help them with the selection of new staff, or with decision-making
about the promotion of existing staff. This is not a very common practice in the
UK or the USA, but in other countries it is more widespread – for instance in
France, where it was found that 6% of major employers made use of astrology in
their selection procedures (Smith and Abrahamson, 1992).

It is clear that astrology is fairly widely accepted as a method of classifying
people, and astrologers do have a very real influence over some people's lives.
Consequently, psychologists have become interested in finding out whether
there is any truth in astrology. If astrologers are genuinely able to provide us

with accurate and predictive information about the character and behaviour of individuals simply from a consideration of their time, date and place of birth, then psychologists would obviously want to make use of this approach. On the other hand, if astrology does not offer any valid information, then its use in real-life applications such as staff selection or decision-making should obviously be discouraged. It is for this reason that psychologists have seen a need to investigate the validity of astrologers' claims.

The origins and rationale of astrology

Astrology has been in existence for several thousand years, and was practised in the ancient Egyptian, Greek and Roman civilizations. The people of those early times were greatly preoccupied with cyclic events such as the passing of the seasons, because they had a profound effect on people's lives, notably on their crops and therefore on their very survival. Since the stars and planets were found to move in regular and predictable cycles, they too were assumed to control events on earth. In those early times most things were assumed to be under the control of the gods, and since the stars and planets were assumed to be some kind of manifestation of the gods, it seemed reasonable to suppose that they might influence a person's destiny, especially those stars which were overhead at the moment of birth.

Over the last few centuries astronomers have discovered the true physical nature of the stars and their movements, and as a result we no longer regard the stars and constellations as representing the divine. Astrologers adapted to these new findings by suggesting other theories – for instance, that the stars might exert their influence by their gravitational pull, citing the moon's influence on the tides as a fairly compelling example. However, this theory also lacks plausibility since it has been shown that the gravitational forces exerted by the stars and planets are incredibly small, so that a newborn baby would actually be subjected to greater gravitational forces from nearby objects, such as the midwife.

One of the greatest problems for astrological theory lies in trying to explain why the moment of birth should be of such crucial significance. Thousands of years ago the moment of birth may have seemed to be a defining moment – the moment when life actually begins. Today we know that it is merely a point in the gestation period, whose timing is made all the more arbitrary by the possibility of premature or even induced birth. It is probably fair to say that no one has been able to provide any plausible explanation for the theory that the position of the stars at the moment of birth should influence our character or our destiny (Kelly, 1998). Even so, this does not mean that astrology has been disproved. There are many valid phenomena for which we do not yet have an explanation, and it would be unwise and even unscientific to dismiss them all on that basis. Although astrology lacks a plausible scientific rationale, astrologers claim that it has been found to work for thousands of years, and the possibility remains that they could be right. The rest of this chapter will therefore be concerned with reviewing the research conducted by psychologists to test the claims made for astrology. First, however, we shall consider just what it is that astrologers do in fact claim.

The claims made for astrology

Astrologers believe that a person's character and destiny are affected by the stars, and in particular by the position of the stars at the moment of their birth. Moreover, this influence is believed to be both powerful and lasting. In other words, the position of the stars at the moment when one is born is considered to shape the kind of personality that one will have for the rest of one's life. The best-known form of astrology, and the one that will be most familiar to those who read their horoscope in the newspaper, divides people's birth dates into the 12 signs of the zodiac, which are 12 bands (or 'houses') through which the sun passes during the course of a year. A person's zodiac sign therefore indicates the position of the sun at their particular moment of birth, for which reason these 12 signs are also known as 'sun signs'. This means, for example, that if one is born when the sun is in the house of Pisces, then one's personality will always tend to show Piscean qualities. You probably already know your own sun sign, but if not (or if you want to look up someone else's sign), the generally accepted birth dates for each sun sign are given in Table 5.1 below.

Table 5.1: The 12 sun signs and their associated birth dates

1. Aries	21 March–20 April
2. Taurus	21 April–21 May
3. Gemini	23 May–21 June
4. Cancer	22 June–23 July
5. Leo	24 July–23 August
6. Virgo	24 August–23 September
7. Libra	24 September–23 October
8. Scorpio	24 October–22 November
9. Sagittarius	23 November–21 December
10. Capricorn	22 December–20 January
11. Aquarius	21 January–19 February
12. Pisces	20 February–20 March

The 12 sun signs can also be divided into four main groups as follows:

1. fire signs (Aries, Leo, Sagittarius);
2. earth signs (Taurus, Virgo, Capricorn);
3. air signs (Gemini, Libra, Aquarius);
4. water signs (Cancer, Scorpio, Pisces).

People born under fire signs are considered by astrologers to be fiery in nature, tending to be energetic, optimistic, enthusiastic and aggressive. Those born under earth signs are said to be down-to-earth types who are practical, dependable, logical and cautious. People born under air signs are considered to be light-hearted, friendly, open-minded and very changeable. Finally, those born under water signs are said to be imaginative, artistic, sensitive and emotional. At a more fundamental level these 12 sun signs are divided into two basic groups, known as the 'active' signs (fire and air signs) and the 'passive' signs (earth and water signs). The active signs (also known as 'positive' or 'masculine' signs) are characterized by energetic, impulsive and outgoing tendencies, whereas the passive signs (also known as 'negative' or 'feminine' signs) denote a more restrained, cautious and withdrawn character. In some ways this distinction reflects the contrast between people who are ruled 'by their heart' or 'by their head'. It could also be said to mirror the more scientifically based distinction between 'extravert' and 'introvert' personality types – a dichotomy which is of some interest to psychologists because it is measurable and thus open to scientific testing (see below for a discussion of the findings). It will be noted that the positive and negative signs alternate with one another when the signs are listed in their chronological sequence. The broad groupings of positive/negative signs and earth/water/fire/air signs are regarded as offering only a very general indication of personality, and for a more detailed analysis of the individual it is necessary to consider each sun sign separately, as each is considered to have its own more specific qualities. The characteristics attributed by astrologers to the 12 sun signs are summarized in Table 5.2.

Table 5.2: Characteristics associated with the 12 sun signs

Aries	Assertive, extravert, energetic, determined, ambitious, courageous, impulsive, impatient
Taurus	Reliable, practical, materialistic, persistent, open, honest, generous, sensitive, easily upset
Gemini	Versatile, lively, witty, sparkling, articulate, communicative, changeable, moody, highly strung
Cancer	Sensitive, sentimental, emotional, affectionate, nurturing, shy, timid, hesitant
Leo	Confident, proud, warm, friendly, extravert, loud, courageous, strong-willed, egocentric, bossy
Virgo	Analytical, conscientious, discerning, fussy, perfectionist, critical, quiet, secretive
Libra	Fair-minded, indecisive, imaginative, intuitive, self-indulgent, charming, agreeable, outgoing
Scorpio	Emotional, strong-willed, forceful, courageous, aggressive, reserved, secretive, possessive
Sagittarius	Optimistic, impulsive, outspoken, inquisitive, restless, freedom-seeking, open-minded, unreliable
Capricorn	Cautious, practical, logical, reliable, honest, fair-minded, loyal, capable, reserved, insecure

| Aquarius | Open-minded, imaginative, creative, inquisitive, opinionated, idealistic, outgoing, likes change |
| Pisces | Creative, artistic, intuitive, romantic, unworldly, vague, sensitive, shy, emotional, easily hurt |

The sun sign descriptions listed in Table 5.2 represent a combination of the views of a number of different astrologers, in an attempt to achieve a rough consensus, bearing in mind that different astrologers are not always in complete agreement about the exact qualities associated with each sun sign. The main sources of these descriptions were Harvey and Harvey (1999) and Huntley (2000), and readers seeking a more detailed account of astrology should refer to these books.

Some astrologers are rather scornful of the sun-sign approach, and insist that precise details of not only the date of birth but also the exact time and place of birth are essential for the construction of an accurate astrological chart. However, although it may be argued that a precise horoscope requires precise birth details, there is still general agreement among astrologers that the broad characteristics associated with the 12 sun signs are fundamental to any astrological reading. The outline of sun-sign astrology given here is essentially no more than a brief summary of the main points. This chapter is not intended to be a complete manual of astrology, and the brief list of sun-sign character descriptions given in Table 5.2 is intended merely as a rough guide to basic astrological ideas, sufficient to allow an evaluation of the scientific studies that are discussed below.

Scientific studies of astrology

Astrology is essentially an art rather than a science, based on theories and beliefs that were proposed centuries ago. Modern astrologers claim that these theories have been supported by observations over many years, and that they have stood the test of time. They also claim that their experience confirms that most people do seem to fit the characteristics attributed to their sun sign. However, this is not reliable scientific evidence. In recent years psychologists have introduced a more objective approach to astrology, by devising experiments which enable them to test the claims and predictions of astrology scientifically.

From the psychologist's viewpoint the most interesting claim made for astrology is that it enables us to predict an individual's personality and abilities simply from the time and date of their birth. If this is true, then we might reasonably expect to find measurable differences between people born under different signs, using an objective test of personality such as a questionnaire. Another claim made by astrologers is that an individual's birth sign can be useful in guiding them towards the type of career to which they might be best suited. This theory, too, can be put to the test by finding out whether people born under certain signs really are more successful in particular professions. Finally, some astrologers claim that they can predict future events. Once again, it should be possible to find out whether their predictions actually come true. Can astrologers really live up to their claims? Most of these are testable, and the findings of such tests of astrology will be considered in the remainder of this chapter.

Astrology and personality

There are a number of ways in which we can assess personality, most of which rely on one person making a subjective judgement about another person, as for example in the case of a job interview, or a rating given by a friend or previous employer. Because these subjective judgements are prone to all kinds of errors and biases, psychologists have come to regard questionnaires as a more dependable way of assessing personality, because questionnaires are objective. Each individual answers the same set of questions, and there is a standardized scoring system, so they will obtain exactly the same score regardless of who administers the test. A questionnaire is basically a means of obtaining a self-rating from the person being tested, but in a very controlled and standardized way. Questionnaires are by no means infallible, but they are the best method of measuring personality that is currently available. For this reason, personality questionnaires have been widely used to test the claims of astrology.

In one early study conducted by Mayo and colleagues (Mayo *et al.*, 1978), a total of 2,324 subjects completed the Eysenck Personality Inventory (EPI), a widely used questionnaire that measures both extraversion and emotionality. The birth dates of the subjects were then used to sort them into the 12 signs of the zodiac, in order to determine whether there were any differences in personality scores between one sun sign and another. The hypothesis proposed by astrologer Jeff Mayo (who was one of the authors) was that the 'active' signs (i.e. fire and air) would be more extravert than the 'passive' signs (i.e. earth and water). Remarkably, this is exactly what was found in the study, although the differences between adjacent signs were actually very small. Since the active and passive signs alternate as one works through the calendar, the average E-score (i.e. extraversion) for each of the 12 signs of the zodiac showed an alternating pattern.

At first glance these findings appear to offer some support for astrology, but subsequent studies have failed to replicate them, and in fact none of the more recent studies have found significant personality differences of any kind between any of the sun signs (Jackson and Fiebert, 1980; Saklofske *et al.*, 1981; Shaughnessy *et al.*, 1990; Dahlstrom *et al.*, 1996). An explanation was finally found for the original findings of the study by Mayo *et al.* (1978). Most of the subjects in their experiment were found to have been very knowledgeable about astrology. A person who knows that their personal sun sign is characterized by extraversion may come to believe that they are more extravert than is in fact the case. In other words, they make a 'self-attribution' based on their knowledge of astrology, and this will affect their answers on a questionnaire. Clear evidence that this was indeed the correct explanation was soon obtained. Eysenck and Nias (1982) were able to demonstrate that the small E-score differences between adjacent sun signs completely disappeared when the study was repeated on children, or on adults who had no knowledge of astrology. Clearly, therefore, the effect was associated with the knowledge and expectations of the test subjects. More recent studies have confirmed this finding. Van Rooj (1999) selected 12 sets of traits which fitted the 12 sun signs. Each set consisted of six traits, thus giving a total of 96 trait words. A sample of 422 subjects was asked to select which of those 96 traits best applied to them. Those subjects who had some knowledge of astrology were found to be more likely to select the trait words which fitted their sun sign, but subjects without any knowledge of astrology did not do so. Indeed, for the latter group there were no differences at all between the selections made by subjects representing the different sun signs. Once again the findings offered no support for astrology, but again there was evidence for a self attribution effect. This phenomenon in itself is of considerable significance to the psychologist, providing a cautionary note for all who study the paranormal. Specifically, we can learn that experimental results may be significantly influenced by the knowledge and expectations of the subjects tested. At a more general level, we should be wary of accepting a 'paranormal' explanation for our experimental findings without first eliminating all of the possible 'normal' explanations.

Matching birth charts with test scores

Carlson (1985) took a different approach to evaluating astrology, by testing the ability of astrologers to match up questionnaire data with astrological data for the same person. Carlson tested 116 subjects who knew the precise time, date and location of their birth, which were used to construct their astrological birth chart. The same 116 subjects then completed the California Personality Inventory (CPI), a widely used personality questionnaire which yields a profile consisting of 18 scores. A team of professional astrologers was presented with the birth chart of one subject, and was then given the same person's CPI profile together with two other CPI profiles chosen at random. The astrologers' task was to decide which one of the three CPI profiles matched up with the birth chart. This same procedure would then be repeated for the next subject, and so on throughout the entire sample.

The results clearly demonstrated that the astrologers were unable to match up the charts with their corresponding questionnaire scores beyond the level that would be expected by chance. Moreover, in a further experiment it was found that the subjects themselves were unable to recognize their own astrological personality profile based on their birth charts, again from a choice of three, where the other two choices represented different people but of the same sun sign. Incidentally, the same subjects performed equally poorly in recognizing their own CPI scores, so if the results offer little comfort to astrologers, they offer little more to psychologists. Carlson's study is worth considering in detail because it is one of the most carefully designed astrology trials ever conducted, and there is much to be learned from it. In the first place Carlson used a 'double-blind' design, which means that neither the astrologers nor the experimenters knew which were the correct test profiles, since the identity of the subjects was kept secret until after the experiment had been completed. Carlson also took steps to overcome the criticisms that had been made of many previous studies, by involving professional astrologers in the design and planning of the study. One criticism they made of previous studies was that these had usually grouped all subjects under the 12 sun signs, which the astrologers felt was not sufficiently precise or discriminating. To overcome this criticism, Carlson used the team of professional astrologers to produce individual birth charts for each of the 116 subjects, based on their exact time, date and place of birth. This study was designed and conducted to exacting scientific standards, and its failure to find any support for astrology is consequently all the more significant.

Astrology and profession

Many astrologers offer guidance about the type of job or career to which an individual is suited, and in some countries astrologers are actually employed to help with personnel selection. The claim that astrology can predict career success is therefore a matter of real practical importance, and as such it should be open to testing. One criterion of career success is the achievement of fame in one's chosen occupation. This was the criterion selected by Michel Gauquelin (1955), who looked up the birth dates of 20,000 famous French people in order to determine whether fame in a particular field was associated with any particular sun sign. For example, astrologers have suggested that Scorpios and Leos tend to make good soldiers, Sagittareans make good lawyers, and Capricorns make good politicians. In fact Gauquelin found no support for any of these predictions, nor was there any significant link between sun sign and fame in any particular profession. However, when he looked at the actual time of day when famous people tended to be born, he discovered that there did appear to be some variations from a random distribution. Famous sportsmen and soldiers were more likely to have been born at two particular periods of the day, which roughly corresponded to the times when the planet Mars was either on the rise or at its highest point. There were similar albeit smaller effects for a few other professions.

Gauquelin's findings were seized upon by astrologers as proof of their skills, but this response was hardly justified. Although Gauquelin had found some apparent variations from a random distribution of birth times, they offered no support whatsoever for conventional sun-sign astrology, as Gauquelin himself admitted. Furthermore, the variations were fairly small, and some critics have argued that they may have been nothing more than chance fluctuations, or else a consequence of some social or biological factor which was totally unrelated to astrology. Since Gauquelin's findings have not been replicated by subsequent studies, they have now been largely dismissed by the scientific community.

More recently, another study of the relationship between profession and sun sign has been conducted, this time using a far larger sample of subjects. Alan Smithers (1984) obtained his data from the 1971 British population census, which provided him with birth dates and occupations of no less than 2.3 million British adults, representing roughly 10% of the British working population. For each occupational group Smithers calculated the total number of people born under each sun sign. Examples of his findings for two of the occupational groups (coalminers and secretaries) are shown in Figure 5.1.

(a) Coalminers (n = 19,859)

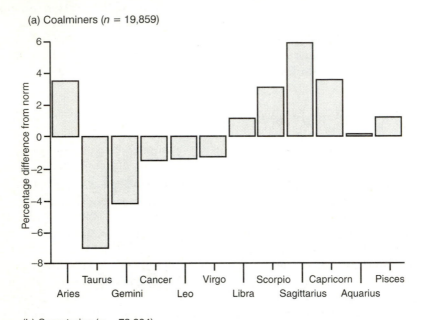

(b) Secretaries (n = 72,884)

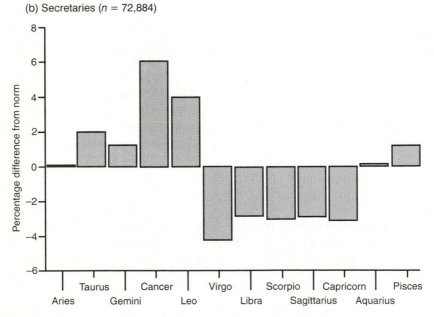

Figure 5.1 Frequency of sun signs.

The distribution of sun signs for the various professional groups caused considerable surprise, since there were some signs which occurred far more frequently than others. Furthermore, these differences reached the level of statistical significance in many cases, and the peak sign varied from one profession to another. These intriguing results raised the question of whether or not these sun-sign peaks might be the result of an astrological influence. In order to answer this question, Smithers recruited a team of 15 professional astrologers, who were asked to predict (without seeing the data, of course) the sun sign which they felt was most likely to predominate in each of the 27 main professions represented in the survey. Unfortunately, the astrologers were unable to agree on their predicted sun sign for most of these professions. In fact, there were only 10 professions for which a consensus could be reached. Their choices for these 10 professions are shown in Table 5.3.

Table 5.3: Sun signs predicted by astrologers as being appropriate for 10 occupations (Smithers, 1984)

1. Author/journalist	Gemini
2. Baker	Taurus
3. Car mechanic	Aries
4. Civil engineer	Capricorn
5. Clerk/cashier	Virgo
6. Coalminer	Scorpio
7. Hairdresser	Libra
8. Optician	Virgo
9. Secretary/typist	Virgo
10. Taylor/dressmaker	Libra

When Smithers examined the actual distribution of sun signs in members of these 10 professions, he found that the astrologers had only guessed the correct sun sign in 1 out of 10 cases. For the profession 'authors and journalists' the astrologers had predicted that Geminis would predominate, and this was indeed the most frequently occurring sign. However, for the other nine professions the most frequently occurring sun sign was not the one suggested by the team of astrologers. A success rate of one 'hit' out of 10 guesses was approximately what would be expected by chance, so there was no evidence that the astrologers had achieved anything better than a random guess.

The sun-sign distributions of the two professions shown in Figure 5.1 are fairly typical of Smithers' data. For coalminers the most frequently occurring sun sign was found to be Sagittarius, but the team of astrologers had predicted that Scorpios would be most likely to take up this occupation. For secretaries the most frequently occurring sign was Cancer, whereas the astrologers had predicted a predominance of Virgos, which in this case actually turned out to be the least frequently occurring sign. Smithers concluded that his data offered no support whatsoever for sun-sign astrology. One argument against this conclusion (Harvey, 1984) was that those employed in a particular profession are not necessarily the people most suited to it, since many people do not actually choose the occupation that they enter. However, if astrological forces really did exert significant control over people's aptitudes, then we would expect some effect to be apparent in their choice of occupation.

Although Smithers' data offered no support for conventional astrology, an explanation was still needed for the non-random distribution of sun signs in many of the occupational samples. As noted above, certain sun signs occurred more frequently than others, often to an extent that reached the level of statistical significance. Moreover, different sun signs predominated in different professions. This phenomenon had been observed in several previous studies, and it had often been cited as evidence of astrological influences, albeit ones which differed from the accepted tenets of astrology. In fact there turned out to be a far simpler explanation.

When seasonal birth trends were examined, some quite large variations were found between different social classes, which fitted in remarkably well with the occupational data. In particular, it was found that for most manual workers there was a pronounced peak in the birth rate in late autumn, whereas for non-manual workers the peak birth rate occurred in the spring (Smithers, 1984; Smithers and Cooper, 1984). If we return to the data shown in Figure 5.1, it is now possible to see these two trends clearly, with an autumn peak for coalminers and a spring peak for secretaries. In fact, these seasonal class trends provide a complete explanation for all of the apparently non-random variations in Smithers' data. This is a finding of considerable significance, because it illustrates how very easily a variation from the norm could be attributed to the stars when in reality it is merely reflecting a social trend. This general principle applies not only to Smithers' data, but probably also to that of other studies. The moral of all this is that we should never attribute a discrepancy in the data to astrological influences without first considering all of the other possible causes.

Predicting future events

Some astrologers claim that they can predict future events from the stars. This certainly does not seem very likely, but a slightly more plausible version of this claim is that although the event itself may not be fated (or indeed inevitable), the stars could still determine the basic conditions which make it more likely to occur. On a similar basis, I could predict that there will be more people in the UK wearing overcoats next winter than there were in midsummer. This prediction is not certain to come true either, but if it does not then many people will be very cold.

One of the reasons why astrologers so often seem to get their predictions right is that confirmation tends to be selective. The predictions that come true tend to be widely publicized, whereas the predictions that fail tend to be forgotten. The famous American astrologer, Jean Dixon, made three major predictions in the mid-1950s. The first was that President Kennedy would die young (he did). The second was that the Russians would reach the moon before the Americans (they did not). The third was that World War III would begin in 1958 (again not so, as far as I recall). Many people were impressed that Dixon had predicted John Kennedy's death, but her less successful predictions went largely unnoticed. In an effort to obtain more scientific evidence about the accuracy of such predictions, Geoffrey Dean (1986) examined the predictions made by a number of professional astrologers for the coming year. In total, 3,000 separate predictions were made, but less than 2% of them actually came true. Furthermore, the few that did come true were mostly the ones that were most vague and most obvious – for example, 'Tension will continue in the Middle East' and 'There will be a tragedy in the Eastern USA next spring'. It would be a reckless person indeed who chose to bet money against either of these events occurring, either in that year or in any other year.

Conclusions

From the studies reviewed above it must be concluded that no evidence has been found to support astrology. This is not quite the same as saying that astrology has been disproved, as the existence of astrology is essentially non-falsifiable. It is impossible to prove that something does not exist or that it is never true, and this is as true for astrology as it is for Santa Claus or the unicorn. Therefore there will always exist a faint possibility that there are some valid astrological effects. However, we can say that any such effects, if they do exist, are so small that they cannot be detected by any known method, so they can probably be safely ignored for all practical purposes. Astrologers have been shown to be unable to predict personality, career aptitude or future events with anything beyond a chance level of accuracy. It would therefore be unwise to base any major decisions on astrological predictions. It can also be stated quite clearly and unequivocally that astrology should never be used in personnel selection, as it has no proven validity as a measure of personality or aptitude. Using astrology for selection purposes would be both unfair and unacceptable.

In reply to these findings, astrologers have argued that the methods employed by psychologists are not suitable for testing astrological claims. It has been argued that personality questionnaires only measure very broad traits, and that they lack the sensitivity required to detect the more subtle aspects of human character that are described by astrology. Astrologers have also protested that one's choice of profession does not imply suitability, since many people do not have much choice in what they do for a living (Harvey, 1984). Psychologists have argued that astrology is formulated in such a way that it can never be subjected to any completely acceptable scientific test, and therefore can never be refuted (Kelly, 1998). For example, astrologers tend to make statements and predictions which are vague and non-specific, so that there will always be some way of reconciling their predictions with actual events.

Given that there is no scientific evidence for astrology, it seems strange that so many people are prepared to believe in it. This apparently irrational belief is of interest to psychologists in its own right, and several studies have been conducted which help to shed some light on the phenomenon. Snyder and Schenkel (1975) asked a large number of people for their time and date of birth, and then presented each of them with a personality description allegedly based on their horoscope. In reality, all of the subjects had been given exactly the same personality description, but despite this most subjects agreed that the profile described them quite accurately. In a similar experiment, French *et al.* (1991) found that most subjects accepted a description of their personality as being 'good' or even 'excellent', despite the fact that it contained both extremes of each personality dimension (e.g. 'at times you are extraverted...while at other times you are introverted'). These experiments illustrate the so-called 'Barnum effect', named after the famous showman who claimed that people will believe anything about themselves so long as it includes 'a little something for everybody'. The trick is to say things with which virtually anyone could identify (e.g. 'you feel at times that some people do not appreciate you enough...'), and to keep the content as vague and non-specific as possible. Astrologers also tend to focus on the more flattering aspects of the reader's personality, so that individuals are being told what they want to hear. If you are not convinced that these tactics really work on people, you might like to try reading through the star columns of your daily newspaper. If you try hard enough you will find some snippets in all 12 zodiac signs which you can recognize in yourself.

One possible motive for accepting the tenets of astrology so uncritically is that most individuals seek both an understanding of their lives and an insight into the minds of other people. The rather limited knowledge offered by psychologists is not enough for many people, who find it frustrating to have no satisfactory framework which enables them to make sense of others. Those who simply cannot accept our incomplete knowledge of people and events will readily grasp at a system such as astrology which promises to give them the insights that they require.

The available scientific evidence offers no support for astrology whatsoever. This being the case, it would be unwise and in many cases unacceptable to use astrology when making real decisions about people's lives (e.g. in personnel selection or career guidance). On the other hand, there is probably no harm in reading your horoscope in the newspaper if you want to, and you may even find that it sometimes comes true.

Suggested further reading

Carlson, S. (1985) A double-blind test of astrology. *Nature* **318**, 419–25.
Kelly, I.W. (1998) Why astrology doesn't work. *Psychological Reports* **82**, 527–46.

An experiment in astrology

This is your opportunity to participate in a research project.

The authors invite you to participate in a study about beliefs in astrological phenomena. Please send your answers to the questions below to the authors. All information received will be treated in the strictest confidence.

Please mark your letter 'Astrology Experiment' and send it to:

Dr D. Groome
Department of Psychology
University of Westminster
309 Regent Street
London W1R 8AL.

1. Please state your date, time (if known) and place of birth.
2. Please state your gender.
3. Please describe your current occupation. If you have been unemployed within the last 6 months, please describe your most recent occupation.
4. Do you believe that the positions of the stars or planets can influence people's personality? (Yes/No)
   If you answered Yes to question 4.
   Using a scale from 0 to 100, please indicate for each of the following how strongly you think they shape personality where (0 = not at all and 100 = completely).
   (a) Genetic make-up.
   (b) Life events (e.g. upbringing, education, friendships, moving house, upsets, etc.).
   (c) Positions of the stars.
   (d) Positions of the planets.
5. Do you believe that the positions of the stars or planets can influence major historical events? (Yes/No)

Thank you for participating.

Part III

Unusual experiences

> *We have been looking for the key to understanding ourselves in the brilliance of the day. But it may not be there.*
>
> (Robert Ornstein)

6 Unconscious awareness

Tony Towell

> *Experience is never limited, and it is never complete; it is an immense sensibility, a kind of huge spider-web of the finest silken threads suspended in the chamber of consciousness, and catching every air-borne particle in its tissue.*
> (Henry James, *Partial Portraits: The Art of Fiction*, 1888)

As elegant as these opening words are, we may well ask whether James incorrectly specified the domain within which the spider's web of experience is woven. Does it really make sense to restrict the sum total of our experiences to that which is consciously discerned? This chapter will address what is currently known about the types of knowledge that we can apprehend whilst remaining oblivious from a conscious perspective that we possess it, as well as considering the types of brain mechanisms (and the contexts) that may make this possible. Non-conscious processing refers to the processing of information without our conscious awareness. It has long been appreciated that we have more information at our disposal than we are capable of attending to, and the assumption is that outside the constraints attention we are engaged in non-conscious passive processing. Historic non-conscious processing has been implicated in psychopathology i of repressed memories (Freud, 1901), and with the advent of r nology and clever experimental paradigms it now seems clea conscious processing can influence our behaviour in a numb ways. In this chapter I shall present evidence from thre namely conscious awareness during anaesthesia, ele markers of non-conscious processing, and blindsight reveal the considerable impact that non-conscio scious experience. I shall also speculate o of non-conscious processing and briefly review some of the theories which attempt to explain consciousness.

Conscious awareness during anaesthesia

Since the introduction of general anaesthesia around 160 years ago there have been numerous reports of conscious awareness during general anaesthesia. For instance, in an experimental study 10 patients were exposed during deep surgical anaesthesia to a suggestion indicative of an anaesthetic crisis: 'Just a moment! I don't like the patient's colour. Much too blue. His (or her) lips are very blue. I'm going to give a little more oxygen.' The anaesthetist then paused, hyperventilated the lungs and then after a moment or two said, 'There, that's better now. You can carry on with the operation.' One month later the patients were hypnotized and regressed to the operation. Four of them were able to reproduce the words spoken by the anaesthetist, four became anxious and awoke from hypnosis, and two did not reproduce the suggestion (Levinson, 1965). The suggestion made during the operation was accompanied by changes in the electroencephalogram (EEG), which has been used in many subsequent studies in an attempt to monitor consciousness during surgery with anaesthesia (see below). The introduction of paralysing muscle relaxants into routine major surgery, together with the trend towards lighter anaesthesia, has increased the risk of unplanned intra-operative 'wakefulness', in which patients may be unable to indicate their predicament to theatre staff because of paralysis. The overall incidence of awareness has been estimated to be between 0.2% and 0.9%, but this is an underestimate for Caesarean section where exact operative details have been reported in 0.9% and 'dreams' in 6.1% of a sample of 3000 women (Lyons and Macdonald, 1991). In a study that aimed to obtain the patients' point of view, the collective experiences of 187 patients who self-reported suffering awareness during general anaesthesia were analysed. Of this sample, 108 patients had undergone Caesarean section, 104 patients had experienced pain and 71 patients had perceived sound (Cobcroft and Forsdick, 1993). However, only 19 cases resulted in litigation or an official complaint.

The isolated forearm technique (IFT) has been used to study awareness ˙uring anaesthesia. During the anaesthetic regime, one forearm is protected ˙n neuromuscular block with a tourniquet, and at intervals the patient is ˙to squeeze the anaesthetist's hand in a specified way. Because of the ˙g practical problems the technique has not been as widely adopted ˙ve been expected. First, the patient's arm is free to interfere with ˙ anaesthetic is light enough for spinal reflexes to be preserved. ˙are documented incidences of false-negative results (i.e. ˙was awake but unable to obey commands). Third it is ˙ify the false-negative and false-positive rates after oper- ˙owerful amnesic properties of the anaesthetic drugs ˙ul during an operation but has no recall after i˙

said not to have suffered awareness but to have experienced amnesic wakefulness. There have even been requests by patients to be awake during surgery. For instance, when one patient became wakeful during a general anaesthetic for Caesarean section, through the IFT she indicated her wish to remain awake. She felt no pain, and after the operation she was able to remember the experience, being told about the delivery and hearing the baby cry (Tunstall, 1980).

Explicit memory refers to the conscious retrieval of prior information, as demonstrated during standard recall and recognition tasks. We have reviewed above several studies that demonstrate the occurrence of explicit memory after surgical procedures. However, the demonstration of implicit memory is more difficult to achieve and it decreases with increasing hypnotic state (Munte *et al.*, 2000). Implicit memory refers to non-conscious retrieval of past experience demonstrated by facilitation in test performance on tasks that do not require intentional recollection of previous experiences. The testing of implicit memory is not straightforward, and it has been assessed by the frequency of story-related free associations to target words from stories read during the anaesthetic, by the reading speed of old (presented during anaesthetic) compared to new stories, and by word stem completion priming tasks. Using these paradigms, limited evidence of implicit memory during anaesthesia has been shown.

Electrophysiological markers of non-conscious processing

The EEG offers a millisecond-by-millisecond analysis of brain function, and it has the highest temporal resolution of any existing functional brain measure. It is a measure of the potential difference between two or more points on the scalp recorded via electrodes. When the EEG is time-locked to a stimulus onset and this is repeated several times, it is possible to record an evoked potential (EP). Evoked potentials have been used extensively as a tool to study early brain processing of stimuli that are thought to be non-conscious. Libet and colleagues demonstrated that electrical stimuli applied directly to the exposed somatosensory cortex of the brain did not cause an immediate sensation. One would expect a verbal report of the sensation within 100 ms of the stimulus, taking into consideration the short conduction time of the sensory pathways (20–30 ms). Stimuli were perceived around 500 ms later, and these researchers therefore concluded that before conscious awareness of a stimulus can occur, it is necessary to achieve a state which they termed neuronal adequacy, which takes up to 500 ms to develop (Libet *et al.*, 1979). More recent work on the somatosensory pathways has suggested a minimum value of 230 ms for the latency of conscious sensation (Gomes, 1998). Whatever the value, it is also clear that there are long readiness potentials occurring about 1–2 s before the initiation of either planned or unplanned movements, which presumably reflect the non-conscious preparation to move. The case of a simple but fast reaction time recorded around 250 ms after the stimulus would be interpreted as a non-conscious and automatic response. Choice reaction times with longer latencies represent conscious processing of stimuli.

Event-related potentials

Event-related potentials (ERPs) are of longer latency than evoked potentials, and are elicited following performance on a task such as target detection. For instance, ERPs can be recorded by presenting the subject with a series of identical stimuli (usually tones known as standards) that are occasionally interspersed by acoustically deviant stimuli (deviants) in an oddball paradigm. The resultant ERPs are classified by polarity and latency such as N1, P2 (i.e. a negative and positive potential recorded at approximately 100 and 200 ms, respectively, following the stimulus). Auditory ERPs to tones have been studied in patients under anaesthesia during surgery with limited success, showing evidence of unconscious auditory processing (van Hoof *et al.*, 1997). More novel paradigms have used syllable stimuli. For instance, in a 7-year-old child undergoing an experimental neurosurgical procedure to treat a severe epileptic aphasia (loss of language), evoked potentials were recorded to syllables /ba/ as standard and /da/ as deviant. These EPs constitute evidence of continued processing of language functions even in an anaesthetized brain (Boyd *et al.*, 1996).

Another approach to the study of non-conscious and preattentive processing has been to use paradigms that are assumed not to require active attention, such as the mismatch negativity (MMN). The latter is a cortical evoked potential that provides an objective measure of the automatic, preattentive processing involved in auditory discrimination and perception (Naatanen, 1995). It is the difference between the standard and deviant responses, and is typically derived by subtracting the standard from the deviant waveforms. The MMN is seen as a negative deflection occurring around 100 ms to 250 ms after the stimulus. It can be elicited in response to any discernible change in a repetitive sound, even in individuals who are unable or unwilling to co-operate. Most of the early work on MMN has presented two tones that differ in frequency, although more recently tones that differ in duration and/or frequency have been used (Liasis *et al.*, 2000). MMN has also been recorded to speech sounds in an attempt to test for higher-order phonemic processing (Liasis *et al.*, 1999). Irrespective of the stimuli used, the MMN is thought to reflect early stages of auditory short-term memory such as the echoic memory. It can be used to probe the functional state of the auditory cortex, and is enhanced in states of higher vigilance, is attenuated by sedative drugs and alcohol, and its presence appears to be a good prognostic indicator of outcome of coma (Kane *et al.*, 1993). MMN amplitudes are also attenuated in patients with Alzheimer's disease, Parkinson's disease and schizophrenia, especially when long inter-stimulus-intervals (ISIs) are used (Naatanen, 1995). Functional brain imaging studies of MMN suggest a primary source in the auditory cortex on the superior surface of the temporal lobe, with some evidence of a later right prefrontal source which may be involved in the switch of attention towards previously unattended auditory stimuli (Alho *et al.*, 1994).

Prepulse inhibition of the startle response

The orbicularis oculi eye muscle blink reflex measures the startle response to sudden, unexpected sensory stimuli. It is thought to reflect neuronal excitability at brainstem levels and it does not involve higher brain functions (Ellrich and Hopf, 1996). It is possible to modulate the blink reflex and startle response by the presentation of a weak stimulus (prepulse) prior to a stronger blink-inducing probe stimulus. The assumption here is that the prepulse stimulus is preattentive and at very short latencies may be non-conscious. It has been widely reported that the timing of the prepulse stimulus can facilitate or inhibit the amplitude and latency of the blink reflex in normal adults (Graham and Murray, 1977). Inhibition of blink amplitude is known as prepulse inhibition (PPI), and it is achieved using prepulse stimuli of around 30–240 ms, being maximal at 120 ms (Graham and Murray, 1977). PPI is thought to alter gains in the neural structure of the reflex path, and therefore to influence reflex amplitudes which can be viewed as a form of sensorimotor gating (Swerdlow *et al.*, 1992). Absent or abnormal PPI has been demonstrated in patients with post-traumatic stress disorder, schizophrenia and schizotypal personality disorder, which is thought to reflect the impaired habituation and increased central nervous system arousal observed in these conditions. However, the position with regard to longer intervals (>120 ms) between the conditioning prepulse and probe stimulus is less clear, because it is possible that additional cognitive/attentional factors may be involved in the modulation of the blink reflex (Davidson and Sutton, 1995). As one would expect, it is also possible to modulate the blink reflex and startle response by both manipulation of attentional direction (Anthony and Graham, 1985) and emotional valence (Lang *et al.*, 1990), and these techniques have been used in the psychophysiological assessment of emotion and psychopathy (Swerdlow *et al.* 1992).

Blindsight

Blindsight is the phenomenon whereby patients with damage to their primary visual cortex retain the ability to detect, localize and discriminate visual stimuli that are presented in areas of their visual field in which they report that they are subjectively blind. Blindsight was first reported by Holmes (1918), and has since been studied extensively by Weiskrantz (1986). It may be that there are two categories of blindsight – one being present in visually guided behaviour in normal subjects as well as brain-damaged patients, while the other is only present following cortical lesions. The evidence of blindsight has been used to argue that we can see things and have perceptual belief without the distinctive visual awareness that accompanies normal sight. In other words, there is a sharp dissociation between visual performance and visual awareness.

Recently it was demonstrated that a blindsight subject recognized facial expressions presented in his blind field. This is consistent with perception of emotional expressions in the absence of awareness in normal subjects, which has been demonstrated in functional neuroimaging experiments and is thought to activate the amygdala via a colliculopulvinar pathway similar to that proposed in blindsight subjects (de Gelder *et al.*, 1999).

A similar analogue to blindsight has been reported in the auditory domain. A patient with total deafness caused by a bilateral lesion in the temporal lobes and central pontine area retained some ability to respond reflexively to sounds. When attempts were made to restore awareness of sound and voluntary responses to sounds by drawing attention to orienting head movements, performance improved and the patient began to respond successfully in a forced-choice paradigm. However, even with confidence in detection and localization of sounds she remained unaware of their meaning (Garde and Cowey, 2000).

Other researchers have pointed out a number of facets of the blindsight phenomenon. These include the proposal that it is very unlikely to result from dissociations within a single system, but rather from the interaction of distinct evolutionary systems. In addition, the spared motor abilities to respond to visual stimuli presented in the blind field indicate that verbal responses of patients result not from degraded vision but from proprioception (i.e. the provision of information about the position, location and orientation of the body), and furthermore that above chance correct verbal responses, being forced guesses are not tentative beliefs (Vision, 1998). That is, awareness does not provide evidence of activation of belief systems.

The notion of blindsight has also been challenged by evidence that patients with occipital damage and contralateral field defects showed residual islands of vision which may be associated with spared neural tissue. However, this cannot be the case where blindsight is detected in patients who underwent the resection or disconnection of an entire cerebral hemisphere (Faubert *et al.*, 1999).

Clinical implications

Therapeutic issues

The assumption that memories which patients cannot consciously recollect may contribute to psychopathology is not new, and it was central to Freud's work on neuroses (Freud, 1901). The repressed memory hypothesis, especially in relation to early childhood abuse, is a highly controversial area.

However, it does appear to be an attractive theory, in part supported by the experimental evidence reviewed here, that it is possible for early experiences to form repressed memories that could modulate psychopathology.

Some researchers have attempted to exploit the treatment potential of non-conscious processing. Successful desensitization of agoraphobic patients has been achieved by presenting films of the phobic stimuli at levels which did not permit conscious perception, and this was experienced as less stressful, with lower measures of muscle tension, sweating, shaking, and breathing difficulties compared to patients receiving supraliminal (i.e. conscious) exposure (Lee and Tyrer, 1980). Another therapeutic strategy that has arisen from the non-conscious processing literature has been subliminal psychody-namic activation. The most common therapeutic phrase in this research has been a 4 ms exposure of 'Mommy and I are one', which is claimed, for example, to facilitate desensitization procedures (Silverman et al., 1974). Impairment of dart-throwing has been achieved by the 4 ms presentation of the phrase 'Beating dad is wrong', and it improved following presentation of the phrase 'Beating dad is OK' (Silverman et al., 1978). Although some of these claims have been replicated, many have not, and it may well be worth screening subjects beforehand in a similar way to that used in hypnosis in order to identify which subjects are susceptible to these manipulations and which are not.

There is also evidence of preattentive priming on stereotypes among thera-pists. Following priming of African-American stereotypes or neutral words using 80-ms flash words, therapist participants were exposed to a vignette introducing Mr X, a patient referred for treatment, and were asked to rate him on various dimensions. Participants who had been primed with stereotyped words rated Mr X significantly less favourably on hostility-related attributes than did participants who had been primed with neutral words (Abreu, 1999).

Understanding neurological and psychological disorders

Non-conscious processing of information has been used to study a number of neurological and psychological disorders, and a few examples are given below. For instance, patients with Alzheimer's disease often show impairment of certain forms of implicit memory, such as word-stem completion priming. In a PET study comparing Alzheimer's disease with controls, the word-stem completion priming deficit was located in the right occipital cortex (area 19) (Backman et al., 2000). By contrast, schizophrenic patients appear to have damaged explicit memory but spared implicit memory (Keri et al., 2000). It has also been demonstrated that low self-esteem and over-concern about body shape and weight are associated in highly restrained eaters at a non-conscious level. After priming low self-esteem, the accessibility of subliminally presented body shape and weight stimuli was increased, but not with a supral-iminal lexical decision task (Meijboom et al., 1999). Panic disorder patients are able to learn panic-related material better than controls on a memory task that requires classification of panic-related words in order to test conceptual information-processing in implicit memory. No memory bias was found on a memory task that tested intentional encoding and explicit recall of panic-related vs. non-panic-related sentences (Neidhardt and Florin, 1999).

Non-conscious processing of information has also been used to explain the development of post-traumatic stress disorder in traumatic brain injury (these are thought to be mutually incompatible disorders) in individuals who are subsequently amnesic, but who were conscious at the time of the traumatic episode. Another pathway to post-traumatic stress disorder may be through subsequent appraisal processes in individuals who were unconscious during the traumatic episode but none the less processed information at a non-conscious level (Joseph and Masterson, 1999).

Explaining consciousness

To explain non-conscious processing we must first be able to explain consciousness. Although there is nothing we are more familiar with than conscious experience, it is proving very difficult to explain. Beyond explaining how information is discriminated, integrated and reported, it is necessary to explain how information is experienced. In other words, there is an explanatory gap between functions and experience. The explanatory methods of cognitive science and neuroscience promise to explain the performance of cognitive functions – and just that. For instance, the neurobiological theory of consciousness advanced by Crick and Koch (1990) identifies 35–75 Hz neural oscillations in the cerebral cortex that those authors claim form the basis of consciousness. These oscillations are correlated with awareness in a number of different sensory modalities, and may activate the mechanisms of working memory. Binding of information between and within modalities is achieved through synchronized oscillations of neuronal groups representing the information. Thus when two pieces of information are to be bound together, the relevant neural groups will oscillate with the same frequency and phase. Ultimately this theory might lead to an explanation of how perceived information is bound and stored in memory for use by later processing, but does it tell us how this information is experienced?

Another theory, namely the cognitive theory of consciousness of Baars (1988), assumes that the contents of consciousness are contained in a global workspace – a central processor that is used to mediate communication between a number of specialized non-conscious processors. When the specialized processors need to communicate information to the rest of the system, they send this information to the workspace, which is then accessible to all of the other processors. This has good explanatory power for non-conscious cognitive functioning, but is ultimately a theory of cognitive accessibility and information-processing, and not of experience itself. In fact, the theories of Crick and Koch, of Baars and of Libet and many others make the case that the most direct physical correlate of consciousness is awareness – the process by which information is made directly available for global control. Given the coherence between consciousness and awareness, it is thus probable that a mechanism of awareness will be a correlate of conscious experience. The search is now on for a theory of consciousness that has biological, psychological and social levels of explanatory power.

Summary and conclusions

The evidence presented so far points to the impact that non-conscious processing can have on our conscious experience. The work on non-conscious processing during anaesthesia is highly disturbing, as we do not know what the impact of this will be on later psychological health. New methods equivalent to the isolated forearm technique are needed to monitor non-conscious processing and awareness during anaesthesia. The newer electrophysiological markers offer some hope in this field, and they can also be used to test hypotheses about consciousness by measuring the high-frequency oscillations that are thought to accompany perception. The blindsight literature offers a biological explanation of non-conscious processing through the processing of information via a primitive subcortical pathway that avoids the primary visual areas. This is strong evidence that high-level subcortical processing influences higher cognitive functions.

The clinical implications of non-conscious processing have not been well studied due to lack of experimental control as well as ethical constraints. However, there are serious concerns for the development of future psychopathology, and strategies need to be developed to address these. Finally, contemporary theories of consciousness are centred on a cognitive science view of information-processing and have limited explanatory power. Theories are needed that have explanatory power across biological, psychological and social domains. In view of this, the areas of affective neuroscience and neurophilosophy have the potential to make a major contribution to our understanding of conscious experience.

Suggested further reading

Kane, N., Curry, S., Butler, S. and Cummins, B. (1993) Electrophysiological indicator of awakening from coma. *Lancet* **341**, 688.

Tunstall, M. E. (1980) On being aware by request. A mother's unplanned request during the course of a Caesarian section under general anaesthesia. *British Journal of Anaesthesia* **52**, 1049–51.

Vision, G. (1998) Blindsight and philosophy. *Philosophical Psychology* **11**, 137–59.

7 Dreams

Antje Mueller and Ron Roberts

> *Put out that light,*
> *Put out that bright light,*
> *Let darkness fall.*
> *Put out that day,*
> *It is the time for nightfall.*
>
> (Stevie Smith, *The Light of Life*)

Introduction

Few topics in psychology have aroused as much interest as dreams, and yet it is true that there are few which illustrate better the gulf that exists between what lay people expect from psychology and what scientific psychology delivers to them. Reasons for this chasm are not hard to find. Freud's theory of dreams (Freud, 1900) was to a large extent the foundation upon which psychoanalysis was constructed. One consequence of this was that the popularization of psychoanalytical thinking led to the widespread dissemination of ideas about dreaming which had and continue to have little empirical evidence in their favour. The negative impact of this was perhaps heightened by the reluctance of analysts to challenge the Freudian orthodoxy on our night life. Jung maintained that his own ideas in no way constituted a theory of dreams (see also Rycroft, 1981), while Freud himself famously remarked that 'The analysts behave as though they had no more to say about dreams, as though there was nothing more to be added to the theory of dreams'.

The unscientific nature of psychoanalytical speculation, coupled with the rise of behaviourism in the 1920s and 1930s meant that dreaming largely remained outside the province of scientific enquiry until the advent of the rapid eye movement (REM) monitoring procedures pioneered by Dement and Kleitman (1957). These established a correlation between the reporting of dreams and the presence of REM sleep – a phase of sleep characterized by a stage 1 EEG (low voltage, mixed frequency; 2–7 cycles per second), bursts of rapid eye movements and suppressed EMG (muscle activity from the neck and chin region reaches its lowest level throughout the night during this phase; see Figure 7.1) (Rechtschaffen and Kales, 1971). Shortly afterwards, Foulkes (1960) found that dream reporting could also be obtained, although less frequently, from the other so-called non-REM stages of sleep. It is now established that dreaming occurs not only in the lighter levels of non-REM sleep, but also during the hypnagogic period of sleep onset, and in 'daydreaming' as studied under laboratory conditions (Foulkes, 1993). However, dream reports from REM sleep have maintained their position as the principal focus of empirical investigations of dreaming. Thus if we wish to enquire into features of dream life, such as lucid dreaming and telepathy, which have attracted the interest of parapsychologists as well as lay people, then we must first become acquainted with what these investigations tell us about the nature of dreaming. In this chapter we shall therefore examine contemporary neurophysiological and cognitive theories of dream production, as well as evolutionary and developmental perspectives. We shall then proceed to discuss both lucid dreaming and the evidence for the existence of extra-sensory perception in dreaming.

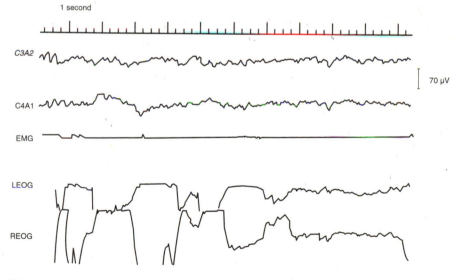

Key
C3A2, EEG left hemisphere; C4A1, EEG right hemisphere; LEOG, left eye movement; REOG, right eye movement; EMG, electromyogram.

Figure 7.1 Electrophysiological characteristics of REM sleep.

Theories of dreaming

Scientists use the term 'dreaming' to refer to any image, thought or feeling attributed by the dreamer to a preawakening state. Their emergence, development and transformation appear to be strongly constrained by both biology and culture (Foulkes, 1993). The experience of dreaming and its recall vary both between and within individuals, as well as across cultures (Von Grunebaum and Callois, 1966). The reporting of dreams in terms of quantity, frequency, quality and type is culturally and historically universal, appearing during ontogeny at about three years of age (see below).

Dream research (both clinical and experimental), faced with the dual tasks of explaining the significance and mode of production of dreams has reached a point of historical hiatus. Research on the psychophysiology of the REM state, once heralded as the means of testing Freudian dream theory and settling controversies about the relationship between mind and brain, is now confronted with disillusionment and lack of funding (Hunt, 1989). It is true that much has been learned about the unique physiology of REM sleep, but the expectation that understanding REM will explain dreaming has been shaken by the growing realization that dreaming involves far more than the specific conditions of the REM state.

Neurophysiological theories

Our current understanding of dreams, their meaning and how to analyse them are all intertwined. In this first section we shall consider dreams as the result of physiological processes occurring in the brain. Both Hobson and McCarely's hypothesis of activation synthesis (Hobson and McCarely, 1977; Hobson, 1988; Mamelak and Hobson; 1989) and Crick and Mitchison's neural network model (Crick and Mitchison, 1983, 1986) attempt to derive the phenomenology of dreams from a knowledge of brain functioning, although each reaches somewhat different conclusions.

Hobson and McCarely followed Freud in spirit by adhering to a belief in the isomorphism of mind and body. However, rather than dreaming being primarily a psychological necessity – a response that deals with occasional neurotic impulses during sleep – they argued that it is in fact the outcome of an automatic, preprogrammed neural process. In their model they describe a functional organization of the brain that is unique to sleep (Hobson and McCarely, 1977; Hobson, 1988; Mamelak and Hobson, 1989). REM sleep, with its characteristic features of cortical arousal, body muscle paralysis, bursts of eye movements and other 'phasic' phenomena, results from activation of the 'REM-ON' area located in the pontine reticular formation (a structure at the apex of the spinal column at the base of the brain). This REM-ON area also cuts off most sensory stimuli from the brain. That is to say, in the absence of motor output and sensory input, the brain is virtually isolated during REM sleep.

Although the motor cortex is highly active, generating activity which would normally result in movement, these commands do not reach the muscles that control the limbs, but are 'switched off' at a relay station at the top of the spinal column, so that we are effectively paralysed during REM sleep. This explains the loss of tone in the neck muscles under the chin, which is used as one of the defining characteristics of REM sleep (Empson, 1989). Parts of the brain that control emotions or store memories may also be activated in the REM state. This may occur either directly via the REM-ON system, or indirectly via activation of motor or sensory systems. In this way, aspects of the person's personality become part of the dream.

When these simultaneously activated systems are synthesized, dreaming is experienced. This process of synthesis is no different to what occurs in the waking brain. Available sensory and motor information is integrated with information on the current affective state, and memories of similar experiences and related meanings are then drawn on in order to understand it (Moorcroft, 1993). During wakefulness the sensory information is strongly related to our motor information and seems 'normal. Our perceptions usually flow smoothly because the sequence of sensory/motor activations follow one another in an orderly fashion. However, when we are asleep, what is activated at one moment may not be related to what is activated next, and thus bizarre shifts occur in dreams. Thus the difference between dreaming and being awake, is not the process of activation and synthesis, but the source of the activation – more external (and sequential) when awake, and almost entirely internal (somewhat random) when in REM sleep.

Hobson and McCarely do not maintain that dreams are meaningless. After all, motivational states, memories, emotions, and even the movement patterns that are activated in an individual's brain during REM are products of their experiences and personality. Although the synthesis of these elements may be unusual, the elements themselves are not. Furthermore, personal characteristics determine the meaning that is attached to a specific stimulus regardless of whether its source is external (as in waking) or internal (as in dreaming). Thus dreams may contain information that is relevant and revealing about the person. However, Hobson and McCarely warn that this should not be carried too far, because it does not follow that each aspect has a symbolic meaning (Moorcroft, 1993). They also suggest that dream sleep may have a functional role in some aspects of the learning process (Empson, 1989).

Crick and Mitchison (the former having attempted one of those risky shifts from a Nobel Prize in microbiology to computer simulations of the mind) have developed a theory that relies in part on the activation-synthesis hypothesis. Crick and Mitchison (1983, 1986) bestow on the activation-synthesis process a function that results in a startling conclusion – we dream in order to forget! They reason as follows. REM sleep is almost universal among mammals. The prevention of REM sleep by selective awakenings results in increased amounts on recovery, as if what had been missed was then being 'made up', suggesting that not only does this sleep stage have its own drive mechanism, but also it may have an important function. However, since most dreams go unremembered, this function either has nothing to do with dreaming or, if dreaming is essential to the process, the forgetting must be a necessary part of it. According to these researchers the random pontine activity that stimulates the cortex during REM sleep has the function of erasing memories, which in their terminology have become 'parasitic'. These are interpretations which, whatever their origin, have no place in our latest view of the world, and are redundant but persistent. This accumulation of nonsense is expressed in dreams which are created only in order to be forgotten (Empson, 1989). According to this theory, recurrent dreams occur because various things (e.g. the dreamer's name being called or certain meaningful contents of the dream) tend to awaken sleepers. The awakened sleeper then attends to the content of the dream, which reinstalls it in memory. This strengthened memory is more likely to be activated again in the future, thereby repeating the process. Thus the theory implies that when we recall our dreams we are defeating their function of weakening associations, and therefore attempts to increase dream remembrance should be avoided (Moorcroft, 1993)!

However, the key assumption in the above models – that dreaming is both meaningless and functionless because it is random – appears to be incorrect. The fact that dreaming is not random at the levels of content or process (e.g. Roberts, 1988) simply reinforces the point that randomness has nothing to do with the meaningfulness or functional significance of dreaming. Crick and Mitchison (1983, 1986) have been widely misunderstood as having proposed an anti-functional theory of dreaming. Although their theory has not received wide support and appears to be incorrect in detail, it has stimulated a considerable rethinking of the functional significance of dreaming, unfortunately providing a rationale for cognitive scientists to eschew an interest in dreaming, except as a means of minimizing error (Foulkes, 1993).

Cognitive theories

Foulkes (1982a, 1985) developed a cognitive psychological model of REM dream production based on the substantive assumption that speech and dreaming may share some common production routines. Thus Foulkes views dreams as originating in the processes of 'inner speech,' a type of psycholinguistics which ends not in speech production but in an alternative secondary visual medium. The core of dream formation now becomes its narrative structure. The dream, for Foulkes, is syntax imposed on diffuse memory activations, but without any underlying intentional semantics. The model proposes that, in the absence of specific semantic intentions to convey unitary messages, the momentary organization and sequential coherence of the dream are largely attributable to syntactic mechanisms. The investment of the latter is not so much in saying any particular thing as in insuring that whatever is said is literally and thematically comprehensible. If the model is correct in proposing a verbal syntactic–lexical–phonetic process that supplies inputs to image generation, then a useful focus for recovering the 'essence' of the dream would lie in applying linguistic analytical schemes, rather than seeking to uncover a single underlying interpretation (Foulkes, 1978).

Although Foulkes considers that a cognitive account of the dream process is independent of any specific psychophysiology of REM sleep, he agrees with Hobson and McCarely (1977) that condensation, sudden displacements and scene changes, and fantastic sensory intrusions and transformations are 'peripherally induced aberrations in the central organization of dreaming' (Foulkes 1982a: 328). Again, the most striking 'cognitive' feature of dreaming is its narrative cohesion, the visual surface of the dream being only a secondary expression of deeper syntax. Thus bizarreness in dreams suggests an error that demonstrates the purely formal or deep-structure aspects of cognition, and is without semantic significance.

Agreeing with Hobson and McCarely (1977), but substituting a central initiation for their peripheral brainstem activation, Foulkes argues that dreams are formed from a 'diffuse mnemic activation' of multiple recent and long-term memory stores that occurs more or less randomly and without any semantic or communicative intent. The organization imposed on these diffusely and simultaneously activated memories is syntactic, not semantic. The result is the structured storyline of the dream, which includes whatever peripherally induced disorientations it could not fully subordinate. The dream lacks semantics and communicative intentionality because, unlike language, we cannot check the result against a preliminary plan or intention. Unlike language, dreams are simply imposed.

Another important cognitive question with regard to dreams is why they are so easily forgotten! A satisfactory answer to this may provide important clues to the process of dream formation. Cognitive psychology conceives of attention as a limited resource, and of any process that cannot deal with all of its potential inputs as an attention-demanding process (Klatzky, 1980). As Foulkes describes dream production, the construction of semantic-syntactic structures for the diverse meaning representations that are active during REM sleep must be highly demanding of attention. This might reduce the attentional allocation to processes that might otherwise be expected to accompany REM dreaming. Thus during REM sleep one is unable to elaborate the current content by interpreting it within the context of the larger body of one's knowledge. Such elaboration is generally lacking during dreaming, and that absence would lead to poor recall.

The substantial differences in the frameworks adopted in neurophysiological and psychological approaches to dream research stand as an object lesson on the necessary relativity and perspectivism of the human sciences. Indeed, part of the promise of the cognitive era in modern psychology is its potential to address the full extent of human symbolic capacity, as reflected in the multiple 'frames of mind' through which human intelligence is manifested – namely language, imagery, interpersonal relationships, mathematics and aesthetics (Hunt, 1989). It would be tragic for a 'cognitive science' to remain focused only on those computational and technical capacities that can be functionally circumscribed and computer simulated – thereby making psychology the unwitting architect of a science of mind that is excessively restricted to the artificial and domesticated.

Evolutionary aspects

The assumption that dreaming has an adaptive value is shared by most researchers in the field (Montangero, 1993, cited in Cavallero and Foulkes, 1993). Indeed, how could biological evolution and ontogenetic development have produced a psychological activity which is so regular and frequent, if it had no adaptive value? One approach to this question has been to consider whether dreaming contributes to learning and memory consolidation. A coherent picture is slowly emerging, based on both animal (Smith and Lapp, 1986; Smith and Kelly, 1988) and human studies of REM sleep (McGrath and Cohen, 1978; Smith, 1993, cited in Moffitt et al., 1993). It has been observed in studies that if the training task is sufficiently difficult, both animals and humans exhibit post-training increases in REM sleep above normal levels. These increases can occur shortly after the end of the training session, but have also been observed many hours and days after the end of training. Furthermore, if REM deprivation is applied at times after training that coincide with these expected increases in REM sleep, learning-memory deficits occur. However, in humans not all learning seems to be sensitive to REM deprivation. Material that is relatively simple, and with which the subject is already familiar, does not appear to be affected. Rather it appears to be material that requires learning and understanding of new, previously unfamiliar concepts that is vulnerable to REM deprivation (Smith, 1993). The suggestion that REM sleep is crucial to memory consolidation is strengthened by the observation that one of the major physiological features of the REM state is the presence of activated hippocampal theta rhythms, which are also characteristically present in wakefulness during exposure to emotionally arousing stimuli (Winson, 1985). The hippocampus itself has already been implicated in the establishment of long-term memories. The question of course remains as to whether it is the non-conscious processes of REM sleep or the conscious experiencing of dreaming during REM sleep that is crucial.

The possibility that dreams provide material for the solution of problems is a fascinating one. Smith (1993) notes that the success of the dream incubation process is markedly enhanced by choosing only those subjects who have already had a dream about the problem they wish to dream more about. The timing of the more valuable dreams is several days later, when a much more helpful, comprehensive dream is often experienced. Consistent with the idea that processing and problem-solving are in progress, the first dream might indicate that the problem has been taken seriously and occupied enough of the individual's time to become a major learning experience. The processing of this experience continues, and of course it could be enhanced by further thought and related daytime activity. Dreams about events that have been in process for some time would be expected to contain more complete solutions or perspectives than the initial dreams about newly considered problems (Smith, 1993). This idea has already been suggested by Cartwright (1977), who in a series of studies found that the first dreams of the night appeared to be directly related to current anxieties, whereas later dreams incorporated emotionally associated experiences from the past, and final dreams of the night appeared to involve contemplation of possible problem solutions. Thus both within a single night and over a period of days there would appear to be continual processing. This processing would take place whether the individual remembered his or her dreams or not.

Griffin (1997) unites these twin strands of learning and problem-solving in his evolutionary account of the function of dreaming. He proposes that REM sleep originally evolved to programme instinctive behaviour, which he describes as genetically anticipated patterns of stimulation. This mechanism for processing anticipated stimulation is then used in later life to deactivate emotionally arousing schemata arising from unresolved problems by representing them as sensory analogues. This is consistent with the increased autonomic arousal and drive expression which follow REM deprivation.

Children's dreams

Our understanding of children's dreams owes a debt to the pioneering work of David Foulkes at the Georgia Mental Health Institute in Atlanta. This began in the late 1960s and continued into the mid-1980s, consisting of major longitudinal and cross-sectional studies. The first longitudinal study utilized sampling of dream reports in both laboratory and home settings (Foulkes, 1982b). Over a 5-year period (1968–1973), a younger group of 7 boys and 7 girls (initially aged 2–4 years) and an older group of 8 boys and 8 girls (initially aged 8–11 years) each spent nine nights per year in a sleep laboratory. In addition, new groups of 7 to 9 year-olds were brought in for comparison with the younger group in the fifth year of the study. A subsequent cross-sectional study involved a total of 80 children, with equal numbers of boys and girls aged 5, 6, 7 and 8 years. Each child spent a total of three non-consecutive nights in the laboratory.

The main aim of these studies was to describe changes in the nature of children's dreams over time, which with the sampling procedure that was used enabled comparisons of dreams from children aged from 2 to 15 years. As well as recording dream reports, a range of additional information was sought, including the results of objective and projective personality tests, behavioural ratings collected from teachers, parents' attitudes to child-rearing, IQ and a variety of cognitive skill tests. During the first three summers observational data was also collected from younger children's play groups. The principal findings were as follows.

First, a comparison of home- and laboratory-collected dreams – which controlled for the method of dream-sampling – found no evidence of bias in the content of laboratory dreams (Foulkes, 1999). Because of their much greater frequency, these laboratory dreams can therefore be said to constitute a more representative sample of children's dream life than those collected at home. In fact, the laboratory dreams of the young children, like those of adults, were found to be mundane and realistic. This result is strikingly at odds with the predictions of Freudian theory, which would lead one to expect the unrestrained expression of instinctual wants and needs, due to the poorly developed egos of children being unable to hold at bay the strivings of the id (Foulkes, 1979).

Secondly, and perhaps more importantly, the dreams unfolding over the course of childhood revealed a clear developmental pattern. This is summarized in Table 7.1. Initially, children's REM periods appear to be 'largely empty of those organized experiences we call dreams' (Foulkes, 1982b: 94). Between the ages of 3 and 5 years they reported REM dreams on average only about 15% of the time, increasing to an average of 31% between the ages of 5 and 7 years (Foulkes, 1999). As children do report dreams between 3 and 9 years of age, they become progressively longer and more complex. For example, whereas at age 3–5 years the reported imagery is generally static (movement verbs are rarely expressed in the reports), by the age of 5–7 years there is a more 'movie-like' quality to the reports, although movement is more often employed by non-self characters. At age 7–9 years, REM reports contained movie-like sequences with the dreamers as actively participating characters. Average recall was now in the region of 43%. By age 9–11 years, report rates approximating to adult levels (79% vs. 85–90% in adults) were found. It was highly significant that neither the rates of dream recall nor the formal properties of the dreams were predicted by personality, behavioural or observational variables, or by verbal skills such as vocabulary or the ability to describe static and moving pictures from memory. However, they were relatively well predicted by visuo-spatial skills, particularly the block-design sub-test of the Wechsler IQ test and other tests involving mental rotation.

Table 7.1: Stages in REM dream development (after Foulkes, 1999)

	0	1	2	3
Approximate age (years)	0–3	3–5	5–7	7–9
Dream frequency	None	Rare	Rare, but increasing	Relatively frequent
Dream form		Isolated event	Simple event sequence	Complex narrative
Dream imagery		Static	Kinematic	Kinematic
Active self-participation		Absent	Absent	Present

What do these findings tell us about dreaming? One inescapable conclusion is that the ability to dream in a form which we as adults would recognize as dreaming is a cognitive accomplishment which takes some years for us to master, and it is linked to our capacity for conscious self-representation – the ability to form in consciousness a representation of our own self. As such it must depend on the evolution and prior development of other cognitive systems (Foulkes, 1993) and it is unlikely to exist in all but the higher mammals in any form that we would recognize as constituting dreaming. The issue of conscious self-representation leads us now to consider a special class of dreams in which the ability to be consciously aware of oneself is not merely a cognitive prerequisite to dream construction, but is actively expressed in real time within it. We speak of course of the lucid dream.

Lucid dreaming

To be aware that what one is experiencing is a dream is a relatively infrequent event. Only around one person in five in the USA reports lucidly dreaming at least once a month (LaBerge and Gackenbach, 2000), during which period on average one would expect between 120 and 150 dreams to have occurred. However, estimates of lifetime prevalence are much higher, ranging from 47% to 100% of the population (Snyder and Gackenbach, 1988). It has been argued that a more precise definition of lucidity is required which includes not just cognizance of dreaming, but also control over the dream material and awareness of memories from waking life. However, such calls have been largely rejected. Compared to non-lucid dreams, lucid dreams have been found to involve higher levels of control, more positive emotions, more scene changes and more physical activity, and to be more vivid (Levitan and LaBerge, 1993).

Of the other well-documented unusual experiences, out-of-body experiences (OBEs) (see Green, 1968), near-death experiences (NDEs) (see Chapter 11) and alien abduction experiences (see Chapter 8) are considered to be related. Three dimensions have been suggested which enable these states to be distinguished, namely a recognition that one's current state of consciousness is different to the usual waking state, a particular belief system to make sense of the experience, and a set of goals which are either concerned with inducing the experience or which delineate the actions/exercises which can be pursued from within the experience. LaBerge and Gackenbach (2000) note that if one compares lucid dreams and OBEs, for example, they share a recognition of the divergent nature of the current state of consciousness, but they differ with regard to the other two dimensions.

Lucidity is often triggered by an awareness of some anomaly in the setting or content of the dream – something which is more likely to be appreciated by people who are familiar with what their dreams are like. Unsurprisingly, therefore, lucid dreams are more often reported by high-frequency dream recallers. In addition, a number of demographic factors have been associated with lucid dreaming. Younger rather than older people, single rather than married people and first-born offspring have all been found to report them more often. No consistent differences have been found with regard to gender, occupation or educational level. With regard to personality attributes there is some evidence that risk-taking, an androgynous sex-role identity and field independence (the extent to which one's perceptions are independent of environmental cues) are associated with the frequency of lucid dreaming, with some (albeit inconsistent) results pointing towards an association with introversion (Snyder and Gackenbach, 1988).

As yet, no simple theoretical framework has been found that can adequately account for these individual differences.

Laboratory studies have found that lucid dreams are more likely to occur late in the sleep cycle. This is perhaps because as the night progresses REM dreams become longer, thus affording the sleeper more time to become aware of cues in the dream which might trigger lucidity. Studies conducted in the laboratory have enabled a unique perspective on dreaming to be obtained by searching for correspondences between events and actions in the dream world and observable events in the real world (Schatzman *et al.*, 1988). This has been made possible by using subjects who are able to signal lucidity in the REM state by making a prearranged sequence of volitional eye movements and forearm muscle contractions.

In a series of experiments, Alan Worsley, an experienced lucid dreamer, first signalled lucidity and then proceeded to carry out a variety of pre-planned action sequences in his dreams. These included counting while writing the numbers on a suitable surface, moving his finger from side to side and following it with his eyes, drawing large triangles on a wall while watching his hand move, and picking up and putting down a shoulder bag. The majority of these attempts showed clear EMG (muscle) or EOG (eye movement) activity in the region of the body corresponding to that moved in the dream. Such correspondences seem to suggest rather strongly that enacted events in the dream world – even in the lucid dream world – unfold not in some transcendental realm but in the workings of the brain and central nervous system. Whether the context in which the dreams unfold can be similarly correlated with specific neural events in the brain is less clear. However, further 'thought' experiments conducted by Worsley whilst in a lucid state may shed some light here as well.

In these experiments Worsley set out to perform a range of activities in order to assess their impact on the dreamed world. These included reading (the longer the material, the more difficult it is to achieve), flicking a light switch in a darkened room (it invariably fails, but gradually increasing brightness is much easier) and firing a gun (a click rather than a bang ensues) (Worsley, 1988). The outcomes of these experiments provide clues as to how and why the dream process operates as it does. In fact Worsley noted the lack of conscious control he had over kick-starting the generation of dream imagery (in any sensory modality) as opposed to modifying it. This is consistent with what we know about the construction of waking perception. For example, if we consider vision, it has long been known that optically stabilizing an image by attaching a small mirror to a contact lens on the eye leads to progressive degradation of the image, and eventually results in a blank homogenous visual field (Gregory, 1977). During wakefulness a continuous stream of new visual information conveyed via saccadic movements of the eyes ensures that this degradation does not occur. In the absence of continuous visual input from the environment during sleep, the dreaming brain also seems to require a compensatory mechanism to inhibit adaptation to the internally generated images. The continuous generation of new imagery fulfils this function and ensures that adaptation to existing visual scenarios cannot take place. Difficulty in reading, thus occurs because images cannot persist for a sufficient length of time before new ones are automatically generated. Sudden effects in other sensory modalities (the gun firing) similarly require an ongoing prior stream of activity to be present. The inability to generate instantly complete, fully formed scenarios similarly informs us that constructing dreams takes time, and that there is an upper limit to the processing power available to do this.

The pivotal role of self-consciousness in lucid dreaming has led some researchers to argue that it should be regarded as a state distinct from ordinary REM sleep – principally because the main characteristics used to define sleep have been the absence of self-consciousness and a lack of awareness and communication with the external world. Further reflection is certainly required here. Unusual and striking as lucid dreams are, the evidence we have reviewed above provides no grounds for believing that there is anything intrinsically mystical about them. Certainly there may well be applications of lucid dreaming to psychotherapeutic practice and the enhancement of general psychological well-being, but we have no reason to doubt that the phenomenon can eventually be accommodated within existing scientific frameworks. If, on the other hand, the presence of extra-sensory perception (ESP) during dreaming can be reliably demonstrated, our current assumptions about the world would face a serious challenge.

Paranormal cognition and dreaming

Dreams have always been a source of wonder and fascination, and from earliest times they have been linked with the supernatural and the sacred. Many esoteric notions have survived to the present day, chief among them being the belief that dreaming permits the boundaries of space and time to be transcended, the future to be divined and the experiences of others to be shared through ESP (see Box 7.1). Certainly the internal logic of remembered dreams seems to defy common sense, entertaining possibilities beyond the bounds of rational thought. Indeed, lucid dreams aside, ordinary reflective self-consciousness – on which much of our everyday rationality and understanding of the world is predicated – appears to be suspended in dreams (Roberts, 1981). This provides fertile ground for the imagination. The big question is whether there is an evidential basis for believing the mind to be capable of paranormal feats during sleep.

> **Box 7.1: Belief in paranormal dreams**
>
> Psychologists have considered ways in which belief in the paranormal ability of dreams can be realized in the absence of real telepathic or precognitive dreams. In one scenario, increased tolerance of ambiguity, coupled with a prior belief in the paranormal, can lead people to believe that accidental hits (i.e. meaningful coincidences between dreamed and real life events) are in fact precognitive dreams (Houran and Lange, 1998). How can this actually occur? If we suppose that the probability of a meaningful coincidence in the

absence of ESP is quite low, let us say for the sake of argument that the probability of this is 1 in every 40,000 dreams. Given that on average we produce around 4–5 dreams per night, then we should expect such a meaningful coincidence to occur once every 8,000–10,000 nights, or approximately once every 22 to 28 years. In a dreaming lifespan of roughly 65 years we might expect two or three such dreams – rare indeed. However, given the population of the UK (the adult working population is approximately 20 million), we might expect by chance some 500 people each night to be dreaming such meaningful coincidences. Given the personal impact that such an event might have, we could expect word of it to spread quickly. In a culture where belief in paranormal phenomena is already established, this would receive continuous support from the misattribution of coincident dreams to the paranormal.

Instances of spontaneous telepathic dreams have been reported for many years, and have been described by many psychotherapists impressed by the material revealed to them by their patients. In fact, a large proportion of all spontaneous cases of ESP have been reported during dreams (Van de Castle, 1977). Foremost among these accounts are themes of death or danger, which seem to provide a rationale for the existence of a primitive extrasensory system that is sensitive to threat. However, impressive as these reports sometimes appear to be, they lack the firm foundation that can be provided by a rigorous, repeatable demonstration of the phenomenon under properly controlled conditions, and moreover where the chances of the phenomenon being explained away on the basis of coincidence can be precisely estimated. Fortunately, during the 1960s a group of researchers at the Maimonides Medical Centre in New York undertook a series of experiments which directly sought to establish whether paranormal cognition could occur in dreaming (Ullmann *et al.*, 1989). These experiments have been the subject of continuing controversy. In total 15 separate investigations (including two pilot studies) were undertaken. The basic experimental paradigm followed by the researchers in eight of the studies is described in Box 7.2, and the results obtained from the eight studies which utilized this protocol are summarized in Table 7.2. For details of the other studies in the series, readers are advised to consult Ullman *et al.* (1989).

Box 7.2: A typical telepathic dream experiment

A percipient subject is first of all prepared for physiological monitoring of sleep. At the beginning of each period of REM sleep, an experimenter in an adjacent room signals to an agent situated at a different nearby location. The agent then concentrates on a randomly chosen picture target (selected only when the agent was physically alone in the room), and he or she attempts to communicate this to the dreamer. Near the end of each REM period the dreamer is awakened in order to report any dream material (this procedure itself is not straightforward, as astute questioning may be needed to elicit the dream material; see Winget and Kramer, 1979). Following awakening in the morning, the dreamer is asked for his or her impressions of what the target might have been. This is conducted by an interviewer who is blind to the identity of the target. Subsequently, several judges independently attempt to match the dream reports to the targets. In the Maimonides studies this was done by ranking the possible targets from most to least correspondence with the dreams. A hit would be designated if the correct target received a mean rank from the judges which fell in the upper half (e.g. with 12 possible targets a hit would require a mean rank of 6 or less).

Table 7.2: Pooled results from eight ESP dream studies (Child, 1985; Ullman *et al.*, 1989)

Study Number	Judges		Dreamers	
	Hits	Misses	Hits	Misses
1	7	5	10	2
2	5	2	6	1
3	4	8	9	3
4	6	2	6	2
5	3	5	5	3
6	8	0		
7	6	2	8	0
8	53	14	42	22

A relatively simple way for statisticians to analyse this data is to use the theory of probability (see Chapter 2) to decide whether the number of hits exceeds what would be expected by chance. If the results obtained from all eight studies are combined, we can see that the judges scored 92 hits and 38 misses (a success rate of 67.6%) and the dreamers scored 86 hits and 33 misses (a success rate of 72.3%), both higher than the rate of 50% that would be expected by chance. The probability of such a result occurring by chance is less than 1 in 7000 for the judges, and less than 1 in 100,000 for the dreamers. These values are way beyond what is normally required to convince scientists that something interesting is going on.

Child (1985) raised the question of why the Maimonides results received so little attention from the wider psychological community. One reason is undoubtedly the failure by researchers in two other studies to replicate the findings, although the procedures followed in one of these studies may have prevented significant results from being obtained (Van de Castle, 1989). However, it must be said that it is difficult to take issue with Child's view that the research community is biased. It really is not plausible to attempt to explain these results away on the basis of either chance, sensory leakage or fraud. At the same time, the original authors have overstated their case. One swallow does not make a spring.

The effort involved in running a sleep laboratory has (perhaps unfortunately) meant that parapsychologists now resort to more accessible (and inexpensive) procedures such as the ganzfeld to investigate psi (see Chapter 10). However, the strength of effects reported in the Maimonides research presents a strong case for the continuation of work on psi and dreaming. Recent work by Sherwood *et al.* (2000) supports this view. In their study, dream reports from the previous night were assessed with regard to their correspondence with four video clips, one of which had been randomly selected as the target and shown repeatedly from 3.00–4.30 a.m. at a remote location. They found that judges were able to successfully match the dreams with the target 43% of the time, a result which significantly exceeded the expected chance rate of 25%.

Before closing this chapter we would like to raise one further issue for consideration. The existence of psi has been postulated as an evolutionarily primitive communication system. However, if it should be found that dreaming is a particularly conducive state for psi, this would raise the questions of how and why such a 'primitive system' came to be associated with a state which is contingent on higher cognitive processes and dependent on the ability to form conscious self-representations. Would it then make sense to regard psi as primitive?

Suggested further reading

Foulkes, D. (1999) *Children's dreaming and the development of consciousness.* Cambridge, MA: Harvard University Press.

Gackenbach, J. and LaBerge, S.(eds) (1988) *Conscious mind, sleeping brain: perspectives on lucid dreaming.* London: Plenum Press.

Ullman, M., Krippner, S. and Vaughan, A. (1989) *Dream telepathy: experiments in nocturnal ESP*, 2nd edn. London: McFarland and Company.

An experiment in dream precognition

This is your opportunity to participate in a research project.

The authors have sealed four postcard-sized pictures in an envelope. Each of these will be numbered. Approximately six months after publication of this book, one of these pictures will be randomly selected to serve as the target.

You are invited to submit the transcript of one dream which you believe will enable the target to be identified. To be eligible for inclusion in the project, this must be sealed in a separate envelope within the main envelope that is addressed to the authors (see Chapter 5, p. 73). At the end of your report you may add any general impressions or associations you have with regard to the dream.

You must also submit a covering letter providing answers to the following questions (all information received will be treated in the strictest confidence).

Please mark your letter 'Dream Experiment'.

1. What was your age last birthday?
2. Please state your gender.
3. Please describe your current occupation. If you have been unemployed within the last 6 months, please describe your most recent occupation.

4. In general how would you rate your health?

(a)	(b)	(c)	(d)	(e)
Excellent	Very good	Good	Fair	Poor
[ ]	[ ]	[ ]	[ ]	[ ]

5. Please rate how confident you are that the dream you have submitted identifies the target.

(a)	(b)	(c)	(d)
Not at all confident	Not very confident	Quite confident	Very confident
[ ]	[ ]	[ ]	[ ]

6. Have you recently been feeling unhappy and depressed?

(a)	(b)	(c)	(d)
Not at all	No more than usual	Rather more than usual	Much more than usual
[ ]	[ ]	[ ]	[ ]

7. Please indicate your level of agreement with the following statements according to the following scale:

   1 = strongly agree, 2 = agree, 3 = neither agree nor disagree, 4 = disagree, 5 = strongly disagree.

   (a) The soul continues to exist although the body may die.

   (b) Psychokinesis, the movement of objects by psychic powers, does occur.

   (c) ESP exists.

   (d) Some people have an unexplained ability to predict the future.

   (e) Your mind or soul can leave your body and travel (astral projection).

   (f) There is a God.

After six months, two independent judges who are blind to the identity of the chosen target will assess the correspondence between each of the possible targets and the dreams submitted.

Thank you for participating.

8 Alien abductions

Christopher C. French

> *Q: Is there intelligent life on Earth?*
> *A: Yes, but I'm only visiting.*
>
> (Graffiti, traditional)

Introduction

Box 8.1: Exercise

Before reading this chapter, set aside some time to write a story in which you are abducted by aliens. Take as much time as you like, and try to include as much detail as you can. Describe both the sequence of events and your reactions to them. Do not read on until you have completed your story.

For those of you who took the time to write the story, perhaps it went something like this. You are driving along in a car at night on a lonely isolated road when you notice a strange light in the sky. At first you do not pay it much attention, but gradually you begin to suspect that the light is actually following your car – and it does not look like any conventional aircraft! As the craft gets nearer to your car, you can see that it is definitely circular in shape. You cannot believe your eyes, as your fear turns to terror. You put your foot on the accelerator, in a desperate attempt to outrun the alien craft. A brilliant beam of light engulfs your car and the engine suddenly cuts out completely. You lose consciousness.

The next thing you remember is that you are lying on your back on some kind of examination table inside a circular, dimly lit room. A number of beings, at least three or four, are standing around you. You try to look closely at their faces, but the whole scene has a strange dream-like quality, as if you had been drugged. The beings appear to be humanoid and around 4 feet tall. They have hairless grey skin and very large heads. Their piercing eyes are large and black, but they have very small noses and mouths. One of them looks you directly in the eye and telepathically tells you not to be afraid. You realize that you are naked and that you cannot move. The aliens carry out a detailed examination using strange pieces of equipment which cause you intense, almost unbearable pain. You cannot scream. They seem to be particularly interested in your genitals and use a probe to extract ova or sperm. Finally, they insert some kind of small metallic implant into your brain by forcing a long probe up your nose. Your mind is filled with such intense pain that you again lose consciousness. When you wake up you are back inside your car beside the road. You look at your watch. Over three hours have passed since you first noticed the strange light in the sky.

Your story is unlikely to have been identical to the one above, but the chances are that there were some strong similarities. In your version, perhaps you were lying in your bed at home when you suddenly became aware that the alien beings had somehow entered despite the fact that all of the doors and windows were locked? Perhaps the aliens somehow transported you back into bed after their unearthly medical interventions. Although there are many variations on the basic theme, alien abduction experiences typically include capture by aliens and medical examination. These days, the aliens most often correspond to the description provided above. Other common although not universal elements in the scenario include tours of the aliens' ship, trips to other planets, and the receipt of messages to humanity, often involving dire warnings of the future destruction of the planet through pollution or nuclear war unless we mend our ways.

It is not difficult to see why most people would come up with a story that is similar to that described above. This standard abduction scenario is now well known in our culture thanks to widespread media coverage such as that provided by the popular series *The X Files* or the films *Communion* and *Fire in the Sky*. Why should psychologists be interested in such flights of fancy? The answer is because thousands of people world-wide are convinced that they really have undergone abduction by aliens, and they have clear and vivid memories to back them up. The media have reported many such claims as fact (indeed, the two films referred to above are both based on allegedly true stories). Knowledge of the typical alien abduction experience has therefore been provided through books, documentaries, chat shows and newspaper and magazine articles. Coverage is typically uncritical and sensationalized. It is tempting to say that you would have to have been living on Mars to have escaped exposure to claims of alien abduction, but presumably it might be a hot topic there, too.

It is extremely difficult to estimate just how many people believe them-selves to be the victims of alien abduction. Thomas E. Bullard (1994) surveyed just 13 UFO investigators and found that between them they had details of around 1700 cases. Whitley Strieber (1987) claims to have received almost a quarter of a million letters from individuals reporting alien contact. It is often claimed that many more people have experienced alien abduction than actually report it. There are at least two reasons for this. First, they may reasonably conclude that they will not be believed, and that they will be ridiculed if they tell others of their bizarre experience. A second and more sinister reason has also been proposed. It is claimed that the aliens are able to directly erase the abductees' memories of the events in question. It is further argued that hypnosis is effective in releasing the victims' memories from this alien-induced amnesic block.

In an attempt to circumvent these problems, Budd Hopkins, David Jacobs and Ron Westrum (1992) took an indirect approach. A random sample of 5947 American adults was surveyed by the Roper organization with regard to unusual experiences. Included in the items presented were five which Hopkins and colleagues claimed were often indicative of an alien abduction experience. The respondents were asked the question 'How often has this experience happened to you?' for the following experiences (the percentages in parentheses indicate the proportion of subjects who said it had happened at least once):

1. waking up paralysed with a sense of a strange person or presence or something else in the room (18%);
2. experiencing a period of time of an hour or longer in which you were apparently lost, but you could not remember why, or where you had been (13%);
3. feeling that you were actually flying through the air, although you did not know how or why (10%);
4. seeing unusual lights or balls of light in a room without knowing what was causing them or where they came from (8%);
5. finding puzzling scars on your body, and neither you nor anyone else remembering how you received them or where (8%).

According to Hopkins *et al.* (1992), if a person answered 'yes' to four or five of the above items (and 'no' to an item allegedly measuring suggestibility), they had probably been abducted by aliens. Of the original sample, 119 individuals (2%) met these criteria. Extrapolating their findings to the American adult population as a whole, these authors claimed that 3.7 million Americans had probably been abducted by aliens. This figure received wide media coverage. Now, if you are the estimated one out of every 50 readers who has answered 'yes' to four or five of the above items, don't panic! The Roper poll gives us much valid and interesting data concerning the frequency of unusual experiences, but the interpretation of the data by Hopkins *et al.* (1992) is totally unjustified. As Philip J. Klass (1997a) points out, if 3.7 million Americans had been abducted between 1961 (when the first such case is alleged to have occurred) and the time when the survey was conducted, the rate of abductions must be about 340 Americans *every single day of the year!* Such a figure must stretch credulity even among those who accept that aliens have the amazing ability to abduct individuals from busy cities without any independent witnesses ever seeing them! Furthermore, as Stires (1997) points out, Hopkins and colleagues made no attempt to validate the claimed association between the unusual experiences and alien abduction. However, even if we accept for the sake of argument that alien abductions really do occur and that they do tend to be associated with the experiences reported above, the interpretation of Hopkins and colleagues is fatally flawed in terms of logic, as has been pointed out by Devereux and Brookesmith (1997). Those authors quote veteran market researcher James R. Adams:

> What [Hopkins *et al.*] are saying is, if abduction, then all these other symptoms. All these other symptoms (or some of them, even), therefore abduction. This does not follow; the logic has what is known as an 'undistributed middle'. If it is raining, the pavements are wet. But the fact that the pavements are wet does not mean that it is raining.
>
> (Devereux and Brookesmith, 1997:170)

Consider another example. Death is associated with lack of movement, failure to respond to mild distracting stimuli, and inability to solve simple problems. By the logic of Hopkins and colleagues, anyone who exhibits these three 'symptoms' is probably dead – whereas common sense suggests that they may be asleep or just watching television!

Amazingly, some estimates are even higher. For example, Jacobs (1992) has suggested that as many as 15 million Americans may have been abducted. Although the number of people with conscious memories of alien abduction experiences is less than this by many orders of magnitude, it is still the case that many thousands of individuals throughout the world *are* convinced that they have indeed been taken aboard an alien spaceship against their will, and have there undergone painful medical procedures. What are we to make of such claims?

Are alien abduction claims deliberate hoaxes?

Uninformed sceptics often assert that those who claim to have been abducted by aliens are simply making the whole thing up. The assumed motivations are both financial (in that claimants may make money from books and film rights) and social (in that they may become celebrated cases and appear at conferences and on talk shows). One or two of the most celebrated cases may indeed be deliberate hoaxes. For example, Philip J. Klass (1989) has raised serious doubts about the sincerity of Travis Walton, whose alleged abduction was the subject of the feature film *Fire in the Sky*. In general, however, even sceptics accept that most claimants are sincere in their beliefs.

Are people really being abducted by aliens?

If the claimants are not deliberately lying, should we then conclude that they really have experienced contact with extraterrestrial beings? Those who support the 'ET hypothesis' would answer this question in the affirmative. Furthermore, they would argue that we need not rely solely on the testimony of abductees to support the ET hypothesis. However, much of the evidence presented in support of the hypothesis is weaker than the uncritical media coverage typically implies. Unfortunately, a full discussion of such evidence is beyond the scope of the current chapter. The reader is referred to Bartholomew and Howard (1998), Brookesmith (1996), Devereux and Brookesmith (1997), Frazier *et al.* (1997), Klass (1983) and Sheaffer (1998) for excellent critical considerations of the ET hypothesis in general. Even such celebrated cases as the alleged crash of a flying saucer and recovery of alien bodies near Roswell, New Mexico, in 1947 are in fact based on incredibly weak evidence (see Klass, 1997b; Korff, 1997).

Much of the general evidence relating to the ET hypothesis is not relevant to the specific topic of alien abductions, but some of it is. In particular, it is often claimed that the reason behind the abductions is that the aliens are engaged in a sinister cross-breeding project, the aim of which is to produce hybrid creatures which are half-human, half-alien (e.g. Hopkins, 1987; Jacobs, 1998). In support of this hypothesis, it is claimed that female abductees often report becoming pregnant even though they may have no memory of having engaged in normal sexual activity. After a few months their pregnancies mysteriously 'disappear'. It is claimed that the aliens have abducted the victim initially to artificially inseminate her, and have then abducted her again to remove the hybrid embryo or fetus some months later before it has reached full term. Some abductees even claim that they have been briefly re-united with their typically pale and sickly offspring during subsequent abductions. Many researchers claim to have several records of so-called missing embryo/fetus syndrome in their files. Despite this, not one convincing documented case has ever been presented to the wider scientific community. There are many reasons why a woman might think she was pregnant when in fact she was not, but the available evidence in no way supports the idea of an alien cross-breeding programme (Randle *et al.*, 1999).

It is also claimed that aliens frequently implant small devices into the bodies of their unwilling victims. The exact purpose of these implants is unclear, although it has been suggested that they may enable the aliens to track the abductees in order to facilitate future abductions. If such an implant could be retrieved and subjected to scientific analysis, the results could potentially provide strong support for the ET hypothesis. If it were concluded that the implant was of alien design and construction, the implications would be staggering. Unfortunately, however, this has not been found to be the case. Despite repeated promises from UFO researchers, no such implant has ever been produced. On occasion, items which abductees sincerely believed to have been alien implants have been analysed, but they have all turned out to have mundane explanations. For example, in one case an 'implant' turned out to be a dental filling (Blackmore, 1999)! More often the implant is mysteriously spirited away (presumably by the aliens?) before proper analysis can take place.

Overall, therefore, there is no strong evidence to support the ET hypothesis. This does not mean that there is no intelligent life elsewhere in the universe. Indeed, many of those who express the gravest doubts about the notion that aliens are regularly abducting earthlings are at the forefront of the search for extraterrestrial intelligence by other means (e.g. Sagan, 1997). Many scientists believe that, given the sheer immensity of the universe, it is highly probable that intelligent life does exist elsewhere, but the evidence that earth has already been contacted by aliens is far from convincing. Therefore, if abductees are not deliberately lying, and yet they are almost certainly wrong in thinking that they really have had a close encounter with aliens, how are we to account for their claims?

Psychological approaches to alien abduction

Psychopathology

As was stated earlier, media coverage of abduction claims is usually uncritical and sensationalized, but when a sceptical approach is taken there is often an unfortunate tendency to ridicule the claimant. The implication is that 'normal' people do not claim to be abducted by aliens, and those that do are therefore 'crazy'. Does the available evidence support this view?

Although limited, the available data suggest that psychopathology is no more common among those claiming alien contact than among the general population. Spanos *et al.* (1993) compared people who had reported intense UFO-related experiences (e.g. missing time, or seeing and communicating with aliens) with those who had reported non-intense experiences (e.g. seeing unidentified lights in the sky) and with control groups who did not report any UFO experiences. The groups were not found to differ on objective measures of psychopathology (although it is unclear how many actual abductees were included in the study). Parnell and Sprinkle (1990) administered the widely used Minnesota Multiphasic Personality Inventory (MMPI) to 225 individuals who reported UFO experiences, and concluded that there was no evidence for serious psychopathology in the group as a whole. The conclusion that abductees do not show higher levels of psychopathology was also reached by Bloecher *et al.* (1985) with regard to nine abductees, by Rodeghier *et al.* (1991) with regard to 27 abductees, and by Mack (1994) for his 76 abduction cases. Bartholomew and colleagues analysed the biographies of 152 subjects who reported temporary abductions or repeated UFO contact, and found them to be 'remarkably devoid of a history of mental illness' (Bartholomew *et al.*, 1991:215).

Having said that, the data do suggest that abductees are not psychologically representative of the population as a whole. In the study by Parnell and

Sprinkle (1990), those individuals who claimed to have communicated with aliens 'had a significantly greater tendency to endorse unusual feelings, thoughts and attitudes; to be suspicious or distrustful; and to be creative, imaginative, or possibly have schizoid tendencies' (Parnell and Sprinkle, 1990:45). Rodeghier *et al.* (1991) reported relatively high levels of loneliness and unhappiness, and poorer sleep patterns. Mack (1994) reported high levels of childhood trauma, as did Ring and Rosing (1990a). The latter investigators also reported that, as children, abductees were more sensitive to 'non-ordinary realities'. Stone-Carmen (1994) found that a staggering 57% of her sample of abductees reported suicide attempts.

Fantasy-proneness

One personality characteristic in particular has been the focus of research in this area, namely fantasy-proneness. This construct was first described by Wilson and Barber (1983) in a study investigating hypnotic susceptibility. Fantasy-prone personalities are typically excellent hypnotic subjects, but are also noted for their profound fantasy lives. They spend a great deal of time fantasizing, and they report that when they imagine something it appears to them 'as real as real'. The hallucinatory nature of their fantasies leads to frequent confusion between imagination and reality. In line with typical abductees, these individuals often report paranormal experiences of various types, and they often believe themselves to be psychic. In Wilson and Barber's sample of 22 fantasizers, no less than 13 individuals reported having experienced false pregnancies. Despite the fact that they report having been heavily engaged in fantasy since early childhood, they usually lead perfectly ordinary lives, and often keep their fantasy lives secret. Interestingly, a much higher incidence of childhood trauma was reported by the fantasy-prone group compared to a control sample. In general, this picture has been supported by subsequent investigations (e.g. Lynn and Rhue, 1988).

Given the overlap between the characteristics of the fantasy-prone personality and the typical abductee, it is often asserted that fantasy-proneness plays an important role in explaining reports of alien abduction (e.g. Nickell, 1997; Bartholomew and Howard, 1998). To the sceptical mind, it is precisely those people who cannot easily distinguish between fantasy and reality who one might expect to report abductions by aliens. However, the evidence supporting such a link is at best mixed (Newman and Baumeister, 1996a,b; Newman, 1997; Appelle *et al.*, 2000). Studies which present data supporting the link tend to be based on biographical analysis. For example, Bartholomew *et al.* (1991) reported that 132 of the 152 cases whom they analysed showed one or more major characteristics of fantasy-proneness (for full details see Bartholomew and Howard, 1998). The characteristics noted include reports of psychic phenomena, out-of-body experiences, healing, apparitions, hypnotic susceptibility and physiological effects. A similar analysis by Nickell (1997) of the 13 cases presented in detail by Mack (1994) concluded that all of these cases displayed several major characteristics of fantasy-proneness.

However, attempts to test the hypothesis directly by measuring fantasy-proneness with questionnaires have not provided much support. Spanos *et al.* (1993) found no significant differences in scores on the Inventory of Childhood Memories and Imaginings (the most commonly used measure of fantasy-proneness) between individuals who had reported UFO experiences and control groups. However, among those who had reported UFO experiences, the intensity of the experience was correlated with their scores on the questionnaire. Rodeghier *et al.* (1991) found no evidence for higher levels of fantasy-proneness among a group of abductees using the same measure. Ring and Rosing (1990a), using a measure which they devised themselves, reported that their UFO reporters (including abductees) were not in general more fantasy-prone than controls. However, as reported above, as children they were more sensitive to 'non-ordinary realities'. This was assessed by endorsement of such items as those dealing with being 'aware of non-physical beings' during wakefulness and seeing 'into "other realities" that others didn't seem to be aware of'. In the absence of any objective proof that these 'non-physical beings' and 'other realities' actually exist, it is obviously a matter of opinion as to whether or not one accepts that these individuals are not fantasy-prone. To many observers it would appear parsimonious to assume that these subjects may have such high levels of fantasy-proneness that they were simply unaware that they were confusing fantasy with reality. It should also be borne in mind that abductees may well be reluctant to endorse items which indicate that they often confuse reality and imagination, given the extraordinary nature of their claims.

Dissociation and childhood trauma

The fantasy-proneness hypothesis is also indirectly supported by studies which show that some factors which are known to correlate significantly with fantasy-proneness appear to be associated with abduction claims. For example, the level of dissociative tendencies (i.e. the tendency for some mental processes temporarily to 'split off' from the normal stream of consciousness) has been shown to be higher in abductees than in non-abductees by Powers (1994). The tendency to dissociate is known to be associated with a history of childhood trauma (including sexual, physical and emotional abuse), which in turn is correlated with fantasy-proneness. It has been argued (e.g. Lynn *et al.*, 1997) that the tendency to dissociate is a defensive mechanism which allows traumatized children to escape the unbearable reality of their lives by entering a more acceptable fantasy world.

It is therefore of considerable interest that several studies have found the incidence of reported childhood trauma to be higher among abductees than among the general population. The work of Mack (1994) and Ring and Rosing (1990a) has already been referred to in this context. Research into paranormal belief in general shows that it is associated with both fantasy-proneness and reported childhood trauma (e.g. Irwin, 1991; 1993, Lawrence *et al.*, 1995). There are several possible interpretations of this reported pattern of correlations. The first one, favoured by many parapsychologists and UFO investigators, is that individuals are more likely to experience genuine paranormal events (including being abducted by aliens) if they have a particular type of psychological make-up, corresponding to that found in fantasy-prone individuals. The second possible interpretation is that described in the previous paragraph, whereby fantasy-proneness and dissociative tendencies develop as a coping mechanism in individuals who are trying to deal with unbearable childhood trauma. The result is people who find it difficult to distinguish fantasy from reality and who report imagined paranormal events (including UFO abductions) as objective reality. The third possibility is that certain adults are fantasy-prone for currently unspecified reasons, and that their reports of childhood trauma are as much a product of their imaginations as their reports of paranormal events. At this point in time, it is not possible to offer a definitive verdict with regard to these possible interpretations.

Hypnotic regression

Another major factor which has been implicated in explaining the formation of false memories of alien abduction is the use of hypnotic regression by investigators such as Budd Hopkins (1987) and John Mack (1994). The public image of hypnotic regression, based on fictional accounts and pseudoscientific documentaries, is that it provides an almost magical key to unlock repressed memories. However, the reality is that hypnotic techniques often encourage the production of fantasy-based narratives which are then believed in as if they were memories of events which actually occurred (e.g. Spanos, 1996). Not surprisingly, therefore, the widespread use of hypnosis has been condemned by many critics as being responsible for the formation of false memories of alien abduction rather than the retrieval of repressed memories of actual events (Klass, 1989; Baker, 1992; 1997a,b; Newman and Baumeister, 1996a,b, 1998; Randle *et al.*, 1999). It should be noted that hypnosis is by no means the only way in which false memories can be formed (see Box 8.2).

Thomas E. Bullard (1989) claimed that hypnosis was employed in about 70% of the 'well-investigated, high-quality cases' in his sample. He presented an interesting analysis of these accounts – for example, comparing abduction accounts produced under hypnosis with those recalled naturally. He claimed that they were very similar, providing evidence (he claimed) that hypnosis had not influenced the retrieval of memories. However, it is unclear why Bullard would expect a large difference between hypnotically and non-hypnotically produced accounts in terms of their actual content. The content of the accounts is likely to reflect a complex mix of culturally derived knowledge, personal idiosyncrasies of the claimant (e.g. the incorporation of dream fragments) and the subtle (or sometimes not so subtle) influence of the hypnotist in question, when hypnotic regression had been employed. The result is likely to be accounts that are generally quite similar, but which represent variations on a theme. This is precisely what Bullard's analysis shows. Hypnosis is likely to have the effect of increasing the abductee's conviction that the apparent recollections are memories of real events, but it will not necessarily have a huge influence on the content of those memories.

Box 8.2: False memories in other contexts

The topic of 'false memory syndrome' is one of the most hotly debated within psychology (Loftus, 1993; Loftus and Ketcham, 1994; Lindsay and Read, 1995; Ofshe and Watters, 1995; Pendergrast, 1996; Lynn and McConkey, 1998). Current interest has been largely generated by the huge numbers of people apparently recovering repressed memories of childhood sexual abuse upon entering therapy, despite having no conscious recollection of such abuse prior to therapy. Alleged abusers were often being tried and convicted purely on the basis of such recovered memories. Needless to say, the validity of these apparent memories is of crucial importance. Following extensive research by experimental psychologists, it is now clear that it is much easier to induce false memories for whole episodes which never actually occurred than anyone would have believed a decade ago. Hypnosis and other related 'memory enhancement' techniques (e.g. guided imagery) have been shown to be risky in this context. It is unclear what proportion of 'recovered' memories of sexual abuse are false, but the potential dangers are now recognized, and all major psychological and psychiatric associations have issued guidelines in order to minimize the risks.

Although recovered memories of apparent childhood sexual abuse appear plausible to therapists, given the appallingly high levels of childhood sexual abuse within our society, other types of false memories lack such initial plausibility. These include memories of satanic ritual abuse involving claims of bizarre and extreme abuse, including perverted sexual acts, devil worship, human and animal sacrifice and cannibalism (e.g. Loftus, 1993; Ofshe and Watters, 1995; Pendergrast, 1996; Bottoms and Davis, 1997). No forensic evidence has been presented to support such claims (La Fontaine, 1998). Hypnotic regression to 'past lives' appears to provide a means whereby subjects produce fantasy-based accounts which they often believe are real memories of prior incarnations (Spanos, 1996; Mills and Lynn, 2000). The content of hypnotically produced past-life memories is strongly influenced by the subject's expectations and beliefs about reincarnation (Spanos et al., 1994). On some occasions, hypnotic subjects produce detailed, historically accurate information about their past lives. However, further analysis (Harris, 1986; Baker, 1992; Spanos, 1996) suggests that such subjects have picked up this information from a variety of sources (books, films, etc.) which they have then forgotten. This phenomenon is known as cryptamnesia (literally 'hidden memories'). Many commentators (e.g. Baker, 1992; Spanos et al., 1994; Spanos, 1996; Baumeister and Sommer, 1997; Paley, 1997; Showalter, 1997) have drawn attention to the similarities between these various examples of false memory. In all cases, the use of memory recovery techniques of dubious reliability is prominent. Furthermore, it is claimed that recovery of such memories will explain and possibly eliminate current psychological problems. The 'memories' are validated by an authority figure, usually a therapist, who will often encourage the claimant to adopt lax criteria in deciding what constitutes a likely memory of a past event (e.g. fleeting mental images or half-remembered dreams will be treated as memories if they fit the hypothesis). Finally, claimants often join support groups in which they feel under social pressure to recover memories in order to gain the approval of their peers.

Bullard (1989) also compared hypnotically generated accounts produced by four different hypnotists. If the hypnotist is shaping the narrative by, for example, asking leading questions, then the accounts produced by different hypnotists might be expected to reflect such an influence. Bullard claimed that the accounts produced by different hypnotists were very similar to each other and did not strongly reflect the influence of the specific hypnotists, but once again this interpretation is open to question. Of the typical traits identified in such accounts, only 30% were similar across all four hypnotists, whereas 50% were dissimilar for at least one. In a more recent survey, Bullard (1994) admitted that investigators do influence the content of the accounts produced, but he insisted that this mainly occurs with regard to peripheral details. Matheson (1998) has argued that the role of the individual hypnotist is much stronger in shaping the final narrative. However, in the final analysis it is unclear how much direct influence from the hypnotist we should expect to see if the core narrative is derived from the generally shared culture in the first place.

Finally, Bullard (1989) compared the accounts of 'real' abductees with those produced by eight subjects whom Alvin Lawson (e.g. Lawson, 1984) had hypnotized and asked simply to imagine that they had been abducted by aliens. Lawson's subjects were in no way suspected to have had genuine abduction experiences. When Lawson's results were first published they caused great consternation among traditional UFO researchers. In Bullard's words, 'Not only did the subjects readily respond to an initial suggestion with an elaborate and detailed story, with little need for prodding along the way, but the contents bore striking similarities to alleged real abductions, both in more obvious matters and in odd, minute details' (Bullard, 1989: 27–8). However, following more detailed analysis, Bullard concluded that the imaginary abductions did not demonstrate the same coherence as the 'real' cases. This difference, he suggests, was most plausibly explained by the assumption that a similar, objectively real experience lay at the core of the allegedly genuine accounts.

A more obvious explanation appears to have been overlooked. As Bullard himself states, Lawson's subjects were selected on the basis of their 'minimal prior UFO knowledge' (Bullard, 1989:27). Is it any surprise, then, that their imaginative narratives strayed further from the cultural template than the 'genuine' abductees who had presented themselves for hypnotic regression to hypnotists specializing in retrieval of alien abduction accounts? It beggars belief to assume that the latter would not have already sought out information on UFO abductions prior to their regression.

Sleep paralysis

The question must be asked why someone might suspect that they had been abducted in the first place without any clear memory of such an event. For many people the answer to this would appear to be a phenomenon known as sleep paralysis. The most frequently endorsed item which Hopkins *et al.* (1992)

claim as evidence of an alien abduction is 'Waking up paralysed with a sense of a strange person or presence or something else in the room'. This is a concise description of the experience of sleep paralysis, which is a standard symptom of narcolepsy, but can occur quite commonly in the general population (e.g. Everett, 1963; Dahlitz and Parkes, 1993). It is known that the muscles of the body are paralysed during REM sleep, presumably to prevent one from performing the movements associated with one's actions in the dream. However, during sleep paralysis one is consciously aware of the fact that one cannot move. Furthermore, there is often a terrifying sense of a malign presence. Fortunately, sleep paralysis is a transient state. Estimates of its prevalence vary considerably, but approximately 25% to 40% of the general population report some experience of it. It may be an isolated or repeated occurrence.

Sleep paralysis is likely to be accompanied by hypnagogic and hypnopompic imagery, which consists of anomalous sensory experiences that occur either preceding sleep or upon awakening, respectively. These sensations include both auditory and visual hallucinations (often of lights or strange figures in the bedroom), pressure on the chest and floating sensations. Although there is a need for further research in this area, progress is being made. Cheyne and colleagues have recently proposed a neurological model of sleep paralysis and associated imagery involving three factors:

One factor, labelled Intruder, consisting of sensed presence, fear, and auditory and visual hallucinations, is conjectured to originate in a hypervigilant state initiated in the midbrain. Another factor, Incubus, comprising pressure on the chest, breathing difficulties and pain, is attributed to effects of hyperpolarization of motor neurons on perceptions of respiration. These two factors have in common an implied alien 'other' consistent with occult narratives identified in numerous contemporary and historical cultures. A third factor, labelled Unusual Bodily Experiences, consisting of floating/flying sensations, out-of-body experiences and feelings of bliss, is related to physically impossible experiences generated by conflicts of endogenous and exogenous activation related to body position, orientation and movement.

(Cheyne *et al.*, 1999:319)

The same core experience has been reported throughout history in many different cultures, although the interpretation of the experience may vary (Hufford, 1982). Despite having a relatively high incidence in the non-clinical population, the existence of sleep paralysis is not common knowledge among the general public. Anyone who has experienced this terrifying (although temporary) ordeal is likely to be keen to explain it. Accounts of alien abduction, including the unusual sensations described above, are far more common in modern Western society (e.g. Whitley Strieber's best-selling book, *Communion: A True Story*) than scientific accounts of sleep paralysis. In the absence of the latter, many people are likely to believe either that they were going mad or that they genuinely experienced intruders from another world. Not surprisingly, they marginally prefer to believe that they are sane. In fact, episodes of sleep paralysis (in non-narcopleptics), although terrifying, are quite harmless and are in no way indicative of psychopathology. At this point, sufferers may well present themselves for hypnotic regression with the strong suspicion that they have indeed been abducted by aliens. A full and detailed account of the standard alien abduction scenario is the most likely outcome. Several commentators insist that sleep paralysis is at the heart of many, if not most, alien abduction claims (e.g. Blackmore, 1994; Newman and Baumeister, 1996a; Baker, 1997b; Randle *et al.*, 1999). Given the fact that many UFO experiences are associated with sleep (e.g. 60% of the intense experiences in the study by Spanos *et al.* 1993), this is a reasonable assertion.

Temporal lobe activity and tectonic strain theory

Although most claims can plausibly be accounted for on the basis of the factors discussed above, how is one to explain the increasing number of cases in which hypnosis was not employed? An interesting hypothesis has been advanced by Michael Persinger to account not only for some UFO abduction experiences, but also for a variety of other ostensibly paranormal experiences (e.g. Persinger and Valliant, 1985; Persinger, 1990). In such cases, he believes, the weird experiences may be due to abnormal activity in the temporal lobes. Such activity is thought to be associated with a variety of mystical and unusual perceptual experiences, including out-of-body experiences. At the extreme end of the continuum of temporal lobe activity are temporal lobe epileptics, who sometimes report that a seizure is preceded by odd sensations, déjà vu, hallucinations and mystical feelings. Persinger has developed a technique whereby he claims that he can induce bursts of firing in the temporal lobes of volunteer subjects. Reports of weird bodily sensations have resulted (e.g. Blackmore, 1994). Persinger and colleagues have recently reported that they were able to induce the subjective appearance of an apparition in a susceptible volunteer using this technique (Persinger *et al.*, 2000). If such an effect is replicated by independent investigators, it could be of tremendous significance in accounting for a whole range of ostensibly paranormal phenomena.

Even more controversially, Persinger (1990) claims that, in susceptible individuals, temporal lobe overactivity can result from magnetic effects produced as a result of the movement of tectonic plates in the earth's crust. The stresses and strains that are produced prior to earthquakes would be expected to produce a high level of such magnetic effects, and Persinger claims that reports of UFO activity correlate with earthquake activity. Furthermore, it is possible that such activity produces strange luminous effects which could account for some UFO reports (Devereux, 1989; Devereaux and Brookesmith, 1997). It is too early to assess fully the validity of Persinger's theory, but it will be interesting to see how many of his ideas stand up to critical scrutiny by others. In support of the general claim that abduction experiences result from unusual mental activity rather than reflecting reality, there are several cases recorded of people reporting full-blown abduction experiences whilst other witnesses could see that the individual in question had not physically gone anywhere. Instead, they appeared either to have lost consciousness or to be in a trance state (for a discussion of such cases see Schnabel, 1994).

Content of alien abduction narratives

The history of folklore strongly suggests that the alien abduction narrative is simply the latest cultural interpretation of core experiences which can be found in many societies throughout history (e.g. Schnabel, 1994; Nickell, 1995; Evans, 1998; Randle *et al.*, 1999). Tales have always been told of strange nocturnal visitations, of abduction, of transformation, and of a return with strange new powers. These tales have always been interpreted within the predominant cultural framework of the particular time and place. Hence in times past, angels, spirits, fairies and demons were held to be responsible. In modern Western culture, beings from advanced technological societies are blamed. But is it possible to account more precisely for the actual content of the narratives? Jung (1959) was probably the first commentator to attempt to interpret the UFO phenomenon in symbolic terms. The content of abduction narratives has also been interpreted in various symbolic ways, including the following.

- *As a memory of birth.* Alvin Lawson (1984) argued that much of the imagery of abduction reflects memories of being born. However, this hypothesis would contradict our current understanding of the development of autobiographical memory, as there is no convincing evidence to suggest that people have reliable memories for any events prior to the age of 2 years (DuBreuil *et al.*, 1998).
- *As a form of sadomasochism.* Leonard S. Newman and Roy F. Baumeister (1996a, b, 1998; Newman, 1997) have drawn attention to numerous parallels between sadomasochistic practices and the contents of abduction narratives (e.g. pain, loss of control and humiliation).
- *As a reflection of ambivalent attitudes towards technology in modern society.* Terry Matheson (1998) has argued that the themes of the abduction 'myth' reflect both our fear of being enslaved by technology and bureaucracy and our hope that, in some inscrutable way, technology may be our salvation.

Each of these interpretations offers more or less plausible symbolic explanations for the abduction narrative. The very fact that three such differing interpretations can be offered (and others could have been provided) highlights the difficulty in providing any kind of definitive explanation of this multifaceted phenomenon.

Conclusion

The evidence relating to the alien abduction phenomenon does not support claims either that individuals really are being abducted by aliens, or that they are in general deliberately lying about their experiences. The most plausible explanation in many cases appears to be that accounts of alien abduction are often based on false memories. The latter are often fantasy-based constructions which the claimant believes reflect actual events and result from the use of hypnosis or other associated techniques of 'memory recovery' (see, for example, Lindsay and Read, 1995). Shared cultural knowledge of the standard alien abduction scenario and experiences associated with sleep paralysis also appear to be important contributory factors. It is possible that fantasy-proneness and temporal lobe abnormalities are also implicated, but further research is required to clarify the exact role that they may play.

Suggested further reading

Appelle, S., Lynn, S. J. and Newman, L. (2000) Alien abduction experiences. In Cardeña, E. Lynn, S. J. and Krippner S. (eds), *Varieties of anomalous experience: examining the scientific evidence*. Washington, DC: American Psychological Association, 253–82.

Devereux, P. and Brookesmith, P. (1997) *UFOs and UFOlogy: the first 50 years*. London: Blandford.

Randle, K. D., Estes, R. and Cone, W. P. (1999) *The abduction enigma: the truth behind the mass alien abductions of the late twentieth century*. New York: Forge.

9 Meditation

Stephen Benton

> *A man, doubtful of his dinner, or trembling at a creditor, is not much*
> *disposed to abstracted meditation.*
> (Samuel Johnson, *Life of Boswell, Volume 3*, 1778)

Altering the balance

When people consider the power of meditation they frequently conjure up examples of memorable feats. So how do we explain the ability of a 46-year-old Hindu, an expert in meditation, to survive for over 5 hours in a sealed metal box? A box not big enough to contain sufficient oxygen to keep a fit person alive for more than 2 hours. During this time he was measured as using less than half the amount of oxygen that is normally needed to keep someone alive, and during a 1-hour period he used less than one-quarter of the amount! This is an example of how powerful the state of meditation can be, yet what is it? And does it perhaps have a less situation-specific role to play? Is the state of meditation to be found somewhere along a continuum of normal relaxation responses or is it a unique state of mind? Does meditation produce beneficial effects for the body and mind and, if so, are they unique in the range of self-regulated and altered states?

Seeing, believing, but not necessarily coping

Like any activity to which we address ourselves, there will be both intrinsic and extrinsic demands. As we focus our attention on the material to hand we simultaneously decide to attenuate other stimuli to which we now need to pay less attention. This chapter is probably a challenge to your attention, and most likely will be of uncertain value...at least at this point. The continued reading and subsequent processing of the following information requires you to apply a selective range of processing, and this cannot occur without your also selectively paying less attention to other ongoing and incoming information. Most of the time, we attenuate a lot of information in order to make the most of a little. It is an uncertain business, and one that is likely to be derailed by extrinsic stimuli (e.g. others' conversations, music, quiet yet unexpected sounds, or loud and disruptive ones), while intrinsic disrupters are legion, ranging from the blossoming and unlooked for word associations to shifts of attention written in the psychophysiology of hunger pangs!

Both the internal and external domain reverberate with unwanted stimuli, which are likely to be experienced as 'noise' around a chosen focus. It is equally likely that this 'noise' may contain, at any given moment, unexpected yet valuable signals. We are able to remain task-focused yet simultaneously maintain a flexible and valid repertoire of behavioural responses because we are able to process information at different levels of awareness. Indications of this capacity are to be found throughout psychology – for example, in memory (Craik and Lockhart, 1972), attention (Broadbent, 1958; Treisman, 1988), perception (Dixon, 1981) and cognitive organization (Collins and Quillian, 1969), all of which help to explain our general capacity to work effectively on a range of tasks that are performed within environments consistently characterized by unpredictable changes in the type and level of stimuli both central and peripheral to focus. This capacity to juggle with competing demands across a cognitive frontier, and to produce adaptive behaviours, is balanced between success and failure through a continuous monitoring of all stimuli that are capable of crossing sensory thresholds of detection.

Our impressions of the world around us flow from this ongoing flux of sensory stimuli, yet our impression is remarkably stable and robust. A number of mechanisms exist that are designed to maintain a constancy of experience (e.g. colour, size, shape, categorical recognition, use of prior information, sense of self, personality etc.). All of these serve as a basis for highlighting stimulus features, with the function of promoting the veridical determination of a stimulus (an object or background) and its appraisal in terms of our behavioural objectives. If this processing fails, then an individual's basis for maintaining a shared perceptual reality – one with reliable points of correspondence with those maintained by others – will degrade. The resultant internal representations, which are the product of cognitive and sensory interactions, will lead to increasingly non-adaptive behaviours. For example, failure to differentiate accurately between redundant and non-redundant stimuli will generate inappropriate and non-adaptive responses. Consequently, any attentional focus would suffer degradation due to poor separation of peripheral and central stimuli.

To guard against potential processing and behavioural 'meltdown', our internal representations are constantly checked and rechecked against a rich and diverse flow of incoming stimuli which interact with the accumulated and evolving constructs which form our personal world view (Bannister and Fransella, 1971). Where discrepancies are signalled, (e.g. between environmental demand and behaviour), immediate refocusing and review will follow. For example a physical reorientation may be required to clarify a sensory stimulus or a semantic search initiated to establish the most likely interpretation of an event, both driven by information search procedures which move between the consciously initiated and the automatic.

In order to clean up a signal and improve our appraisal of it, we are able to initiate a range of search strategies – both sensory and cognitive – interacting and sharing elements of the behavioural puzzle to be solved. More information will be sought and further sensory registration and analysis will serve to refine and redefine internal representations in order to re-establish veridical correspondence. As the numbers of redundant features accrue, we tend to assign increasing certainty to event attributes. The more noise that is identified, the easier it will be to detect a signal, but when uncertainty arises in our experience of a moment and/or a series of moments, we are designed to provide alternative explanations based on the operation of a set of parallel scramble and search procedures. For example, Bentall (2000) describes how auditory hallucinations in some patients may arise from errors in 'source monitoring' of their own thoughts, with 'external' signals (voices) more likely to be detected under conditions of uncertainty. In general, under conditions of suboptimal arousal (anxiety) individuals tend to focus conscious processing around a narrower range of possibilities. However, it should be noted that the semi and automatic search procedures would still be engaged.

We do not have much choice about how much information we register. It is as if we are subject to a continuous and involuntary downloading of information from any environmental website. Our waking behavioural environment is composed of endless links. Each behavioural moment will have a sense of connection imposed upon it by our ability to link current impinging stimuli with past or potential experience. This constant stream of diverse and rich material provides us with a contrast of noise to not-noise events (both real and imaginary). Without this continuous contest for our attention we quickly experience loss and disorientation – a form of deprivation. This is the context of every waking moment.

Thus we are apparently designed to cope with the world, and the melting-pot of its and our needs that mark our moods and thoughts, through a search for information. From increased information and/or better definition of that information will come a match between demand and resource. Effective behaviour is the result of a synthesis from an ongoing, if inconsistent, flux of impinging stimuli. What then can be said of a way of processing information that is predicated upon the idea that less is best, where understanding evolves from accessing that state of mind which is out of reach of the scramble and search operations upon which our cognitive continuity is founded?

What is meditation?

Meditation can be seen as initiating the clearing of the mind through the narrowing of attention to one point – from an object or a sound to a complete stillness where thought rests. It was originally practised in India and the East in the pursuit of enlightenment and 'right' conduct, only arriving in the West during the 1960s, where it was assigned the role of an anti-materialistic philosophy. The clearing of the mind through meditation is one of the oldest forms of human behaviour, and may be described as part of humans' natural response to the world. It is a sense of 'being lost' for a time, not in thought, but rather beyond thought – engulfed in a sense of mood based on internal stillness. How might this natural state be accessed? Could it be attained through prayer, self-hypnosis or even free association?

Meditation and prayer: just another altered state?

The roots of meditation can be found in the formalized set of practices and objectives that occurs in religions all around the world. In this context we are concerned with the question of whether a meditation is a religious act designed to promote 'spiritual growth'. Both Hindu and Buddhist practices have developed meditation into a central role in the pursuit of their spiritual objectives. In the West, prayer is the common way towards contemplation, and while prayer is unlikely to occur without some 'meditative mood', differences do exist (Carrington, 1998). Like meditation, prayer is usually an inward-focusing practice, undertaken in a quiet moment, in a calm environment and alone, or at least in a sense of aloneness. This combined with music, ritual sounds, candlelight and strong incense, or even awe-inspiring architecture, may create a sensory impact that is capable of altering the usual focus of attention. Away from the need to discriminate between regularly competing and contrasting stimuli, the senses are subject to an array of rhythmic interactions across different sensory modalities. The impact is akin to that of a novel sound. Attention can be diverted beyond conscious control, rather like overhearing someone mentioning your name even when you thought you were not listening to them. That semi-involuntary shift of attention – that refocusing away from many stimuli to a few – is a quieting experience. This experience is conducive to a meditative mood, wherein the intonation of phrases and the act of prayer sit. It exists in a form of dissociation, yet is firmly focused on personal meaning. The act of prayer – of focusing upon the inner voice – has been described as the socially endorsed form of meditation for the West (Maupin, 1968).

However, important differences exist between prayer and meditation, even when the objective of prayer is union with God and spiritual renewal. Prayer is usually a goal-directed form of behaviour. The act of prayer is founded upon a dialogue, with the use of inner speech, in order to achieve particular objectives. The communication is framed within the syntax of need, and is articulated through the structure of grammar, each phrase representing an expression to be understood. Lama Surya Das (1997), writing in *Eight Steps to Enlightenment*, emphasizes that meditation exists in the absence of striving and is framed within relatively goalless absorption.

Thoughts and concepts are tricks of the information-handling system outlined above. They represent facets of the mind designed to maintain a working relationship with the daily commerce of life. According to Tibetan teachings, thoughts and concepts are delusions which act to accentuate 'self-absorption', the starting and end point of all appraisals from the point of view of 'me'. Self-absorption acts as a veil through which all information will pass and become tainted, as a result of the motives maintaining the veil and distorting everything. This appears to be one form of cognitive biasing that no amount of corrective information scramble and search could rectify! In his classic work on Hindu practices, written in 1918, Woodroffe considers that our addiction to the view of an 'objective existence' independent of and beyond our self leads to suffering and our consciousness becoming 'veiled or contracted' (Woodroffe, 1972).

Within a meditative state of bliss, such schisms and fractures of reality are made whole and connection is established with the one undifferentiated 'Supreme Spirit'. Until this moment all perception acts to confirm the existence of an independent objectivity, as such perception is the product of a veiled consciousness. It seems that such meditation may be goal aware rather than goal directed. Fundamentally, the choice of vehicle for the journey is paramount, and it appears that neither language nor thought will serve, except as a form for initial momentum.

Self-hypnosis and trance states

Perhaps one altered state is the same as another, the only difference being found in the intensity and duration. Any unexpected event could trip up our attention and send us stumbling off course. This usurpation of our attention is often described as a form of trance-like state, the reasoning being that it involves a rapid and sharp narrowing of attention, creating a focus on a few objects and moments. Consequently, the maintenance of our ongoing weighting of redundant vs. non-redundant information is distorted. Most of us survive such attentional collapses because in the background the analysis of incoming stimuli continues, albeit at an attenuated level. For example, being engrossed in something (e.g. reading a book), fulfils many of the criteria of a trance state. While you are absorbed in reading you might become aware that something around you had changed, and you might then respond by taking stock of your surroundings. Noticing someone looking at you might trigger a 'notion' that something had been said and, having established that possibility, the subsequent priming of an information search. You might then find yourself able to register speech directed towards you and to recall exactly what had been said. Hypnosis can induce such states of focused selectivity, mood and, for that matter, recall (Bower *et al.*, 1981; Baddeley, 1991). So is it possible that self-hypnosis could be the route towards meditation, if in fact it is not meditative in itself?

Although it is acknowledged that meditative and self-hypnotic states share some common ground in terms of trance states, there are important differences between them. One of the key attributes of an effective hypnotic state is the increased receptivity of the subjects to self-administered suggestions. Such suggestions are typically designed to address problem behaviours or behaviours that could be improved relative to some set of attainment criteria. Individuals' subsequent behaviours reflect the goal-directed aims either of themselves or of another. The hypnotic state becomes a necessary part of the progress towards behavioural change or the display of a behavioural indicator of a preferred emotional state (e.g. reduced anxiety). This is unlike meditation, where the striving towards behavioural change is supplanted by a non-striving state. Clearly in practice the meditator makes some *effort* to achieve a state different to that from which they are starting. In some sense the repetition of a mantra would seem to be a form of striving, but importantly the mantra is claimed to be used as a stepping-stone towards release from focused behaviour, unlike the functional trance state of hypnosis (Norbu, 1996).

Measurement of the physiological states that accompany self-hypnosis and meditation has shown them to be different. This issue will be discussed in a later section, but for now let us note that in general meditation induces a lowering of metabolism, whereas self-hypnotic states tend to raise it. This is more clearly the case when individuals are in pursuit of behavioural change which translates into specific achievement-led targets (Macintyre, 1992). However, it is not surprising, given the similarity in subjective impact and state between self-hypnosis and meditation, that the most prominent of relaxation techniques, namely autogenic training, had its origins in the study of hypnosis (Carrington, 1998). However, the potential of a self-induced and self-directed change in physiological activity to enhance a sense of well-being and thereby promote beneficial relaxation has been the focus of research and practice for some time.

Relaxation: autogenic practices

The act of attending to self-induced mental constructs, focused upon sensation, was developed by a Berlin psychiatrist, J.H. Schultz, in 1926, and was reported to produce strong recuperative effects in patients. Schultz is responsible for initiating the world's most widely used and extensively researched method of relaxation training. A physiologist, Dr Oskar Vogt, had reported that patients who had undergone a programme of hypnotic sessions were accessing this state without formal inducement and protocol, and were deriving measurable recuperative benefits. Schultz explored this further and found that simply by focusing the mind on bodily sensations characteristic of self-induced states (e.g. a heaviness in the limbs and a pleasant sense of warmth), patients were still able to show improved recovery. The act of thinking about physiological states – those states that are naturally associated with the body's state of relaxation, led individuals towards deep and beneficial mood states. The typical initial practice helps individuals to focus on various bodily states, such as the weight of an arm or of eyelids, and perhaps breathing sensations. This focus creates a sensory referent that is clear and quite distinct from one's usual perceptions. This difference enhances the shifting of attention and permits an experience that is a blend of modalities (e.g. weight and warmth). These cross-modal combinations reinforce directed attention and enable an increased purchase on an individual's internal state. Developments of this process enable individuals to use 'visualization' in order to create a profound sense of rest. This approach aims to provide a controlled mental landscape that is accessible to the individual, who follows a mental pathway which is coded in imagery. Each step along the way is guided and framed by a state linked to an image, and each successive image is linked to a deeper level of associated calm and relaxation. This approach has widespread appeal and application, and represents the development of a personal 'mantra', except that this time the mantra is coded in visual imagery.

Regular autogenic training of this kind would seem to have much in common with the meditative state. It takes place in a quiet environment with subdued lighting, with the eyes closed and with time given to calm the body. After training, individuals are able to follow their image pathway in a semi-automatic manner, with each step apparently able to go its own way once placed on the path. The experiential outcome of this process is described as a dream-like state and is known as 'passive concentration'. No force of will should be necessary. Each step is apparently a natural consequence of the preceding 'state' and association. This activity appears to meet the criteria for state-dependent conditioning. If so, this is a powerful tool to be used in the pursuit of 'removed perception', each step moving the individual into a territory constructed in accordance with their personal selection of associations.

The route of 'passive concentration' is for personal use only. It represents a construction – a conduit built from one level of perception to the next distinct level – and is achieved by carefully accumulating selected paired associates of image and internal state. The state of relaxation achieved by autogenic training can be deep and beneficial, but it is probably not profound, unless the goal sought (that of relaxation) is in itself profound. The way towards such relaxation is entirely prescriptive, and the question of meditative quality is probably irrelevant to the aims and outcomes. The fundamental question here concerns the issue of natural resonance. The meditative state is a self-energized resonant state defined by a natural configuration of self and 'knowing' (Epstein, 1995). If this is the case, then it would be difficult for exponents of autogenic visualization to gain access to the same state, given that the path they tread is derived from the accumulated baggage of 'paired-association', a subtle and pervasive source of knowledge acquisition (Macaulay *et al.*, 1993). In one sense the difference is probably to be reconciled with the individual's motivation.

The last topic in this section again concerns association. The impact of induced dissociation is a powerful tool in the exploration of altered perception and associated states, and this has long been known in clinical practice. This would seem to be an appropriate place to consider the impact of free association on states and just how close 'free association' may come to meditation.

Free association: structured dissociation

Free association shares a common origin with autogenic training, namely hypnosis. While Sigmund Freud was working with a colleague, Dr Josef Breuer, on the treatment of hysteria he noticed a number of changes in symptoms that were not consistent with existing medical reductionist models of 'dysfunctional' or 'ill' behaviour. They discovered that if patients were able to access repressed material (e.g. memories of events) when under the influence of a light hypnosis, they experienced a cathartic discharge of intense, emotionally charged material (Breuer and Freud, 1893). Freud continued to work with the technique, moving away from the imposition of control by the practitioner to a patient-centred approach. The induced and directed hypnotic trance was replaced by the patient's 'free recall' of material. If the patient was given a place to stretch out and relax in a calm environment of non-judgemental listening, then material sufficient for the analysis, and often cathartic in itself, would flow. Perhaps the unusual behaviour of simply lying on a couch with eyes averted from the doctor (if not closed), and in a wholly receptive relationship with a comparative stranger helps to induce unusual perceptual states. It might be said that such an environment, with minimal demands for external control, is an integral part of the state inducement necessary for the therapy. Perhaps in this case we see the mantra expressed in a set of behaviours that are written in the text of changed physiological activity. The physical context as such helps to trigger some form of inward scramble and search across associations, within memory, that were unlikely to be open to conscious and directed access under the usual processing demands.

Effective as free association can be in releasing repressed and stored material, and in particular the emotional affect with which memories are charged, the process is not meditative. Relaxation plays a role in the process, yet this role is to facilitate the ongoing voiced record of everything reclaimed from memory. All material is encouraged, as in any non-judgemental relationship, yet much material – perhaps key associations – may be missed. Patients are continually seeking a language in which to transmit the recollected experience, while the experience is still associating with other material. The material so generated is used as source material, each association being simply one piece of a puzzle, to be analysed and reassociated after being subjected to the logic of the unconscious. This is in essence a process of reconstruction, based on free-associated elements, each of which acts as a platform, a step, or yet another pathway, only this time it is on the 'royal road' of the unconscious. However, this is not a journey to be undertaken alone. Each step is the product of a conscious analysis performed on conscious elements linked through unconscious associations. The journey is a partnership without which one would need to be conscious of transient and unconscious material simultaneously.

Much research has been conducted into the type and extent of meditative effects on individuals' behavioural capacity and states of mind. The first part of the following section will consider some of the evidence available from the masters of the art. Certain feats of endurance became well established in the late 1960s and early 1970s, and served to usher in serious research into the empirically quantifiable aspects of meditation. This topic will be reviewed in the next section.

Meditation: evidence of its impact

The masters

The example given at the beginning of this chapter – of the man sealed in an airtight box – is just one of an extraordinary range of behaviours exhibited by masters of the art. The results of studies conducted at the Menninger Foundation in Kansas helped to draw attention to apparently inexplicable physiological events. The man in the example was Sri Ramanand Yogi, and such active control over the autonomic nervous system was considered to be sensational (Anand *et al.*, 1961). The view in the West was that control over physiological factors such as body temperature, blood pressure, heart rate and brain waves was internally regulated by physiological processes. These processes were designed to protect the individual from damage by extreme variation, and they necessarily worked within set physiological limits – a pattern of interactive homeostatic processes automatically regulating key bodily activities. The emergence of biofeedback experiments highlighted the potential of 'thought' to change fundamental physiological responses (Green *et al.*, 1970). People were taught to alter their brain waves in response to a conscious decision to do so. With the aid of an EEG machine linked to an acoustic indicator, individuals were able to shift towards the target brain pattern. The sound provided them with a parameter with which to monitor directly the impact of their 'thoughts'. The results obtained certainly gained scientists' attention, and consequently a new generation of technically led investigations into yogic attainment followed.

Having survived the sealed box, and emerged in completely good health, the yogi was then subjected, together with other masters, to a range of tests designed to measure habituation, which is itself fundamental to the maintenance of selective attention. Without the effective functioning of habituation, valid associations between stimuli, affect and effect would need to be relearned as if no prior experience had been registered. All of those stimuli constantly bombarding us, yet not assigned to prime attention space, would intrude and disrupt the working basis for stimulus discrimination. Our selective attention is only able to tune into stimuli because habituation tunes out so much more. In physiological terms, this automatic process allows us to inhibit the orienting response (a heightening of arousal activity when registering new stimuli) (Sokolov, 1963), and thereby permits the cognitive dimension of familiarity and supports the operational ground rules for arbitrating between competing redundancy weightings. This process is as fundamental to effective attention as the autonomic nervous system is to the maintenance of homeostasis.

Researchers have explored how habituation – this fundamental feature of attentional states – would respond during meditation. By recording the brain waves of four yogis, Anand *et al.* (1961) were able to uncover some fascinating insights into the meditative state. Two yogis were studied during a normal resting state, characterized by alpha rhythms, and found that a normal response to distractors ensued. The normal response is for the alpha rhythm to be blocked and a more alert pattern (part of the orienting response) to emerge, which in conjunction with other changes probably prepares for heightened processing of stimuli. However, when the same stimulus was presented again and repeatedly, the yogis did not habituate to it. Each and every presentation led to alpha-blocking, as if it was the first time of presentation. During deep meditation, known as *samadhi*, yogis report that they are completely unaware of either external or internal stimuli. Accordingly, the results showed that none of the distractors that were used induced a block in the alpha rhythm. It was as if the yogis were oblivious to sense impressions, yet the readings showed their brains to be alert!

Scientific interest in transcendental meditation

The primary area of research has been into the physiological composition of a meditative state, no doubt in part stimulated by the feats of expert meditators. In a pragmatic sense, it was equally likely that the sheer volume of research material claiming physiological benefits (e.g. management of stress, improved cardiovascular health and associated performance improvements) from transcendental meditation (TM) helped to galvanize investigations. The initial studies tended to investigate individual physiological parameters such as galvanic skin response (GSR), oxygen intake and heart rate (HR), all of which suggested potential health benefits. A general profile of the physiological findings taken from studies into TM and meditative states (Allison, 1970; Wallace, 1970; Orme-Johnson, 1973; Blanchard *et al.*, 1990) is shown in Box 9.1. A number of studies considered the cognitive impact of meditation, and some of the findings from these have been included (e.g. Pirot, 1970; Frew, 1974; Blasdell, 1978).

Box 9.1: Correlates of transcendental meditation (TM)

- Decreased heart rate, lowered blood pressure, slower breathing and reduced oxygen consumption.
- Increased blood flow to tissues, leading to enhanced removal of waste products and a lower level of lactic acid in the blood.
- Reduced sensitivity to noise, and improved temperature control.
- Possible benefits to immune system (e.g. gum inflammation was reduced after TM).
- EEG changes indicating a more ordered brain function.
- Predominance of alpha waves in the frontal and central regions of the brain during meditation.
- Improvements in concentration focus and span.
- Improvements in manual skill.
- Enhanced accuracy of discrimination (e.g. differentiating between degrees of brightness).
- Faster reaction times for discrimination tasks.

- Long-term meditation was found to decrease resting cortisol levels, even when not meditating, with reduced anxiety and improved memory recall.
- Regular practice of TM increases the stability of the autonomic nervous system.

Psychologists have been accused of having difficulty in moving beyond a black-box mentality, whereby if one is not sure of a mechanism, then one names it, calls it a process and puts it in a black box. Other boxes can then be readily attached, after which one has a 'working model' of the real thing! At last in the case of meditation some of the boxes have been opened. Perhaps the relatively sudden and massive refocusing of scientific interest upon meditation has as much to do with the astonishing ability of yogis to, if not override, then at least 'disengage' from fundamental responding, as it has to do with objective scientific enquiry.

Issues: established and challenged

While the list in Box 9.1 does summarize some of the available research findings about meditation, questions have been raised concerning interpretation. The work of Fenwick (1974) has drawn attention to difficulties in interpretation which arise from contrast effects. The latter refer to how comparisons of reductions in a given physiological activity should be gauged against relevant and relative resting (baseline) levels. If the starting level of activity is unclear, it then becomes difficult to develop any standardized estimate of effect. For example, Fenwick investigated the dramatic decreases in oxygen consumption that are generally reported as evidence of physiological responses to meditation. The reports would typically refer to 'before' and 'after' measures of consumption, thereby contrasting one score with another, with the difference assumed to result from meditation. The average difference for the 'average' meditator was around 18%. Could such a high figure indicate a failure to take adequate account of the contrast? In other words, are the large differences which are observed the consequences of inadequate experimental method?

While working with a group of TM meditators, it was shown that the slightest movement during the pre-meditation period could raise oxygen consumption by as much as 50%. Even closing their eyes or being spoken to could increase consumption, and thereby elevate the 'basal' level (the starting point for calculating any difference). Subjects who were tense before meditation displayed the largest decreases in oxygen consumption during the subsequent meditation period. Moreover, the carbon dioxide output of those who were relaxed before meditation would start to drop even before the meditation period. In order to investigate this further, a group of experienced TM practitioners was recruited and tested just after rising in the morning, and before having eaten. It turned out that this group were already so relaxed that they could not produce any further metabolic change during meditation. This added support to the view that many of the reported decreases in metabolism during meditation may have been contaminated by a contrast effect. Incidentally, the consumption of oxygen in Fenwick's group was recorded to be around 7%! This research certainly contributed to an awareness of the need to compile thorough behavioural profiles of individuals as part of any experiment into meditation. It also generated interest in identifying rogue stimuli that would be likely to contaminate a basal state. Once in place these findings were translated into experimental protocol and were effective in promoting improved reliability across data. In general, the trend of the early findings has not been reversed by the later studies, and the nature of those findings remains as follows. Meditation relaxes people, reduces tension and may bring a number of valuable benefits such as improved immunological functioning, resilience to stress, and enlightenment!

Concluding comments

Much of cognitive psychology is concerned with delineating the sensory and cognitive processes that are engaged in making firm and clear our subjective world – a platform upon which we exercise our internal roles and negotiate exchanges with the external environment. This stable subjective world may properly be called a state of mind, and it has a number of dynamic features, not least of which is the capacity to make firm and reliable the correspondence between sensory registration and cognitive elaboration. Cognitive processes such as elaboration are able to weight and direct sensory encoding in response to past actual and future possible experience. Each of these contexts interacts and forms the platform of subjective stability mentioned above. We learn and develop short cuts towards this information flow and flux, against which we impose our own personal frames of reference. If this sketch of the relationship between individual and environment is feasible, then it is possible that each of us occupies a partial and biased corner of our reconstructed cosmos. Perhaps the mightiest challenge for our heavy-duty information processors is an internal state that places the individual away – out of reach – from those fundamental and defining operations, and even from habituation. What function and role could meditation have? Even if it is devoid of explanation, it has been established that in the domain of mind–body effects it is real and it offers genuine benefits to health.

Suggested further reading

Epstein, M. (1995) *Thoughts without a thinker: psychotherapy from a Buddhist perspective.* New York: Basic Books.

Lama Surya Das (1997) *Eight steps to enlightenment: awakening the Buddha within. Tibetan wisdom for the Western world.* New York: Bantam Books.

Meditation preparations: 10–15 minute programme.

Try to plan your meditation session so that you have already eaten (about an hour before), and avoid stimulants such as coffee or tea. You do need to feel calm, so make sure that you have space and time to allow yourself this feeling.

Meditation requires a concentrated period with few distractions. Choose a quiet room and let others know that you are not to be disturbed.

For the first session, it may help to sit facing a vase of flowers or any other natural object that is pleasing to the eye. The smell of incense may enhance the meditative process. Choose a natural, unobtrusive scent. The aim here is to support a gentle concentration, and a mental–focal point will probably help to calm thoughts.

The use of subdued lighting may also enhance the meditative experience. Face away from any direct light.

Choose a comfortable sitting position, either on a chair or on the floor. Remove your shoes and loosen any tight clothing. Be prepared to change position if the one that you choose becomes uncomfortable. It is more important to be comfortable!

If your concentration is broken by an unavoidable interruption, allow yourself to break your meditation slowly. Yawning and stretching will aid this process. Stretching and relaxing can help you to feel at ease. If possible, return to finish the remainder of your meditation process.

Choose the best way for you to time your meditation period, by having some easy way just to check the time. Try not to twist and turn just to check how the time is going!

As you relax, let your mind scan your body from top to bottom, and feel your muscles relax. Let your breathing become calm and peaceful. Close your eyes (if that is comfortable). Turn your attention inwards, and follow inwards the thought of an object (or focus on the object itself) or a sound or whatever you have selected.

If it is an object, you could explore it in your mind's eye. Perhaps try occasionally mentally rotating the object.

Allow the object to help you to bring your inward focus away from the discursive images and thoughts that are likely to occur. The image of the object helps you to gauge how far you may have wandered from your inward focus. Occasionally concentrate on the image itself.

At the end of your meditation, remain seated with your eyes closed and allow yourself to return gradually to your everyday thoughts. When you are ready, open your eyes. The process of rubbing your hands together lightly and then running them over your face produces a warm bodily effect that helps to bring you back to your present state. Remember to rise slowly.

10 Paranormal cognition

Caroline Watt

> *She predicted all the earthquakes and other natural disturbances; the*
> *one and only time snow fell in the capital, freezing to death the poor*
> *people in the shantytowns and the rose bushes in the gardens of the*
> *rich; and the identity of the murderer of schoolgirls long before the*
> *police discovered the second corpse; but no one believed her.*
> (Isabel Allende, *The House of the Spirits* 1986:96
> Reproduced with permission of Alfred A Knopf, a division of
> Random House Inc.)

Introduction: the what, why and how of research into paranormal cognition

What are paranormal phenomena? UFOs? Bigfoot? Mind-reading? Ghosts? Spoon-bending? By 'paranormal', I do not mean 'supernatural' or 'beyond nature', where the phenomena are by definition incompatible with scientific theorizing and investigation. Rather, I mean that the phenomena appear to suggest that organisms can interact with their environment in ways that are not explicable within current scientific understanding. This does not mean that paranormal phenomena can never be understood, but it may mean that some of our present scientific knowledge and theories would need to be adjusted to accommodate them. We do not yet know exactly how paranormal phenomena operate. Indeed, there is still some debate as to whether such phenomena even exist. The particular paranormal phenomenon that I shall concentrate on in this chapter is extra-sensory perception (ESP), of which a further definition and examples are given below.

We can distinguish between paranormal *phenomena*, where there is a claim that a real anomalous effect is occurring, and paranormal *experiences*. In the latter, there may or may not be a real anomalous effect, but the individual has interpreted their experience as a paranormal one. Even if paranormal phenomena do not exist, paranormal experiences do, as surveys have shown that a considerable number of people report experiences which they interpret as paranormal in nature.

This chapter is about 'paranormal cognition', a term that implies some kind of information-processing model of paranormal phenomena. That is, the term suggests that individuals are somehow perceiving, processing and responding to information that is acquired without the mediation of their known senses. I shall consider research in parapsychology that throws some light on paranormal phenomena from a cognitive perspective, and I shall set out some of the evidence which parapsychologists claim supports the existence of genuine paranormal phenomena. Even if it turns out that paranormal phenomena can be explained by normal mechanisms, because many people have experiences which they interpret as paranormal, scientists have a responsibility to try to understand them. This is *why* parapsychologists conduct research into paranormal phenomena, but what about the *how*?

Before we proceed further, let me define some technical terms. Parapsychology is the scientific study of paranormal phenomena and experiences. The neutral term 'psi' is often used to describe these phenomena and experiences, which may be further subdivided into two main categories, namely extra-sensory perception (ESP) and psychokinesis (PK). ESP refers to apparent mind-to-mind communication. For example, when you are asleep you may have a dream about your brother in Australia, and when you wake up the telephone rings and it is your brother, saying that he had been in an accident and had been thinking about you. Some people would interpret this anecdote as an example of extra-sensory communication between you and your brother, while others would say that the coincidence between the dream and the phone call is just down to chance (see Chapter 7). If you frequently dream about your brother then it is more likely that your dream will coincide with his phone call by chance alone. PK refers to apparent mind over matter. For example, a gambler may wish for a particular outcome when throwing dice. He might throw hard for a 'six' and soft for a 'one' face uppermost. If a hard throw coincides with a six face, in line with the gambler's intentions, an observer might conclude that the gambler used PK to alter the way in which the dice tumbled. Alternatively, it is possible that the desired outcome came about by chance alone, as this outcome would occur anyway on average in one throw out of every six.

Unlike PK experiences, which are quite rare, ESP experiences are relatively common. One random postal questionnaire survey found that 36% of respondents believed in ESP and 25% had experienced it (Blackmore, 1984). However, as the above examples illustrate, it is difficult to obtain an accurate understanding of what causes such spontaneous paranormal experiences. Our perception and memory are notoriously inaccurate, as they are biased by our expectations and beliefs. Therefore our interpretation of events may be distorted or imprecise. If you have a strong *belief* in ESP, you may interpret an ambiguous occurrence (e.g. a coincidence between a dream and a telephone call) as being due to ESP. On the other hand, if you have a strong *disbelief* in ESP you may reject the ESP interpretation as improbable or impossible, and assume that there is an alternative interpretation.

In addition, it is very difficult to estimate the role that chance plays in many spontaneous paranormal experiences. Striking coincidences *will* happen by chance alone, but when such a coincidence happens to you personally, it can be very impressive and meaningful. For these reasons, although spontaneous paranormal experiences are valuable in giving us a picture of how these experiences occur naturally, parapsychologists also conduct research under laboratory conditions in order to gain a better understanding of psi phenomena. This chapter will focus on ESP phenomena because of their apparent similarity to other more orthodox forms of perception and cognition. So how does laboratory research into ESP proceed?

In the laboratory, parapsychologists are able to isolate and manipulate variables so as to eliminate alternative normal explanations and focus on paranormal explanations. For example, an ESP experiment might involve three individuals – first, a sender who will view a randomly selected 'target' picture and attempt to concentrate on it and send it psychically to the receiver, second, a receiver who will relax and describe the images that come to mind, and third, an experimenter who supervises and conducts the experiment. In order to rule out the possibility that normal sensory channels may allow communication from the sender to the receiver, each one is isolated in a separate sound-shielded non-adjacent room monitored by the experimenter. As a result, shouting or stamping by the sender will not be heard or felt by the receiver. The target (e.g. an art print or a short video clip) is randomly chosen by a computer after the sender has been placed in the sending room. Therefore only the sender knows the identity of the target. This eliminates the possibility that the experimenter may deliberately or unconsciously pass on cues to the receiver about the identity of the target. At the end of the sending period, the receiver looks at the target and three decoy targets, not yet knowing the identity of the actual target. The receiver chooses which of the four target possibilities is closest to their mental impressions. The aim is to determine whether the receiver can correctly identify the target on the basis of there being a stronger correspondence between that picture and the receiver's impressions, compared to the other three pictures.

Because the target is randomly chosen from a larger number of possible targets, we can calculate the likelihood of the receiver correctly identifying the target by chance alone. For example, if the target is chosen from a total of four possibilities, then the likelihood of correctly identifying the target is one in four(25%). Standard statistical procedures are then used to estimate the likelihood that the results obtained from a number of sending sessions are due to chance alone. If the results exceed what would normally be expected by chance, and other normal means of knowing about the target have been eliminated, then parapsychologists claim that evidence of some additional means of communication – ESP – has been provided. However, a single statistically significant experiment is not sufficient evidence for the existence of a genuine ESP effect. Scientists require that the effect can be independently replicated – that is, that it can be found by other scientists in other laboratories.

These are some of the ways in which parapsychologists attempt to use laboratory conditions to evaluate the possibility that genuine ESP communication occurs. For a more detailed consideration of how to conduct methodologically sound ESP research, see the guidelines by Milton and Wiseman (1997).

In this chapter I shall first consider the use of techniques related to altered states of consciousness to study ESP. Next, the line of research that suggests there are similarities between subliminal perception and extra-sensory perception will be reviewed. These two research areas have been selected because they provide good examples of the model whereby paranormal cognition operates like our other normal cognitive processes. This suggests that it is appropriate and useful to consider the cognitive perspective in order to increase our understanding of paranormal phenomena. Finally, I shall consider some philosophical and methodological issues that have been raised by research into paranormal cognition.

Altered states of consciousness and ESP

Probably the strongest evidence for ESP comes from a line of research that uses altered states of consciousness (ASC) to facilitate ESP performance. The idea underlying this work is that normally we live in very distracting, noisy environments, both externally and internally. The ESP information may be akin to a weak signal. If it were a strong signal, then we would know all about ESP already, and there would be no debate as to its existence. In order to help the receiver to detect the weak ESP signal among the distracting noise, parapsychologists use noise reduction techniques such as helping the receiver to relax physically and mentally. This is known as the 'noise reduction' model of ESP (Honorton and Harper, 1974; Braud, 1975).

Parapsychologists use ASC techniques to study ESP because they noticed several converging lines of evidence which suggested that such states of consciousness facilitated ESP. In the late nineteenth century, many 'spiritual mediums' claimed to be able to obtain information paranormally by going into a trance. More recently, there have been claims that ESP performance could be enhanced by using hypnosis (Honorton and Krippner, 1969). Furthermore, large-scale surveys of spontaneous psychic experiences have found that about two-thirds of cases occurred while the experient was in the dream state (Rhine, 1969). Throughout history there have been accounts of ESP information occurring in dreams. When parapsychologists tested for ESP using sleep laboratories, they were encouraged by obtaining positive results (Ullman *et al.*, 1973). However, it proved to be expensive, inconvenient and time-consuming to conduct dream–ESP research.

As an alternative approach, parapsychologists decided to use a mild sensory isolation procedure called the 'ganzfeld'. In this procedure, the receiver is seated for about 30 minutes in a comfortable reclining chair, wearing headphones that play a relaxation tape followed by white noise (a sound like radio static that becomes quite monotonous). The receiver wears goggles and is bathed in red light. The sensation produced by this procedure is of complete, unpatterned stimulation – indeed the word 'ganzfeld' comes from the German for 'entire field'. Under these conditions the receiver becomes pleasantly relaxed and may even begin to experience hypnagogic imagery – the kind of vivid imagery that may occur when one is drifting off to sleep. The ganzfeld stimulation helps to reduce sensory distractions and focus the receiver on their internal impressions. The task is for the receiver to identify the ESP target correctly, on the basis of the similarity between the receiver's mental impressions and the target that the sender is simultaneously viewing while the receiver is relaxing in the ganzfeld. The target is usually visual (e.g. an art print or a video clip), although other targets such as musical pieces have been used, and it is randomly chosen from a large pool of potential targets. The receiver wears a microphone to record their commentary. At the end of the sending period, these impressions are compared with four target possibilities, and the judging proceeds as described above.

Using this technique, parapsychologists have obtained success rates that significantly exceed the 25% rate one would expect by chance alone when choosing from four alternatives. Many argue that the ganzfeld research provides evidence for ESP (e.g. Utts, 1991; Bem and Honorton, 1994), although the interesting debate over how to interpret the evidence is still raging (see Box 10.1) because not all experiments have produced positive results. The Koestler Parapsychology Unit (KPU) at Edinburgh University is the UK's premier centre for ganzfeld research. Of the six ganzfeld studies conducted since the Unit's inception, four have provided statistically significant positive results. One would expect only one out of 20 studies to be significant by chance alone. Therefore the results of the KPU ganzfeld studies cannot be explained as chance coincidence, and this provides evidence in support of the hypothesis that ESP exists.

Box 10.1: The ganzfeld debate

For the last 15 years there has been an often heated debate over how to interpret the results of ESP experiments using the ganzfeld technique. Meta-analysis is an important statistical tool for evaluating the results of groups of studies that seem to demonstrate a weak effect. In meta-analysis, one combines a number of studies using similar methods in order to evaluate the overall size of the effect, and also to detect trends in the combined data that might not be visible in individual studies. The debate over ESP in the ganzfeld began in 1985 when Ray Hyman, a critic of parapsychology, published a meta-analysis of ganzfeld studies that found an overall success rate of 31%, where 25% would be expected by chance. Hyman concluded that this positive effect was due to an 'error some place' – that is, to methodological weaknesses rather than extra-sensory perception. In response, Charles Honorton, a successful ganzfeld experimenter, conducted his own meta-analysis of ganzfeld studies and found a 43% success rate. This, he claimed, indicated that the ganzfeld ESP results were a step towards replicability of psi effects. A third meta-analysis was conducted by an independent methodologist, Robert Rosenthal, whose conclusions agreed with those of Honorton.

Rather than engaging in further argument over how to interpret past ganzfeld studies, Honorton and Hyman published a joint communiqué in which they agreed upon a set of methodological guidelines to which future ganzfeld studies should adhere (Hyman and Honorton, 1986). Honorton then proceeded to devise an automated ganzfeld system, and a series of 11 experiments with 8 different experimenters was conducted at Honorton's laboratory, adhering to the methodological guidelines and using the new system. A meta-analysis of these new studies found a 33% success rate overall, a result that would be expected by chance less than one in 10,000 times, which was claimed to provide replicable evidence of psi (Bem and Honorton, 1994).

At this point, it seemed as if the debate had been settled. A series of studies had been conducted according to methodological guidelines laid down by a prominent critic, and the analysis of these studies had shown a statistically significant positive effect. However, a further meta-analysis was recently conducted on the ganzfeld studies that were carried out after the closure of Honorton's laboratory and published prior to February 1997. This included 30 studies from 7 independent laboratories, and the results showed only chance success rates. That is, the 'new-generation' studies appeared to provide no replicable evidence for psi (Milton and Wiseman, 1999). Since then, some more positive studies have emerged. Thus, as you can imagine, the debate continues! One thing is clear from the debate. There is still much disagreement among parapsychologists about the features of a 'standard' ganzfeld. For instance, should ganzfeld experiments using auditory targets be regarded as distinct from ganzfeld experiments using visual targets? (Edge and Schmeidler, 1999; Milton, 1999). This disagreement reflects the fact that there is a need for systematic research into what features of ganzfeld experiments are important in eliciting ESP.

Researchers are not simply interested in demonstrating the existence of ESP (proof-oriented research). They also need to understand how ESP operates (process-oriented research). For example, what types of people perform particularly well at ESP tasks? What is the mechanism that allows ESP to operate? Is extra-sensory information processed in the same way as other types of sensory information? Progress in answering these process-oriented questions has been slow, but some patterns are beginning to emerge. For instance, a ganzfeld study in the USA using students from the Juilliard School for the Performing Arts in New York found remarkably high success rates. In total, 50% of targets were correctly identified, compared to the 25% that would be expected by chance (Schlitz and Honorton, 1992). These results would be found by chance only once in 100 times. This led to the prediction that creative participants would perform well in subsequent studies. Three of the six KPU ganzfeld studies used creative participants, and these confirmed the prediction, with success rates of 41% (Morris *et al.*, 1993), 33% (Morris *et al.*, 1995), and 47% (Dalton,

1997). The study by Dalton (1997) explored the question of creative participants in greater detail by systematically comparing the success rates of
different types of creative individuals. Dalton found that musicians had the
highest success rate, followed by artists. Actors and writers had the lowest
success rates, but these were still significantly higher than would be
expected by chance. Using questionnaire measures of personality and
creativity, this study is a good example of how parapsychologists try to
build an understanding of the reasons why particular participant characteristics are associated with ESP success.

ESP research using the ganzfeld technique illustrates the types of
methods that parapsychologists are using in order to understand more about
extrasensory perception. The noise reduction model has led to a fruitful line
of research using altered states of consciousness techniques to facilitate ESP
performance. Once reasonable levels of ESP performance are obtained
under laboratory conditions, parapsychologists can begin to investigate how
ESP works. Research with the ganzfeld and other techniques has indicated
that ESP impressions can be vague and fleeting. It is rare for a receiver to
give an exact and unambiguous description of the ESP target. This suggests
that ESP impressions resemble weak sensory impressions, where one
obtains only incomplete information which may be distorted or only
partially represented in conscious awareness. In fact, some parapsychologists have explicitly suggested the hypothesis that ESP information is
processed similarly to subliminal or weak sensory information. The next
section describes this line of research.

Subliminal perception and ESP

Subliminal perception (SP) refers to the perception and processing of information below the 'limen' or threshold of conscious awareness. Nowadays,
cognitive psychologists who are studying this phenomenon use the terms
'preconscious processing' or 'perception without awareness', because
research has shown that there is no such thing as a fixed and easily measured
sensory threshold. Moreover, modern cognitive psychologists perhaps wish
to distance themselves from the early subliminal perception studies, many of
which had methodological flaws. Some rather extravagant claims can be
found – for example, that audio tapes containing subliminal suggestions can
produce weight loss or influence consumers' buying preferences. There is
scant evidence that gross human behaviour can be influenced by such
complex subliminal messages. Nevertheless, there is good evidence that individuals can perceive and process simple information, such as a single word or
a simple line drawing, that is presented at levels that are too weak for
conscious awareness.

Many parapsychologists have noted similarities between SP and ESP. For
a detailed review of this research see Nash (1986) and Roney-Dougal (1986).
Experimental findings in both parapsychology and subliminal perception

research indicate that there are wide individual differences in apparent 'sensitivity' to subliminal and extra-sensory stimulation. A state of dispersed attention or relaxation is known to facilitate sensitivity to subliminal stimulation. Likewise, ESP seems to be facilitated by an increased awareness of internal processes, feelings and imagery, by relaxation, and by a passive and non-analytical state of mind. These similarities have led to speculation that, once the extra-sensory information has reached an individual, it is processed in very similar ways to subliminal information. That is, both extra-sensory and weak-sensory information initially arrive at an unconscious or preconscious stage of processing. Both types of information then have the potential to emerge into consciousness, subject to various types of distortion and transformation along the way. The area in which most research has been conducted into distortions and transformations of weak sensory material is that of defensiveness.

Defensiveness can be defined in several ways. The concept has its origins in psychoanalytical theory, in which the ego uses defence mechanisms to protect itself against anxiety. In contrast, focusing more on the process of defences than on the goal of defences, the cognitive approach conceptualizes defence as the cognitive reappraisal of threatening situations, leading to a reduction of subjective threat. However, most conceptualizations of defensiveness share the general notion of the delayed or distorted perception of potentially threatening information.

Although paper-and-pencil measures of defensiveness do exist, the measure that we are most concerned with is the Defence Mechanism Test (DMT). In this test, simple pictures depicting a potentially threatening situation are shown for extremely short durations, and after each exposure the participant is asked to describe what they thought they saw. The rationale behind the test is that, at such short durations, individuals can perceive little if anything of the stimulus picture, so they will project something of their own fears and attitudes into their descriptions, in the form of distortions and transformations. A trained scorer checks the individual's descriptions for signs of various types of defensiveness.

Martin Johnson was the first parapsychologist to test the idea that individuals who are defensive to weak sensory information may also be resistant to extra-sensory information. As he put it, 'people who are prone to draw their preconscious blinds in matters of visual perception might act somehow similarly towards perceptions which are extra-sensory' (Carpenter, 1965: pp. 70–71). His expectations were confirmed. Individuals who showed defensive reactions on the DMT tended to have lower ESP scores than individuals who were not defensive. This led to a series of studies, conducted in Iceland, USA and Holland, comparing DMT and ESP performance. A meta-analysis of these studies (Haraldsson and Houtkooper, 1992) found positive evidence for a DMT-ESP correlation, suggesting that there was indeed a link between subliminal perception and extra-sensory perception. This provided formal confirmation of the speculations and observations of parapsychologists that there appeared to be a similarity between SP and ESP.

I consider that this was an important finding, as it suggested that ESP information was processed according to normal psychological principles. However, there was a need for independent replication of the DMT-ESP studies, and replication attempts were hindered by difficulties in administering the DMT. I therefore developed an alternative measure of defensiveness that enabled objective scoring of individuals' reactions to weak sensory stimuli. In two studies I found that defensive individuals tended to have lower scores on the ESP task than individuals who were not defensive (Watt and Morris 1995). This finding is a conceptual replication of the DMT–ESP studies, and it provides converging evidence of the similarity between SP and ESP. It underlines the claim that normal cognitive processes may be applied to information that is of extra-sensory origin.

I have focused here on research with altered states of consciousness techniques and research comparing subliminal with extra-sensory perception, but these are not the only areas in which parapsychologists are applying psychological principles to the study of paranormal phenomena. For example, a new line of research is now developing using the concept of 'Shannon entropy', making predictions based on the assumption that anomalous cognition (another term for ESP) operates in part like visual processing (May *et al.*, 2000). The gradient of Shannon entropy refers to the change in level of information content across a target. This research arose from the observation that dynamic target material, (e.g. video clips) tends to be associated with higher ESP scores than unchanging or static target material (e.g. simple art prints). The visual system reacts more to changes in brightness across the visual field than to overall brightness. Analogously, the researchers postulated that anomalous cognition might be sensitive to changes in the target information, but not to the overall level of target information, suggesting that anomalous cognition operates like other sensory systems. Two studies conducted by May and colleagues confirmed these hypotheses, and other researchers are now beginning to use targets with known Shannon entropy properties in order to replicate independently and expand this line of research.

Although the means by which extra-sensory information reaches an individual are still unknown, and may be found to violate currently known physical principles, the evidence just described suggests that the processing of ESP information occurs in line with established psychological principles. This holds some promise that in time it may be possible to reach an understanding of psi with a model that can to some extent integrate psi within existing frameworks. Further discussion of the similarities and differences between psychology and parapsychology can be found in Schmeidler (1988).

Philosophical and methodological issues

There are a number of complexities in parapsychological research, some of which are to do with philosophical issues, while others are more methodological in nature. All of them tend to illustrate how challenging parapsychological research can be. The expertise that parapsychologists develop in responding to these challenges can be usefully applied to other similar fields (e.g. in behavioural research).

Probably the greatest challenge facing parapsychologists is to find replicable evidence for psi. It is difficult to do this, given that psi seems to be a weak and unreliable effect, and that parapsychology is a relatively small field with only limited resources to tackle its problems. Like psychology, its studies involve human participants, and when humans are involved it is neither easy nor even realistic to come up with well-established 'laws' of behaviour, unlike the situation in the physical sciences. This makes replicability difficult – a problem that is faced by behavioural research in general. However, parapsychologists have been among the first to realize the utility of tools such as meta-analysis in dealing with replicability issues. Along with meta-analysis has come an understanding of the importance of related concepts of statistical power and effect size. Parapsychologists have been quick to realize that a measure of effect size is a more accurate indicator of whether or not a study has replicated a claimed effect than the all-or-nothing indicator of statistical significance.

Another reason why replicability in parapsychological research is difficult is that the experimental system in parapsychology is an open one. This is true of any research involving human participants, because the participant is not an isolated entity that the experimenter observes impartially. Instead, the participant is trying to make sense of the experimental situation and respond in what they think is an appropriate manner. The experimenter can unintentionally affect the participant's behaviour, thus introducing a source of bias into the results. The way researchers deal with this problem is to conduct their research 'blind' – that is, keeping both participants and experimenters unaware of the experimental manipulations, so that their expectations cannot influence their behaviour. However, consider the implications of psi research. What if ESP really exists? What if the participant can read the experimenter's mind? What if the experimenter can use PK to influence delicate physical instruments directly? If this is the case, the experimental environment is even more open than was previously thought. If psi is a genuine effect, this has the startling implication that all research is vulnerable to unintended exchange of information and influence. It might be impossible to use completely blind methods, because these could be penetrated by ESP. This would mean that all experimental findings could be affected, perhaps with the person having most motivation to find a certain outcome (usually the experimenter) being most likely to influence the experiment.

This scenario does not mean that all experimental research – that is, all attempts to isolate and manipulate variables – is rendered invalid. Instead, it means that researchers have to learn more about how expectancy effects operate, and if psi exists they have to learn more about its limiting conditions. In general, researchers have to become more sophisticated in developing strategies to deal with the study of complex open systems. Parapsychologists are particularly well placed to develop this expertise, as the question of experimenter influence has a particularly high profile in this field. It is already well established that certain experimenters consistently achieve positive results, while others consistently achieve null results. The reasons for this 'experimenter effect' have yet to be established. One possibility is that it is just a chance pattern. If this is so, then the pattern would be expected not to appear consistently in future experiments. Some critics have suggested that the successful experimenters are either fraudulent or sloppy, so their positive results are artefacts. However, there seems to be no consistent evidence to support this hypothesis.

Another possibility is that parapsychology's experimenter effect is due to experimenter psi, with some particularly psychic experimenters being able to influence the outcome of the study according to their desires and expectations. There has been some investigation of this possibility, resulting in evidence that successful experimenters do tend to perform well on laboratory psi tasks. Another possibility is that some experimenters are better at eliciting psi from their participants than others (perhaps they are more enthusiastic and more able to help their participants to relax and be confident that they can perform well). Moreover, some experimenters may be more able to recruit the right type of participants than others. That is, some of them may be particularly talented in recognizing and recruiting participants who are able to perform well under experimental conditions. One ganzfeld experimenter noted that his successful results might have been due to the fact that he had avoided recruiting psychology students as experimental participants, while his less successful co-experimenters did recruit psychology students.

These are all questions that parapsychologists have to deal with, and in the process they may develop an expertise that can be applied to similar fields that present similar problems. Regardless of the reality or otherwise of psi, science has much to gain from investigating paranormal phenomena and experiences.

Acknowledgement

I wish to thank Professor Robert Morris for his helpful comments on an earlier draft of this chapter.

Suggested further reading

Irwin, H.J. (1999) *An introduction to parapsychology,* 3rd edn. Jefferson, NC: McFarland.

Milton, J. and Wiseman, R. (1997) *Guidelines for extrasensory perception research.* Hatfield: University of Hertfordshire Press.

Radin, D. (1997) *The conscious universe: the scientific truth of psychic phenomena.* New York: HarperCollins.

Schmeidler, G.R. (1988) *Psychology and parapsychology: matches and mismatches.* Jefferson, NC: McFarland.

11 Near-death experiences

Chris A. Roe

> *To die; to sleep;*
> *To sleep: perchance to dream: ay, there's the rub;*
> *For in that sleep of death what dreams may come?*
>   (William Shakespeare, *Hamlet,* Act III)

Introduction

Consider the following tale.

A man is dying, and as he reaches the point of greatest physical distress, he hears himself pronounced dead by his doctor. He begins to hear an uncomfortable noise, a loud ringing or buzzing, and at the same time feels himself moving very rapidly through a long dark tunnel. After this, he suddenly finds himself outside of his own physical body and sees his own body from a distance, as though he is a spectator. He watches the resuscitation attempt from this unusual vantage point and is in a state of emotional upheaval.

Others come to meet and help him. He glimpses the spirits of relatives and friends who have already died, and a loving warm spirit of a kind he has never encountered before – a being of light – appears before him. This being asks him a question, non-verbally, to make him evaluate his life, and helps him along by showing him a panoramic instantaneous playback of the major events in his life. At some point he finds himself approaching some sort of barrier or border, apparently representing the limit between earthly life and the next life. Yet he finds that he must go back to the earth, that the time for his death has not yet come [and] he reunites with his physical body and lives. The experience affects his life profoundly, especially his views about death and its relationship to life.

Moody (1975: 21–3)

You might be forgiven for thinking that the above account was taken from a work of science fiction. Indeed, it does read like a work of fantasy, although in fact it is an account by researcher Raymond Moody of a 'prototypical' near-death experience, compiled from accounts given to him by people who had either been clinically dead or come close to death, but who had survived to tell the tale of their experiences. As we shall see, the accounts are given earnestly (indeed, many people are loath to recount their experiences for fear that they will be thought 'crazy'), are fairly consistent across different time periods and cultures, and are treated as genuine experiences by theorists who strive to explain them. In this chapter we shall consider what the main features of near-death experiences seem to be, and whether some people may be more prone to have them than others, and we shall assess the adequacy of the theories that have been put forward to account for them, either in natural or in supernatural terms.

Experiences that include many (but rarely all) of the features described in Moody's prototype are known as *near-death experiences* (NDEs). Greyson (2000: 315) defines NDEs as 'profound psychological events with transcendental and mystical elements, typically occurring to individuals close to death or in situations of intense physical or emotional danger'. This reflects the fact that NDEs have been reported in cases of actual clinical death, where the vital signs are absent for up to 20 minutes (in rare cases), but also seem to be experienced in situations which are only *potentially* fatal (see Box 11.1). NDEs were originally thought to be rare (Moody, 1975; cf. Greyson 2000), but more recent estimates (Sabom, 1982; Ring, 1984; Fenwick and Fenwick, 1996) suggest that up to one-third of people who come close to death have them. Although this figure may be somewhat inflated (Greyson, 1998), there is evidence to suggest that such experiences are not uncommon. For example, Royce (1985) found that 70% of the clergymen whom he surveyed had been given NDE accounts by parishioners, and Gallup and Proctor (1982) reported that 5% of Americans claimed to have had some form of NDE. This relatively high incidence could be explained in terms of improvements in resuscitation methods, which mean that more people survive the kinds of close brush with death (e.g. heart attack, drowning, road traffic accident) that would previously have been fatal. It could, of course, simply reflect the fact that the notion of NDEs has entered popular culture and may provide the basis for some fantasized experience produced while unconscious or in crisis.

Box 11.1: Are people who have NDEs really 'dead'?

The near-death experience is carefully named, since the experience is not restricted to those who have actually 'died'. NDEs have been reported by people who have been pronounced clinically dead but subsequently resuscitated, by individuals who actually died but were able to describe their experiences in their final moments, and also by individuals who in the course of accidents or illnesses simply feared that they were near to death (Greyson, 2000). In all three types of case it could be claimed that the experience has more to do with the process of dying than with the end point of death itself. Part of the problem lies in the way in which we 'diagnose' death. According to Roberts and Owen (1988), there is a long history of misdiagnosis of death. Initially, death had been determined by checking for a pulse or respiration, and by checking the pupils for a reaction to light. Later, after the invention of the stethoscope, attention concentrated on the heart. However, with the advent of cardiopulmonary resuscitation it became clear that people who had been pronounced dead could be brought back to life (Sabom, 1998). Attention has therefore now switched to brain function. Yet in the same way a lack of cortical activity and even brainstem quiescence may be symptomatic of dying but need not be an indicator of death. In each case there may be a suspicion that some vestige of life may be going undetected which is capable of maintaining some kind of phenomenological experience. These shifts in focus demonstrate how difficult it is to identify any single event as defining death. Rather, death is a process that takes time, and if the appropriate action is taken then the dying process can be reversed. Roberts and Owen adopt an extreme definition of death, which they describe as being 'characterised by irreversible loss of organ functions and is a one-way permanent state' (Roberts and Owen, 1988: 610). According to this definition, no one reporting an NDE has died (since their dying was reversible), and therefore all NDE reports refer to the experiences of people who have remained alive.

If the NDE genuinely indicates what happens after we die, as many who have reported it believe, then we might expect to find differences between those who were actually near death and those who only thought that they were. Moody (1975) claims that in such cases the NDE is less complete than when the person is clinically 'dead'. However, Greyson (1983) found little difference in the content or sequence of NDEs occurring in the dying compared to those who only believed themselves about to die. Owens and colleagues (1990) compared NDEs in patients whom they believed would have died without medical intervention with those in patients who believed that they were near death but in fact were not. The only differences in the experiences were in terms of enhanced perception of light and more lucid clear thinking. The fact that virtually identical NDEs can be induced by perceived threat needs to be taken into account in any potential explanation.

The person most closely associated with bringing the near-death experience to popular attention, and indeed for coining the phrase, is Raymond Moody. His interest in the phenomenon stems not from direct experience, since Moody has not had an NDE himself, but from his time as an undergraduate studying philosophy. One of his professors described to him what had happened after he had 'died' and been resuscitated. Some years later while teaching philosophy, one of his students recounted his grandmother's experience, which involved virtually the same series of events. Moody began to take an active interest in such cases, and he found that many of the classes he took would include at least one student who could describe a personal NDE (either his own or that of a close friend or relative). After teaching philosophy for three years he went to medical school with the intention of becoming a psychiatrist, and there he found patients on the wards who had been resuscitated after having 'died' for a short time, who were also able to recall experiences from the time when they were 'dead'. Moody was impressed by the broad similarities between cases even though they involved people from a range of religious, social and educational backgrounds. It is very easy to be blasé about these similarities when thinking about NDEs now, in the twenty-first century, when notions of travelling down tunnels and being met by deceased relatives form part of popular culture (e.g. in movies such as *Flatliners*, television programmes such as *The Simpsons*, and many popular books), to the point where a classic NDE is almost archetypal. However, at the time many of the common features were quite unexpected, and they certainly did not conform to stereotypical views of what might happen after death. As the number of cases increased, Moody found that he had enough material to be able to give public talks on the subject, and members of the audience at these lectures would often volunteer further cases. By the time his first book *Life After Life*, was published in 1975, he had amassed over 150 cases.

In this book, Moody identified 15 elements that seemed to recur in NDE reports (see Box 11.2). When considering these we must bear in mind that they have been drawn from a variety of cases, and this sketch is not representative of any one particular case. In fact, no single experience included more than 12 of these 15 elements, and no single element was always present, so we cannot claim from this that some elements are more central or more characteristic of the NDE than others. In addition, it must be noted that there is no fixed order to the sequence in which these features appear in an NDE. The purpose of Moody's book was to draw attention to the fact that people were reporting such experiences, and to convince serious researchers that the topic was worthy of study. At this level it was a great success. The book was an international bestseller (Irwin, 1999) and has been translated into over 30 languages (Roberts and Owen, 1988). A whole new research area of near-death studies has been established, with its own professional body (The International Association for Near-Death Studies) and peer-reviewed publication (*Journal of Near-Death Studies*). However, as Moody himself freely admits (1975: 181), the book was not intended to stand as a scientific study – the collection is no more than descriptive, and it does not permit conclusions to be drawn about which elements are more common or which seem to be precursors of others.

Box 11.2: Key features of the near-death experience (Moody, 1975)

The inherent ineffability of the experience: People find it difficult to put into words what has happened to them.

Overhearing the news of their own death: Often some clear statement that others believe them to have died, which may come as a surprise to them.

Feelings of peace and quiet: In some cases euphoria, and these feelings can be in stark contrast to the intense pain that is experienced immediately prior to the NDE.

The noise: Often a rather unpleasant buzzing or rushing sound.

The dark tunnel: More often a sensation of being pulled rapidly through a dark space than a vision of an actual tunnel.

Out of the body: A sense of being outside one's body and looking down at it.

Meeting others: Awareness of others, perhaps (but not always) deceased relatives.

The being of light: A light that is typically dim initially but which becomes intensely bright and enveloping.

The review: A panoramic review of one's major life events.

The border or limit: A 'point of no return' at which one must 'decide' whether to return to the body.

Coming back: A sense of making the decision to return.

Telling others: Reticence about describing the experience to others due to fear of appearing insane.

Effects on lives: Subtle but profound changes in views on life and other people.

New views on death: Reduced fear of death, but also greater valuing of life.

Corroboration: Independent confirmation of elements of the NDE by others.

Kenneth Ring (1980) took things a stage further by conducting a more systematic survey using a structured interview and measurement scale that he had devised. This was administered to 102 people who had been near death, of whom 48% reported an NDE of some description. Ring used their accounts to identify a 'core experience' which consisted of five stages. Not only did these tend to unfold in a particular order, but the earlier stages seemed to be more common than the later ones, as one might expect if some people are revived earlier than others. However, we need to be aware that this series of stages is better described as a trend rather than as an invariant sequence. For example, Greyson (1998) reports on some experiences which were 'out of sequence'.

The five stages of the NDE

1. Feelings of deep peace and well-being

The first and most common stage, reported by 60% of Ring's NDE subjects, involves a sense of bliss or peace. This feeling is often characterized by an absence of fear and/or pain (which may have been the dominant emotions prior to the NDE, e.g. during cardiac arrest). Heim's (1892) autobiographical account of his own experience after falling from a mountain to what he believed would be his certain death is a good example:

> No grief was felt nor was there any paralysing fright. There was no anxiety, no trace of despair or pain, but rather calm seriousness,

profound acceptance and a dominant mental quickness. The relationship of events and their probable outcomes was viewed with great objective clarity, no confusion entered at all.

(Heim, 1892, cited in Roberts and Owen, 1988: 607)

Although for some individuals the feeling is tinged with sadness or lone-liness (Irwin, 1999), for others the experience is not simply one of emotional detachment, but of ineffable euphoria:

I felt embraced by such feelings of bliss, that there are no words to describe the feeling. The nearest I can come to it in human terms is to recall the rapture of being 'in love', the emotion one feels when one's first-born is put into one's arms for the first time, the transcendence of spirit that can sometimes occur when one is at a concert of classical music, the peace and grandeur of mountains, forests and lakes or other beauties of nature that can move one to tears of joy. Unite all these together and magnify a thousand times and you get a glimpse of the 'state of being' that one is in.

(Grey, 1985, cited in Blackmore, 1993: 94)

2. A sense of separation from the body

The next most common experience among Ring's respondents was a sense of being disconnected from the body, often with accompanying sensory experiences. In total, 37% of the NDE subjects reported this, of whom about half were able to see their own body – usually from a bird's-eye view. At times this provided them with an excellent view of the medical staff's attempts to resuscitate them:

The next thing was I was above myself near the ceiling looking down. One of the nurses was saying in what seemed a frantic voice, 'Breathe, Dawn, breathe.' A doctor was pressing my chest, drips were being disconnected, everyone was rushing around. I couldn't understand the panic. I wasn't in pain.

(Fenwick and Fenwick, 1996: 35)

Emotional reactions to seeing one's own body have varied from a desperate desire to return to it (but without any idea of how this could be achieved) through to complete disinterest. 'I could see my own body all tangled up in the car amongst all the people who had gathered around, but you know, I had no feelings for it whatsoever. It was like it was a completely different human, or maybe even just an object' (Moody, 1975: 40–41).

In some cases the 'person' who is having the out-of-body experience feels as if they do not have any 'body' at all, but rather exist as a kind of pure consciousness. Others do describe what could be called a spiritual body which is invisible and inaudible to others, unable to be touched and virtually weightless.

3. Entering darkness/passing through a tunnel

To the general public the image of travelling along a dark tunnel towards a bright light seems to capture the essence of the NDE. Indeed, in about a quarter of Ring's NDE cases, either before or after the out-of-body experience the respondent described feeling as if they were drifting or even moving rapidly through a dark space (Ring, 1980). Although this was referred to as a tunnel in Moody's prototype, the experience is only sometimes described as being tunnel-like in any literal sense. In fact it is much more commonly thought of as a kind of enveloping space or velvety blackness that gives only a vague sense of being enclosed, rather than there being perceptible tunnel walls. For example, one NDE subject describes their experience as follows: 'I went through this dark vacuum at super speed. ... I felt like I was riding on a roller-coaster train at an amusement park' (Moody, 1975: 32).

4. Seeing the light

For 16% of respondents, as they progressed down the tunnel they became aware of a light at its end, to which they seemed to be drawn. As they moved forwards, the light expanded and became brighter until it enveloped them completely. The light was described as brilliant, often golden, but did not seem to dazzle or hurt the eyes in the way that a real bright light might do if viewed normally. There is a common belief among NDE subjects that the light is actually some kind of being, and it is often associated with a religious figure such as Jesus. One's prior religious beliefs do not seem to affect the likelihood or form of such an encounter, although clearly they may affect the interpretation of it, so that atheists still see the light, but they do not associate it with a particular God (Greyson and Stevenson, 1980; Sabom, 1982). Communication with this being does not seem to involve speech, but is somehow more direct. NDE subjects have great difficulty in articulating what was actually communicated, although they frequently say that it seems to centre on the life of the person, offering them an opportunity to reflect on what they have and have not done (athough this does not seem to involve any kind of critical judgement), and to decide whether to return to their body.

A panoramic life review may follow in which key events in the NDE subject's life are played out to them. Its exact nature can vary. For some it follows a chronological order, starting with their earliest memories, whereas for others it seems to come all at once. Some subjects view the events as spectators, while others review the scene from the perspective of different actors, having an empathic sense of the consequences for others of their actions. The memories themselves are primarily visual, but they seem to be more vivid than normal, and to evoke the emotions of the time. The events do not seem to be random, but rather to have been chosen to illustrate certain lessons, such as when they were particularly unkind to others, or equally when they were particularly benevolent, or where the course of their life changed, (e.g. with the birth of a child). Some subjects experience the life review in the company of the being of light, whereas others are left to reflect alone. Again the emphasis seems to be on understanding rather than on judgement.

5. Entering the light/beautiful garden

Around 10% of Ring's NDE subjects reported that on entering the light they found themselves in some other world, which was often so indescribably beautiful that experients did not want to return from it. It was often classically 'heavenly', consisting of a lovely garden with beautiful music, etc; rather than stereotypically 'heavenly', with clouds, angels, and Pearly Gates (Irwin, 1999), although the latter have been reported on occasion (Sabom, 1982). While here the NDE experients may be greeted by deceased relatives and friends, or by people who are unknown to them but who are described as 'guardian spirits' or 'helpers'. These companions are usually present to reassure them or to facilitate the decision as to whether to return to the body. While in this transcendental realm, the NDE experient may approach some kind of natural border, such as a river, a wall with an archway, a fence with a gate or simply a line. This takes on symbolic meaning to them and they become convinced that if they pass across this border they will not be able to return. This typically results in the decision to go back. Most subjects do not recall the 'journey' back, but find that they must have lapsed into unconsciousness only to awaken back in their body. However, some do recall being drawn rapidly back into their bodies, and this may be achieved with a jolt.

Correlates of the NDE

If we are to understand the causes of the near-death experience, it would be useful to consider what type of person reports having such experiences and under what circumstances. This should help us to discriminate between some of the explanations that have been put forward.

Effects of type of life threat

Surprisingly, physiological details of the close brush with death seem to play only a minor role in the form of the NDE (Ring, 1980; Siegel, 1980; Twelmlow and Gabbard, 1984). We have already seen (see Box 11.1) that there are only modest differences between those who were actually near to death and those who simply thought that they were. When looking at different types of life threat it appears as if those who were chronically ill prior to the NDE were more likely to experience positive emotions and apparitions, whereas those who had a sudden threat to life reported a more typical core NDE (Grosso, 1981). Similarly, Noyes and Kletti (1977) found that features such as hallucinations of beings (guides or relatives) and also panoramic life reviews were more common in cases of drowning or terminal illness than after falls and accidents. Greyson (1985) found that sudden life reviews rarely occurred among people who had long been expecting death, presumably because such individuals had already had the opportunity to take stock and prepare for death.

Demographic and personality factors

The incidence of the NDE does not seem to be related to such demographic factors as age, gender, socio-economic status, ethnicity or marital status, although these factors may be related to the actual content of the NDE (Roberts and Owen, 1988; Irwin, 1999). However, there are demographic differences in the type of brush with death that is most likely. For example, males may be more likely than females to have a road accident (Twelmlow and Gabbard, 1984; Irwin, 1999). Children's NDEs seem to follow the adult pattern with only minor deviations. For example, they tended to be greeted by deceased pets rather than by relatives (Morse and Perry, 1990), which tends to argue against an explanation in terms of social conditioning. Although few differences have been found with regard to general personality dimensions, Locke and Shontz (1983) found that NDE experients scored higher on an absorption measure compared with those who had experienced an out-of-body experience. Greyson and Stevenson (1980) found that NDE experients reported more prior mystical-type experiences than comparison groups, and Ring and Rosing (1990b) suggested that the incidence of childhood trauma was higher in NDE experients. They speculated that this might lead to higher levels of absorption and dissociation, but not necessarily to fantasy-proneness.

Cultural differences in the content of NDEs

The central features of the NDE have been recorded throughout history and across various cultures and religious groups. Holk (1978) found descriptions in the beliefs of Bolivian, Argentinian and North American Indians, and accounts from China, Siberia and Finland that included a sense of joy and peace, being out of the body, being reunited with ancestors, perceiving a light, and reaching a border or dividing line. According to Greyson (2000), accounts similar to that of Moody can also be found in the folklore and writings of European, Middle Eastern, African, Indian, East Asian, Pacific and Native American peoples.

However, there are some differences in the specific details. For example, Schorer (1985/86) found that North American NDEs included moccasins, snakes, eagles, and bows and arrows as dominant imagery, whereas Pasricha and Stevenson (1986) found that Asian Indians were sent back to live because of an apparent supernatural bureaucratic mistake rather than through their own conscious choice, or because of earthly commitments. Osis and Haraldson (1977) found in their reports of encounters with 'God' that no Hindus reported seeing Jesus and no Christians reported seeing a Hindu deity. However, we have already noted that NDE experients rarely recognize the entity by their physical appearance, so this cultural difference in labelling may simply be a consequence of the inexpressible nature of the experience. If a Christian experiences being in the presence of an all-powerful and benign entity, this may naturally be described as Christ, and need not suggest an encounter with someone in human form who resembles ecclesiastical representations of Christ (e.g. with long robes and flowing beard). Despite some cross-cultural variations in specific NDE content, it is worth noting that people do report elements that run counter to their cultural expectations (cf. Ring, 1984; Abramovitch, 1988), and that individuals who have never heard of the NDE (e.g. most of Moody's original sample) still tend to describe the same features (Sabom, 1982). This may suggest that whereas the process may be universal, the specific imagery and interpretation that are ascribed to an NDE are determined by the expectations and beliefs of the individual.

Theories of the NDE

Spiritual theories

The first theory we shall consider is that NDEs arise as the mind or spirit separates from the body near the point of death, since this seems to be the most popular interpretation among members of the general public (Kellehear *et al.*, 1990). Roberts and Owen (1988) claim that many studies of the NDE are based implicitly on the notion that such experiences can most economically be understood in terms of the existence of an afterlife, and popular interest in the phenomenon is based on the hope that it might provide an empirical basis for what they had previously accepted as an act of faith. Notable subscribers to this view are Ring (1980, 1984) and Sabom (1982, 1998). But what would stand as evidence for the NDE being a literal experience of an afterlife? It would be extremely difficult to operationalize and test an immaterial interpretation using materialist scientific methods.

One possible strand of support could come from claims that certain early stages are objectively real. If this could be demonstrated, then it might indirectly strengthen the case for regarding later stages as similarly real. The autoscopic experience (i.e. seeing one's body from afar) is the most promising stage on which to focus, since during this experience some people claim to have witnessed resuscitation procedures or their loved ones being comforted in nearby rooms. Is there any evidence to suggest that these experiences could not have occurred as a result of some vestigial sense of hearing and a good imagination? Sabom (1982) claims that patients who have been resuscitated have seen things during their NDEs that they could not possibly have reconstructed from the available sensory information or from a general knowledge of resuscitation. Blackmore (1993) has criticized this evidence, although unconvincingly, whilst others have offered further impressive cases that are equally difficult to explain away (e.g. Moody and Perry, 1988; Ring and Lawrence, 1993; Ring and Cooper, 1997, 1999). However, none of these cases need imply survival if we allow for the existence of ESP. It may seem as if we are replacing one mystical unknown with another, but in fact there is some good evidence to suggest that at least under some circumstances people may gain access to information that is not available to them via the normal sensory channels or inference (Bem and Honorton, 1994; Radin, 1996).

Spiritual theories do not readily explain why there should be cases in which the threat to life was only perceived rather than actual (why should there be mistakes?), although this may simply reflect prejudice about the form that an afterlife should take. Parsimony dictates that the spiritualist interpretation should be set aside until it can be shown that explanations in terms of more mundane mechanisms, with roots in the principles of psychology and psychopharmacology, are inadequate. If these latter theories can account for the data equally well, then they should be preferred because they do not require us to invoke any new or mysterious mechanisms.

Psychological theories

Depersonalization

Perhaps the first explanation of the NDE to be proposed was by Pfister (1930, translated by Kletti and Noyes, 1981), who attempted to account for the experiences of Heim's mountaineers when they were falling, they thought, to their deaths. He suggested that when confronted with the prospect of their own imminent demise, they might have attempted to escape from this unpalatable thought by retreating into a more positive fantasy experience in an effort to protect themselves from the emotional shock. Noyes and Kletti (1976, 1977) developed this notion further, suggesting that NDEs represent a type of depersonalization. Noyes (1972) proposed that where there is any possibility of avoiding death, physical and mental alertness increase and attention becomes focused on survival, but where death seems inevitable, fear is replaced by a sense of peace and resignation, with the panoramic life review perhaps reflecting a need for premature grieving for one's own death. This accounts very well for some of the features of the NDE, such as the sense of being out of one's body and the general sense of detachment from proceedings, but does not accord with the higher level of alertness that is usually experienced, since depersonalization is usually rather dream-like and involves a loss of sense of self (Irwin, 1999).

The NDE as a remembrance of the birth experience

It has been suggested that the shock of being close to death may evoke powerful memories of another occasion of great stress, namely one's own birth (Grof and Halifax, 1977; Sagan, 1979). In this account the dark tunnel down which one is passing represents the birth canal, the light is the theatre into which one is being born, and the authoritative presence may simply be the adult medical staff or parent. However, this explanation has a number of weaknesses. If we consider the birth experience, the birth canal is nothing like a tunnel, even if the fetus were actually looking face-first and open-eyed into it (which of course they are not), not least because for the fetus it is a very tight squeeze, whereas it is more common for NDE experients not to be able to touch the sides of the tunnel along which they travel. Birth is not a gradual floating sensation, but rather it consists of a succession of 'pushes'. The process of birth is typically very stressful for the child, in contrast to the serenity and joy of the NDE. In any case, Becker (1982) has shown that newborns simply do not have the visual–spatial or cognitive capacity to recall the birth experience in the way that would be needed to spark the NDE, and Blackmore (1983) found that tunnel experiences were just as common among those born by Caesarean section, who would not have had the original birth experience.

Organic theories

Endorphins

Extreme stress and fear can lead to the release of endorphins. These are naturally produced opiates that can reduce pain perception and induce pleasant sensations. It may be that endorphins are also released near death, and they might therefore be responsible for the positive emotions and calm that are often reported. It is interesting to note that drugs which negate the effects of neurochemicals such as endorphins may give rise to NDEs that are more negative in nature (e.g. Judson and Wiltshaw, 1983). Jansen (1997) has similarly argued that the naturally occurring anaesthetic ketamine can trigger experiences of lights, tunnels, and so on. However, these compounds have a number of effects that are not characteristic of the NDE. For example, ketamine experiences are often fearful rather than positive (Strassman, 1997), they have an unreal quality that is not found in NDEs (Fenwick, 1997), and the analgesic effects associated with them last much longer than the few minutes or seconds of an NDE (Sabom, 1982).

Cerebral anoxia

It has been noted that the final common pathway to death is cerebral anoxia (lack of oxygen supply to the brain) (Rodin, 1980). The types of effects that are produced by anoxia, which include a sense of well-being and power, suggest that the NDE might best be explained as the result of an anoxic brain. It is interesting in this context to consider the research conducted by Whinnery (1990, 1997). This examined experiences reported by pilots who had briefly become unconscious during the periods of rapid acceleration which occurred in the course of certain manoeuvres. Loss of consciousness occurs because the accelerating forces can substantially reduce the blood flow to the head, inducing a type of anoxia. Whinnery found that a number of the features reminiscent of NDEs are reported, such as tunnel visions, bright lights, floating sensations, out-of-body experiences and euphoria, and even the report of 'dreams' that sometimes include visions of beautiful gardens and meeting (live) family members (Blackmore, 1993). Perhaps we are dealing with a similar phenomenon in the NDE. For this interpretation to be tenable, we need to be sure that anoxia is a necessary precursor of the NDE, and there is some evidence to suggest that it is not. According to Greyson (2000), the only study to date that has actually measured blood levels of oxygen and carbon dioxide during NDEs was by Sabom (1982), and this found no significant differences in the experiences of individuals with and without anoxia. This finding has been questioned on the grounds that general blood measures (taken, say, from an easily accessible artery) are not good indicators of blood oxygen levels in particular regions of the brain. More accurate measures are clearly needed. However, there are many instances of NDEs where we can be fairly sure that anoxia is unlikely, particularly where there is only a perceived threat to the person's life (e.g. with Heim's mountaineers). This does not rule out anoxia as a possible cause of some of these effects, but it does rule it out as the *only* cause.

Temporal lobe seizures

Sabom and Kreutziger (1982) considered the idea that hypoxia (impaired oxygen supply to the brain) can give rise to temporal lobe epilepsy, which has features similar to the NDE, such as the panoramic life review and the changes in affect. However, these researchers noted qualitative differences in the reports of the two types of experience which led them to conclude that this was not an adequate explanation. Seizure-induced perceptions also tend to feature auditory imagery more frequently than visual imagery (Irwin, 1999), whereas in the NDE it is not uncommon for the person to experience no sound at all, and the memories that are invoked tend to be random and not particularly meaningful, quite unlike the life review reported by NDE experients (Noyes and Kletti, 1977).

Hallucination

Some medications and some physiological malfunctions can give rise to hallucinations. Could these form the basis for reported NDEs? Although this hypothesis is superficially plausible, those whom we can be sure have not taken drugs or suffered injury or malfunction have NDEs that are essentially the same as those whom we are less sure about (Greyson, 2000), suggesting that this is not the key factor. In fact, there is evidence to suggest that drug- or metabolically induced delirium may actually be an *inhibitor* of NDEs (Osis and Haraldson, 1977). In any case, hallucinations induced in various other ways typically include confused thinking, disorientation and fear together with rather bizarre and idiosyncratic visions. This is in stark contrast to the common pattern of events found in NDEs that includes particularly lucid thinking and calmness, or even euphoria.

The 'dying brain' hypothesis

Perhaps the best known and most popular explanation of the NDE is Blackmore's (1993) account of the dying brain. She suggests that different elements of the NDE may need to be explained by different psychological or physiological mechanisms. She differentiates between the features of the tunnel, light and noises that she thinks are probably caused by hypoxia and other threats to the brain, and the affective features of peace and well-being, which are due to the action of endorphins. Some of these features have already been considered above, so we shall concentrate here on her explanations of the tunnel and out-of-body experiences.

Tunnel and light phenomena are claimed to be the result of neuronal disinhibition in the visual cortex. In this brain area, the natural state for cells is to fire, and they have to be suppressed from firing via inhibition. If the inhibitory cells responsible for this control are more sensitive to oxygen depletion, then the first consequence of anoxia may ironically be an *increase* in cell firing. Given that light receptors in the retina are more densely packed in the middle of the visual field, and more of their impulses survive to be represented in the cortex, then this increasing activity may be experienced as a light at the centre of the visual field which becomes increasingly bright and large as more cells start to fire (Blackmore and Troscianko, 1988). This expansion may naturally be interpreted in terms of movement towards the circle of light. When many cortical cells are firing, this could give the impression of a brilliant light, but since the eyes are not involved in its perception, the experience would not be painful. Again the problem here is in accounting for such experiences among people who are clearly not anoxic.

Blackmore (1993) argues that the out-of-body experience can be explained in terms of our ordinary sense of self (as located in our heads just behind the eyes) in fact being a *construction*. Rather than being real in any sense, this is simply the best model of reality we have, given the type of sensory input that we receive. Since vision is the dominant sense for most of us, it seems natural for our 'selves' to be located at a point that appears most sensible from a visual perspective. However, when sense data is in disarray (e.g. when meditating or taking hallucinogenic drugs, or when brain systems are shutting down close to death), then this preferred model may break down and be replaced by another which makes more sense of the remaining information. Blackmore suggests that if the reconstruction relies heavily on memory, then we might expect the model to be in the third person (viewing the scene from outside, typically above our bodies, as often occurs in our dreams). There is some evidence that individuals who normally dream from the third-person, 'bird's eye' perspective are more likely to have out-of-body experiences (Irwin, 1986; Blackmore, 1987), but this relationship does not hold for waking imagery. However, there are features of the experience that would be difficult to explain as simply being due to vestigial hearing and guesswork.

Conclusion

We have seen that a number of theories have been proposed to account for the NDE, but none of them comes very close to providing a comprehensive explanation for all of the features that are typical of the experience. Where these psychological and physiological hypotheses do succeed in explaining elements of the NDE, this is achieved by focusing selectively on some features that can be explained, and ignoring or diminishing the importance of those that cannot. However, while it may be true that these theories are incomplete at best, they may still be able to provide us with a rich source of speculative predictions that can be tested in future investigations. We should bear in mind that inadequate evidence is not the same as absence of evidence, and it is certainly premature to reject the psychological and organic theories in favour of a spiritualistic one. This is particularly so given that we still do not really have an adequate definition of what constitutes an NDE – no single feature seems to be necessary or unique to the experience. Despite the numerous books on the subject, there is still relatively little systematic evidence available, so it should not be too surprising that we are still some way from developing an understanding of the nature and cause of NDEs, and further work is clearly necessary. Whatever the ultimate resolution, it would be fair to say that the NDE is an intriguing and powerful area of human experience that merits our continued interest.

Suggested further reading

Bailey, L.W. and Yates, J. (1996) *The near-death experience: a reader*. London: Routledge.
Blackmore, S.J. (1988) Visions from the dying brain. *New Scientist* **1611**, 43–6.
Blackmore, S.J. (1993) *Dying to live: science and the near-death experience*. London: Grafton Books.
Moody, R.A. (1975) *Life after life*. New York: Bantam Books.

12 Gateways to the mind: society and the paranormal

Ron Roberts

> *It was the best of times, it was the worst of times, it was the age of wisdom, it was the age of foolishness, it was the epoch of belief, it was the epoch of incredulity, it was the season of light, it was the season of darkness, it was the spring of hope, it was the winter of despair, we had everything before us, we had nothing before us, we were all going direct to Heaven, we were all going direct the other way.*
> (Charles Dickens, *A Tale of Two Cities*, 1859)

> *To see what is in front of one's nose needs a constant struggle.*
> (George Orwell, *In Front of Your Nose*, 1946)

In this book we have posed a number of challenges for the reader. Our principal interests have been to review evidence pertinent to several phenomena which have fuelled the endeavours of parapsychologists in recent years and to survey some of the more unusual facets of our experience which more typically attract the interest of non-professional psychologists – or the lay public as they are more commonly known. The phenomena we have included in this volume do not represent an exhaustive list, but focus particularly on what have come to be known in some quarters as *anomalous experiences* (Cardeña *et al.*, 2000), although we prefer the more prosaic term *unusual experiences*. Our purpose is not exhausted by this review. We began by considering some of the conceptual tools which form the arsenal of scientists, and which have usually been omitted in volumes of this nature. We have aimed therefore not only to promote the scientific perspective on unusual experience, but also to provide insights into how the research process is conducted and evaluated – what is in the methodological tool-bag, as it were, to assist the drawing of accurate inference. In Chapter 3, Chris French provided a sobering account of the powerful effects which can follow from belief and expectation, and how our experimental manipulations must take careful heed of these, and indeed attempt to estimate the magnitude of these effects in each experimental context. Serious errors of judgement may ensue if these effects are ignored, and maximum benefits to our well-being may escape us if we fail to make full use of their potential.

An important constituent of the tool-bag, although one which is unpopular in some quarters, is the use of mathematical reasoning. However, without a thorough understanding of the laws of probability it is easy to make large errors in estimating the likelihood of events. Research shows that individuals who believe in the paranormal (so-called 'sheep') are more likely to underestimate the likelihood of a whole range of events occurring due to chance (i.e. they think that these events are much rarer than in fact they are). One influential field of work proposes that attributions of paranormality frequently arise to serve the purpose of explaining coincident events which are not perceived as such.

As we saw in Chapter 1, researchers bring with them a conceptual schema for attempting to validate reports of particular types of experience, and they have a variety of methodological tools (e.g. experimental design, statistical analysis, logical inference) to assist them in this quest. We considered a number of different types of experiential reports in this book, including dreams, near-death experiences, unconscious awareness under anaesthesia, meditative states and alien abduction experiences, which have all come under critical scrutiny. On the basis of the evidence that is available we can be reasonably certain that the various reports accurately describe the quality of experience in unique states of consciousness. However, we must distinguish between describing an experience and interpreting its origin, and we shall return to this issue later. On that basis we must make an exception of putative alien abduction experiences. Although the reports under this heading may stem from temporal lobe abnormalities or arise under conditions of sleep paralysis (Cheyne *et al.*, 1999), the notion that the features reported arise from actual abductions by aliens should at this stage be firmly rejected.

With regard to instances of paranormal cognition, during dreaming and in the ganzfeld the evidence is equivocal but merits continuing attention. However, an assessment that researchers must evaluate the existing evidence carefully and seek further data is not the same as an unequivocal endorsement of the reality of paranormal realms. The information presented in this book must surely alert the open-minded reader to the fact that there are myriad ways in which the inferences that we make may lead to incorrect judgements, no matter how good the intentions behind them may be. Current data on near-death experiences and on unconscious awareness should caution us against rushing to draw conclusions about the limits of cognitive functioning when the brain is under extreme physical duress. Clearly greater knowledge is required in these areas, but the present lack of reliable information should not lead to the automatic conclusion that the information which forms the basis of the experiences reported following such extreme physical conditions must have been conveyed to the recipient by means which defy known physical laws. This view is unwarranted, and would signal an abandonment of the intellectual rigour which has served humanity so well.

Why study the paranormal?

With the world in what some would say is a state of crisis, with increasing inequalities in health and wealth, global ecological catastrophe looming, a new industrial revolution unfolding at a breakneck pace, and a landscape of shifting moral values, why pay attention to the paranormal? Is it not life before death that should warrant all our attention, and not the possibility of life after it?

One strand of opinion maintains that it is precisely these dangers in the material world that lead some individuals to seek solace in an attachment to an eternal, immaterial world. The social marginality hypothesis, as it is known (Wuthnow, 1976), proposes that it is people in socially marginal groups who are more likely to interpret anomalous experiences in terms of paranormal occurrences. According to this view, personal status comes from assigning to oneself a special role – as someone who is different and, who is connected to a paranormal realm. While Targ and colleagues (2000) dismiss this notion on the grounds that political convictions, income or religiosity fail to correlate with the reporting of paranormal experiences, their argument is not that convincing. Precious few studies to date have examined the relationship between paranormal belief and social status, and the fact that divorced and separated people are more likely to report paranormal experiences suggests at the very least that social support (or its absence) may be a key factor in how people interpret some types of unusual experience. A wealth of evidence already points to the absence or relative lack of social supports as a highly influential ingredient in the developmental of mental and physical ill health (Stansfeld 1999). Its potential role in the development of paranormal belief or in unusual stress-induced experiences which may be interpreted as paranormal warrants further consideration.

The challenge posed by these opening words is one that parapsychologists ignore at their peril. Investigation of claims of the paranormal requires keeping an open mind, and an open mind requires periodic self-examination. However, it is a challenge that investigators of paranormal claims are more than able to meet, principally because so much of the work undertaken has yielded important insights about ourselves as human beings, whatever view one holds about the veracity of paranormal claims. These reveal a myriad of ways in which our interpretations of events can be skewed and misguided by prior beliefs and expectations – sometimes fuelled by deliberate fraud on the part of others – as well as misunderstanding of the possibilities afforded by the clustering of chance events. A number of cognitive mechanisms have been identified which can lead to perceptual distortion of essentially random data, leading to mistaken support of the psi hypothesis. These include only attending to events which seem to confirm one's expectations, and ignoring or underplaying evidence which does not.

Of course, the importance of such mechanisms extends well beyond the issue of whether or not the existence of psi abilities can be confirmed experimentally. The history of the twentieth century bears testimony to how organizational and political tyranny has been promoted by the operation of mechanisms to deny truth, distort reality and foster intolerance and hatred towards minority groups. In response to this we must recognize that truth does not and should not amount to certainty. Even the self-correcting mechanisms within science which contribute to public versions of 'truth' within the scientific community are by no means foolproof – in order to have their desired effect they must operate in a reasonably healthy society. If one speaks of the scientific community as an island, then extending this metaphor further we can say that this island cannot exist surrounded by a sea of irrationality. The wider environment must provide a moral and intellectual climate within which the values of the scientific community are nurtured, as well as the means (funding and problems in need of resolution) for its continued existence.

The question of whether the uncritical thinking which has characterized some claims for the paranormal has further adverse social consequences is a vitally important one. However, research on the relationship between paranormal beliefs and social judgements and actions in other areas of life is still in its infancy. Links between the ragbag collection of wild ideas which have moved into the mainstream of western (and notably US) culture and the steady erosion of intellectual rigour are a threat which some have argued that we ignore at our peril (Sagan, 1996; Kaminer, 1999). If we are not careful, a cultural descent into superstition could lead to an intellectual dark age and provide the fertile ground for those despots and tyrants who feed off the cravings for certainty and authority which science, if properly conducted, should challenge.

Of course, sloppy thinking is not a feature of all of the claims which are made in favour of the paranormal, and in this context we must make two comments. First, paranormal belief is itself more complex than it might appear. For example, Holden and French (2000) point to disagreements between researchers regarding the types of beliefs which should be included in any attempt to measure paranormal belief. Some individuals might believe that telepathy is established while rejecting outright claims of alien visitations or ghosts. Should the definition that is used be restricted to those events which, were they to be verified, would necessitate rewriting the laws of nature? Or should it also encompass such phenomena as alien visitations which, although they are currently not an accepted part of the historical record, in themselves pose no threat to established physical laws? Such disagreements aside, many of the scales that have been used have a number of similarities. All of them are agreed that paranormal belief is multifaceted. One of the most influential, namely Tobacyk and Milford's (1983) paranormal belief scale, proposes seven dimensions of belief (traditional religious belief, psi belief, witchcraft, superstition, spiritualism, extraordinary life forms and precognition). Some of these have been found to correlate with measures of critical inference (Tobacyk, 1988), while others have not.

Psi and religion

Commenting on the credulous nature of human beings, the philosopher Bertrand Russell (1950) once remarked that we must believe in something, and in the absence of good grounds for belief, we will be satisfied with bad ones. The question of whether belief in the paranormal is synonymous with credulity and irrationality haunts the discipline of parapsychology. Certainly rational claims can be made on the basis of serious empirical evidence to support such belief, but if we are considering the overall prevalence of paranormal belief, it is difficult to avoid the conclusion that much of this belief is unfounded. Navigating through the complex field of paranormal belief is a difficult enough endeavour. However, we cannot really hope to achieve our goal of understanding this unless we inquire into the functions which such beliefs serve for us as human beings.

How do we explain the ubiquitous nature of such beliefs? Is it enough to invoke the various types of neurological dysfunction, sleep disturbance, psychological and cognitive distortions, prior expectations, misunderstanding of chance, and other such biases which frequently underpin our interpretation of what lies before us? We must seek to understand further why the issue of the paranormal is of so much importance to sceptics and believers alike. To be sure, if the claims are true, sceptics must eat humble pie and revise their understanding of the universe. However, at present even where the evidence seems to be at its strongest (from ganzfeld studies, near-death experiences and dream research) it is not yet compelling. Serious objections have been made in all of these areas with regard to the most appropriate interpretation of the evidence – objections which the parapsychological community have yet to overcome. But should this situation change, it would be fair to ask sceptics what personal relevance this has for them? Which particular branch of their own tree of certainty fears the axe? It is probably fair to say that the determinants of belief or disbelief in the paranormal are inadequately understood. The evidence does indicate that psychologists are around 12 times more likely than natural scientists to consider ESP an impossibility (Wagner and Monnet, 1979). The reasons for this are uncertain, although Child (1985) suggests that psychologists' better understanding of errors in human judgement may be partly responsible. However, more research is needed to clarify matters.

And what of believers? What if they have to accept that the realm of the paranormal exists only in the imagination? The relationship between publicly espoused theory and personal values merits more serious examination. For example, anyone familiar with the behaviourist psychology of B.F. Skinner cannot but be impressed by the contrast between the extreme denial of thought and feeling present in his theoretical accounts of human behaviour and the intensity of emotions in his personal life (Walker, 1984). We know that it is not just the purely scientific merit of an idea which determines whether it gains a foothold in a wider discourse. A complex of personal goals, values, beliefs and expectations which are widely shared at a particular time also seems to be influential. An investigation of the relationship between public and private values in parapsychology is long overdue. Susan Blackmore's (1996) account of her experiences as a parapsychologist are a welcome and brave foray into these relatively uncharted waters.

My own experience suggests to me that belief in the paranormal serves to bolster the religious convictions of large numbers of people, whatever their religious denomination. Conflict between science and religion is nothing new, but in recent years a resurgence of fundamentalist opinion has placed dogma and blind faith ahead of the discomforting world view which modern science seems to offer. The media depiction of science as unfeeling techno-logical (or genetic?) manipulation is surely of some significance here. However, if we truly wish to understand our current malaise, we must look further afield. Modern cosmology and evolutionary theory seem to have placed us here not as a result of some predestined grand design or divine purpose (Dennett, 1995b), but by chance alone in all its wonder, and we have neither gods nor extraterrestrials to comfort us in our hour of need. The coun-tenance of New-Age therapies and mysticism, the rejection of evolutionary theory and disdain for scientific method are unholy palliatives that will not solve the real problems we face. These are how to face, connect with and live with the universe as it is, as opposed to how we would wish it to be. The pain of separation that people feel between themselves and this world which they think science projects requires something new – something different.

Is the paranormal the last battleground between science and religion – a battle which some would say organized religion has been losing ever since Galileo was visited by the inquisition? Although there are few data on this subject, I would conjecture that for many, paranormal cognition would imply the existence of a soul – an immortal one at that – and rejection of it would imply negation of our spiritual nature. Many people appear to be frightened – perhaps understandably so – that science threatens our humanity, and that the relentless march of materi-alism will destroy religion and with it morality, spirituality and the world itself. Some invoke the language of science to bolster their beliefs without under-standing the grammar. Such pseudoscience begins by assuming that desired beliefs are true and then seeks out confirmatory evidence to provide back-up. However, this one-sided accumulation of 'facts' bears no witness to truth. If out-of-body experiences, near-death experiences, mystical revelations, telepathy and apparitions can all be explained through a knowledge of the (far from simple) workings of the brain, where does that leave our conception of ourselves as human beings? What if there is no life after death?

At this juncture in our collective history, parapsychology is indispensable because it offers a gateway not to other worlds but to this one – its questions about the nature of human minds and human brains go right to the heart of our quest to understand ourselves and our place in the world. We have just entered the twenty-first century. As a young boy I remember thinking of this as the far-off future. Now it is here and much has changed – and it seems that nothing is sacrosanct. Is there nothing to hold on to? Many cherished views are being challenged. Surely one of the greatest of these challenges for humanity is to realize that we are mortal beings, alive at this moment, and to consider our presence in a universe without a creator and responsible to ourselves and each other alone. Death is an ever present part of our existence – we have no real need to deny it. We can claim access to our spiritual nature without religion, and without surrendering reason to orthodoxy.

> Our revels now are ended. These our actors, as I foretold you, were all spirits, and are melted into air, into thin air; And, like the baseless fabric of this vision, the cloud-capp'd towers, the gorgeous palaces, the solemn temples, the great globe itself, Yea, all which it inherit, shall dissolve, and, like this insubstantial pageant faded, leave not a rack behind.
>
> William Shakespeare, *The Tempest*, Act IV

Our immortality resides not with our souls but in how we change the world by our presence.

Suggested further reading

Blackmore, S. (1996) *In search of the light: the adventures of a parapsychologist.* New York: Prometheus Books.

Dennett, D.C. (1995) *Darwin's dangerous idea: evolution and the meanings of life.* Harmondsworth: Penguin.

Kaminer, W. (1999) *Sleeping with extra-terrestrials: the rise of irrationalism and perils of piety.* New York: Pantheon Books.

Sagan, C. (1996) *The demon-haunted world: science as a candle in the dark.* London: Headline Books.

Glossary

Some of these definitions have been adapted from Michael Thalbourne's book, *A Glossary of Terms Used in Parapsychology* (Thalbourne, 1982).

autoscopy the experience of seeing one's body as if one was physically removed from it.

blind adjective used especially with reference to a judge or other participant in an experiment to describe the situation where the person is without knowledge of cues or other information which would reveal the true target or its relationship to the responses in a test of psi.

blindsight the phenomenon whereby patients with damage to the primary visual cortex retain the ability to detect, localize and discriminate visual stimuli presented in areas of their visual field in which they subjectively report that they are blind.

chance the constellation of undefined causal factors which are considered to be irrelevant to the causal relationship under investigation, often spoken of as if it were a single, independent agency. The expression 'pure chance' is sometimes used to describe a state characterized by complete unpredictability.

cognition a psychological term that covers all of the various modes of human information-processing, such as perception, memory, imagination and problem-solving, generally used to denote the process, but occasionally used to denote the product.

coincidence two events are said to constitute a coincidence if they occur in such a way as to strike an observer as being highly related with regard to their structure or their meaning. To dismiss such an occurrence as a mere coincidence is to imply the belief that each event arose as a result of quite independent causal chains.

Defence Mechanism Test (DMT)   a so-called projective test of personality developed by the Scandinavian psychologist Ulf Kragh. Inspired by Freudian theory, it is said to be a means by which an individual's characteristic mechanisms for coping with anxiety can be determined.

double-blind   refers to the fact that neither the patient nor the person administering the treatment knows whether the patient is receiving the active treatment or the placebo treatment until the experiment is over.

endorphins   opiates naturally produced by the brain that can reduce pain perception and induce pleasant sensations.

extra-sensory perception (ESP)   paranormal cognition; the acquisition of information about an external event, object or influence (mental or physical, and past, present or future) other than through any of the known sensory channels.

ganzfeld   a special type of environment (or the technique for producing it) consisting of homogeneous, unpatterned sensory stimulation. The consequent deprivation of patterned sensory input is said to be conducive to introspection of inwardly generated impressions, some of which may be extra-sensory in origin.

hypnagogic imagery   the type of vivid imagery that may occur when one is drifting off to sleep. This is to be distinguished from hypnapompic imagery, which occurs as one is waking up.

mantra   an aid to meditation, usually a ritual verbal incantation for eliminating attention to the events that usually occupy the stream of consciousness.

paranormal   term applied to any phenomenon which in one or more respects exceeds the limits of what is deemed to be physically possible on current scientific assumptions.

parapsychology   term coined by Max Dessoir and adopted by J.B.Rhine to refer to the scientific study of paranormal phenomena (i.e. psi). Except in the UK, it has largely superseded the older expression 'psychical research'.

phenomenology   a branch of philosophy concerned with the study of things as they are perceived and experienced.

placebo   any therapy that is prescribed for its therapeutic effect on a symptom or disease, but which is actually ineffective or not specifically effective for the symptom or disorder being treated. The placebo effect is the non-specific, psychological or psychophysiological therapeutic effect produced by a placebo.

postmodernism   a critical cultural movement contending that we have gone beyond the world view of modernism (associated with increasing certainty of knowledge, social progress and progression toward truth in science). Postmodern critiques contend that no set of values, morals and judgements can lay claim to special status compared to others. With regard to the practice of science, this has led to arguments that no system of knowledge has a privileged position for describing and characterizing the world.

probability   one widely used definition of probability is based on possibility. The probability of an event is the total number of ways that the event can occur, divided by the total number of possible outcomes. Another definition is based on frequencies of events. Defined in this way, the probability of an event is the frequency of the event divided by the frequency of all types of events in which it could have occurred.

psi   a general blanket term, proposed by B.P. Wiesner and seconded by R.H. Thouless, used as either a noun or an adjective to identify paranormal processes and paranormal causation.

psychokinesis (PK)   paranormal action, a term introduced by J.B. Rhine to refer to the direct influence of mind on a physical system without the mediation of any known physical energy.

repeatable   as applied to experimental findings, repeatable phenomena are those which can be produced by any competent independent investigator by following a particular standardized procedure.

replication   (1) an experiment which is designed to yield the same findings as a previous experiment or series of experiments. (2) the event of conducting a replication study. (3) more strictly, an experiment which does in fact replicate the findings of its predecessor(s). In the latter sense an experiment that attempts to replicate previous findings but which fails is only an attempted replication.

subliminal   term coined by F.W.H. Myers to refer to events occurring below the threshold of conscious awareness.

subliminal perception   the reception, without awareness, of a stimulus.

sun signs   the best-known form of astrology divides people's birth dates into the 12 signs of the zodiac, which are 12 bands through which the sun passes during the course of a year. A person's zodiac sign indicates the position of the sun at their particular moment of birth, for which reason these 12 signs are also known as 'sun signs'.

supernatural   a theological and folkloristic term for paranormal, generally avoided by parapsychologists because of its implication that psi is somehow outside or over and above nature.

target   in a test of extrasensory perception, the object or event (physical or mental) that constitutes the information to be paranormally acquired by a percipient. In a test of psychokinesis, the physical system, or a prescribed outcome thereof, which the subject is attempting to influence or bring about.

validity   broadly speaking, validity is concerned with the ability of a model (or construct) to represent reality. Various types of validity exist. Discriminant validity refers to the extent to which a scale discriminates between people who differ in their degree of a particular attribute. Construct validity refers to the degree to which a new measure agrees with existing measures of the same construct.

References

Abramovitch, H. (1988) An Israeli account of a near-death experience: a case study of cultural dissonance. *Journal of Near-Death Studies* **6**, 175–84.

Abreu, J.M. (1999) Conscious and nonconscious African-American stereotypes: impact on first impression and diagnostic ratings by therapists. *Journal of Consulting and Clinical Psychology* **67**, 387-93.

Adams, J. (1998) *Risk*. London: UCL Press.

Ader, R. (1997) The role of conditioning in pharmacotherapy. In Harrington, A. (ed.), *The placebo effect: an interdisciplinary exploration*, Cambridge, MA: Harvard University Press, 138–65.

Alho, K., Woods, D., Algazi, A., Knight, R. and Naatanen, R. (1994) Lesions of the prefrontal cortex diminish the auditory mismatch negativity. *Electroencephalography and Clinical Neurophysiology* **91**, 353–62.

Allende, I. (1986) *The house of the spirits*. London: Black Swan.

Allison, J. (1970) Respiratory changes during the practice of the technique of transcendental meditation. *Lancet* **7651**, 833–4.

Anand, B.K., Chhina. G.S. and Singh, B. (1961) Studies on Sri Ramannand Yogi during his stay in an air-tight box. *Indian Journal of Medical Research* **49**, 82–9.

Anthony, B.J. and Graham, F.K. (1985) Blink reflex modification by selective attention: evidence for the modulation of 'automatic' processing. *Biological Psychology* **20**, 43–59.

Appelle, S., Lynn, S.J. and Newman, L. (2000) Alien abduction experiences. In Cardeña, E. Lynn, S.J. and Krippner, S. (eds), *Varieties of anomalous experience: examining the scientific evidence*. Washington, DC; American Psychological Association, 253–282.

Baars, B.J. (1988) *A cognitive theory of consciousness*. Cambridge: Cambridge University Press.

Backman, L., Almkvist, O., Nyberg, L. and Andersson, J. (2000) Functional changes in brain activity during priming in Alzheimer's disease. *Journal of Cognitive Neuroscience* **12**, 134–41.

Baddeley, A. (1991) *Human memory: theory and practise*. Hillsdale, NJ: Lawrence Erlbaum Associates.

Baggally, W.W., Johnson, A., Feilding, E., Taylor M. and Lobb, J. (1906) Sittings with Mr Chambers. *Journal of the Society for Psychical Research* **12**, 197–203.

Baker, R.A. (1992) *Hidden memories: voices and visions from within.* Buffalo, NY: Prometheus.

Baker, R.A. (1997a) The aliens among us: hypnotic regression revisited. In Frazier, K. Karr, B. and Nickell J. (eds), *The UFO invasion: the Roswell incident, alien abductions, and government coverups.* Amherst, NY: Prometheus, 210–27.

Baker, R.A. (1997b) No aliens, no abductions: just regressive hypnosis, waking dreams, and anthropomorphism. In Frazier, K. Karr, B. and Nickell, J. (eds), *The UFO invasion: the Roswell incident, alien abductions, and government coverups.* Amherst, NY: Prometheus, 249–65.

Bannister, D. and Fransella, F. (1971) *Inquiring man.* Harmondsworth: Penguin.

Bartholomew, R.E. and Howard, G.S. (1998) *UFOs and alien contact: two centuries of mystery.* Amherst, NY: Prometheus.

Bartholomew, R.E., Basterfield, K. and Howard, G.S. (1991) UFO abductees and contactees: psychopathology or fantasy-proneness? *Professional Psychology: Research and Practice* **22**, 215–22.

Baumeister, R.F. and Sommer, K.L. (1997) Patterns in the bizarre: common themes in satanic ritual abuse, sexual masochism, UFO abductions, factitious illness and extreme love. *Journal of Social and Clinical Psychology* **16**, 213–23.

Becker, C.B. (1982) The failure of saganomics: why birth models cannot explain near-death phenomena. *Anabiosis: Journal of Near-Death Studies* **2**, 102–9.

Beecher, H.K. (1955) The powerful placebo. *Journal of the American Medical Association* **159**, 1602–6.

Bem, D.J. and Honorton, C. (1994) Does psi exist? Replicable evidence for an anomalous process of information transfer. *Psychological Bulletin* **115**, 4–18.

Benson, H. (1997) The nocebo effect: history and physiology. *Preventive Medicine* **26**, 612–15.

Bentall, R. (2000) Hallucinatory experiences. In Cardeña, E. Lynn, S.J. and Krippner S. (eds), *Varieties of anomalous experience: examining the scientific evidence.* Washington, DC: American Psychological Association, 85–120.

Blackmore, S.J. (1983) Birth and the OBE: an unhelpful analogy. *Journal of the American Society for Psychical Research* **77**, 229–38.

Blackmore, S.J. (1984) A postal survey of OBEs and other experiences. *Journal of the Society for Psychical Research* **52**, 225–44.

Blackmore, S.J. (1987) Where am I? Perspectives in imagery, and the out-of-body experience. *Journal of Mental Imagery* **11**, 53–66.

Blackmore, S.J. (1988) Visions from the dying brain. *New Scientist* **1611**, 43–6.

Blackmore, S.J. (1993) *Dying to live: science and the near-death experience.* London: Grafton Books.

Blackmore, S. (1994). Alien abduction: the inside story. *New Scientist* **144**, 29–31.

Blackmore, S. (1996) *In search of the light: the adventures of a parapsychologist.* New York: Prometheus Books.

Blackmore, S.J. (1997) Probability misjudgement and belief in the paranormal: a newspaper survey. *British Journal of Psychology* **88**, 683–9.

Blackmore, S. (1999). *The meme machine.* Oxford: Oxford University Press.

Blackmore, S. and Troscianko, T. (1985) Belief in the paranormal: probability judgements, illusory control, and the 'chance baseline shift'. *British Journal of Psychology* **81**, 455–68.

Blackmore, S.J. and Troscianko, T. (1988) The physiology of the tunnel. *Journal of Near-Death Studies* **8**, 15–28.

Blanchard, E.B., Appelbaum, K.A., Raduiz, C.L. *et al.* (1990) Placebo-controlled evaluation of abbreviated progressive muscle relaxation and of relaxation combined with cognitive therapy in the treatment of tension headache. *Journal of Consulting and Clinical Psychology* **58**, 210–15.

Blasdell, K.S. (1978) The effects of transcendental meditation techniques upon a complex perceptual–motor task. In Orme-Johnson, D. and Farrow, J.T. (eds), *Scientific research on the transcendental meditation program: collected papers*. Livingston Manor, NY: Maharishi European Research University Press, 322–5.

Bloecher, T., Clamar, A. and Hopkins, B. (1985) *Summary report on the psychological testing of nine individuals reporting UFO abduction experiences.* Mount Rainier, MD: Fund for UFO Research.

Bottoms, B.L. and Davis, S.L. (1997) The creation of satanic ritual abuse. *Journal of Social and Clinical Psychology* **16**, 112–32.

Bower, G.H., Gillingham, S.G. and Monteiro, K.P. (1981) Selectivity of learning caused by affective states. *Journal of Experimental Psychology: General* **110**, 451–73.

Boyd, S., Rivera-Gaxiola, R., Towell, A., Harkness, W. and Neville, B. (1996) Discrimination of speech sounds in a boy with Landau–Kleffner syndrome: an intra-operative event-related potential study. *Neuropediatrics*, **27**, 1–5.

Boyle, M. (1990) *Schizophrenia: a scientific delusion.* London: Routledge.

Braud, W.G. (1975). Psi-conducive states. *Journal of Communication* **25**, 142–52.

Breuer, J. and Freud, S. (1955, first published 1893) Studies in hysteria. In Strachey, E.J. (ed.), *Standard edition of the complete psychological works of Sigmund Freud.* Vol. 11. London: Hogarth.

Broadbent, D.E. (1958) *Perception and communication.* Oxford: Pergamon.

Brookesmith, P. (1996). *UFO: the government files.* London: Blandford.

Brown, W.A. (1998a) Harnessing the placebo effect. *Hospital Practice* **33**, 107–16.

Brown, W.A. (1998b) The placebo effect. *Scientific American*, **278**, 68–73.

Brugger, P., Landis, T. and Regard, M. (1990) A 'sheep–goat effect' in repetition avoidance: extrasensory perception as an effect of subjective probability? *British Journal of Psychology* **76**, 459–68.

Buckman, R. and Sabbagh, K. (1993) *Magic or medicine? An investigation into healing.* London: Macmillan.

Bullard, T.E. (1989) Hypnosis and UFO abductions: a troubled relationship. *Journal of UFO Studies*, **1**, 3–40.

Bullard, T.E. (1994) The influence of investigators on UFO abduction reports: results of a survey. In Pritchard, A. Pritchard, D.E. Mack, J.E. Kasey, P. and Yapp, C. (eds) *Alien discussions. Proceedings of the Abduction Study Conference.* Cambridge, MA: North Cambridge Press, 571–619.

Burger, E. (1986) *Spirit theatre.* New York: Kaufman and Greenberg.

Cardeña, E., Lynn, S.J. and Krippner, S. (eds) (2000) *Varieties of anomalous experience.* Washington, DC: American Psychological Association.

Carlson, S. (1985) A double-blind test of astrology. *Nature* **318**, 419–25.

Carpenter, J.C. (1965) An exploratory test of ESP in relation to anxiety proneness. In Rhine, J.B. and associates (eds), *Parapsychology from Duke to FRNM.* Durham, NC: Parapsychology Press, 85–120.

Carrington, P. (1998) *The book of meditation: the complete guide to modern meditation*, 2nd Edn. Shaftesbury: Element.

Cartwright, R. (1977) *Night life: explorations in dreaming*. Englewood Cliffs, NJ: Prentice-Hall.

Cavallero, C. and Foulkes, D. (eds) *Dreaming as cognition*. London: Harvester Wheatsheaf.

Chalmers, A.F. (1999) *What is this thing called science?* 3rd edn. Buckingham: Open University Press.

Cheyne, J. A., Rueffer, S. D. and Newby-Clark, I. R. (1999) Hypnagogic and hypnopompic hallucinations during sleep paralysis: neurological and cultural construction of the night-mare. *Consciousness and Cognition* **8**, 319–37.

Child, I.L. (1985) Psychology and anomalous observations: the question of ESP in dreams. *American Psychologist* **40**, 1219–30.

Cobb, L.A., Thomas, G.I., Dillard, D.H., Merendino, K.A. and Bruce, R.A. (1959) An evaluation of internal mammary artery ligation by a double-blind technic. *New England Journal of Medicine* **260**, 1115–18.

Cobcroft, M.D. and Forsdick, C. (1993) Awareness under anaesthesia: the patient's point of view. *Anaesthesia and Intensive Care* **21**, 837–43.

Collins, A.M. and Quillian, M.R. (1969) Retrieval time from semantic memory. *Journal of Verbal Learning and Verbal Behaviour* **8**, 240–48.

Craik, F.I.M. and Lockhart, R.S. (1972) Levels of processing: a framework for memory research. *Journal of Verbal Learning and Verbal Behaviour* **11**, 671–84.

Crick, F. and Mitchison, G. (1983) The function of dream sleep. *Nature* **30**, 111–14.

Crick, F. and Mitchison, G. (1986) REM sleep and neural nets. *Journal of Mind and Behaviour* **5**, 81–98.

Crick, F. and Koch, C. (1990) Toward a neurobiological theory of consciousness. *Seminars in the Neurosciences* **2**, 263–75.

Dahlitz, M. and Parkes, J.D. (1993) Sleep paralysis. *Lancet*, **341**, 406–7.

Dahlstrom, W.G., Hopkins, D., Dahlstrom, L., Jackson, E. and Cumella, E. (1996) MMPI findings on astrological and other folklore concepts of personality. *Psychological Reports*, **78**, 1059–70.

Dalton, K. (1997) Exploring the links: creativity and psi in the ganzfeld. In *The Parapsychological Association 40th Annual Convention: Proceedings of Presented Papers* Durham, NC: Parapsychological Association, 119–34.

Davidson, R.J. and Sutton, S. (1995) Affective neuroscience: the emergence of a discipline. *Current Opinion in Neurobiology* **5**, 217–24.

Dawkins, R. (1998) *Unweaving the rainbow*. London: Allen Lane.

Dean, G. (1986) Does astrology need to be true? *Skeptical Enquirer* **11**, 257–73.

de Gelder, B., Vroomen, J., Pourtois, G. and Weiskrantz, L. (1999) Non-conscious recognition of affect in the absence of the striate cortex. *Neuroreport* **10**, 3759–63.

Delanoy, D.L. (1987) Work with a fraudulent PK metal-bending subject. *Journal of the Society for Psychical Research* **54**, 247–56.

Dement, W.C. and Kleitman, N. (1957) The relation of eye movements during sleep to dream activity: an objective method for the study of dreaming. *Journal of Experimental Psychology*, **53**, 339–46.

Dennett, D.C. (1995a) *Consciousness explained*. Harmondsworth: Penguin.

Dennett, D.C. (1995b) *Darwin's dangerous idea: evolution and the meanings of life*. Harmondsworth: Penguin.

Devereux, P. (1989) *Earth lights revelation*. London: Blandford.

Devereux, P. and Brookesmith, P. (1997) *UFOs and Ufology: the first 50 years*. London: Blandford.

Diaconis, P. (1985) Statistical problems in ESP research. In Kurtz, P. (ed.), *A skeptics handbook of parapsychology*. Buffalo, NY: Prometheus Books, 569–84.

Dimond, E.G., Kittle, F. and Crockett, J. E. (1960) Comparison of internal mammary artery ligation and sham operation for angina pectoris. *American Journal of Cardiology* **4**, 483–6.

Dingwall, E. (1921) Magic and mediumship. *Psychic Science Quarterly* **1**, 206–19.

Dixon, N.F. (1981) *Preconscious processing*. Chichester: John Wiley & Sons.

DuBreuil, S.C., Garry, M. and Loftus, E.F. (1998) Tales from the crib: age regression and the creation of unlikely memories. In Lynn, S.J. and McConkey, K.M. (eds), *Truth in memory*. New York: Guilford Press, 137–60.

Edge, H. and Schmeidler, G.R. (1999) Should ganzfeld research continue to be crucial in the search for a replicable psi effect? Part II. Edited ganzfeld debate. *Journal of Parapsychology* **63**, 335–88.

Ekman, P. (1985) *Telling lies: clues to deceit in the marketplace, politics and marriage*. New York: W.W. Norton and Co.

Ellrich, J. and Hopf, H.C. (1996) The R3 component of the blink reflex: normative data and application in spinal lesions. *Electroencephalography and Clinical Neurophysiology* **101**, 349–54.

Empson, J. (1989). *Sleep and dreaming*. London: Faber and Faber Ltd.

Epstein, M. (1995) *Thoughts without a thinker: psychotherapy from a Buddhist perspective*. New York: Basic Books.

Ernst, E. and Resch, K.L. (1995) Concept of true and perceived placebo effects. *British Medical Journal* **311**, 551–3.

Ernst, E. and Abbot, N.C. (1999) I shall please: the mysterious power of placebos. In Della Sala, S. (ed.), *Mind myths: exploring popular assumptions about the mind and brain*. Chichester: John Wiley & Sons, 209–13.

Evans, H. (1998) *From other worlds: the truth behind aliens, abductions, UFOs and the paranormal*. London: Carlton.

Everett, H.C. (1963) Sleep paralysis in medical students. *Journal of Nervous and Mental Disease* **135**, 283–7.

Eysenck, H.J. and Nias, D.K. (1982) *Astrology. Science or superstition?* London: Maurice Temple Smith.

Faubert, J., Diaconu, V., Ptito, M. and Ptito, A. (1999) Residual vision in the blind field of hemidecorticated humans predicted by a diffusion scatter model and selective spectral absorption of the human eye. *Vision Research* **39**, 148–57.

Fenwick, P.C. (1974) Metabolic and EEG changes during transcendental meditation. Paper presented at conference on *Transcendental Meditation: Research and Application*, Institute of Science and Technology, University of Wales, Cardiff.

Fenwick, P. (1997) Is the near-death experience only N-methyl-D-aspartate blocking? *Journal of Near-Death Studies* **16**, 43–53.

Fenwick, P. and Fenwick, E. (1996) *The truth in the light: an investigation of over 300 near-death experiences*. London: Headline Books.

Feyerabend, P. (1975) *Against method: outline of an anarchistic theory of knowledge*. London: New Left Books.

Fitzkee, D. (1945) *Magic by misdirection*. Oakland, CA: Magic Limited.

Foulkes, D. (1960) Dream reports from different stages of sleep. *Journal of Abnormal and Social Psychology* **65**, 14–25.

Foulkes, D. (1978) *A grammar of dreams*. New York: Basic Books.

Foulkes, D. (1979) Home and laboratory dreams: four empirical studies and a conceptual re-evaluation. *Sleep* **2**, 233–51.

Foulkes, D. (1982a) A cognitive–psychological model of REM dream production. *Sleep* **5**, 169–87.

Foulkes, D. (1982b) *Children's dreams: longitudinal studies*. New York: John Wiley & Sons.

Foulkes, D. (1985) *Dreaming: a cognitive–psychological analysis*. Hillsdale, NJ: Lawrence Erlbaum Associates.

Foulkes, D. (1993) Data constraints on theorising about dream function. In Moffitt, A., Kramer, M. and Hoffmann, R. (eds), *The functions of dreaming*. New York: State University of New York Press, 11–20.

Foulkes, D. (1999) *Children's dreaming and the development of consciousness*. Cambridge, MA: Harvard University Press.

Frazier, K., Karr, B. and Nickell, J. (eds) (1997) *The UFO invasion: the Roswell incident, alien abductions, and government coverups*. Amherst, NY: Prometheus.

French, C.C. (1996) Psychic healing. In Stein, G. (ed.), *The encyclopedia of the paranormal*. Amherst, NY: Prometheus Books, 597–604.

French, C.C., Fowler, M., McCarthy, K. and Peers, D. (1991) A test of the Barnum effect. *Skeptical Enquirer*, **15**, 66–72.

Freud (first published 1900) (1976) *The interpretation of dreams*. Harmondsworth: Penguin.

Freud, S. (1901) *The psychopathology of everyday life*. London: Hogarth.

Frew, D.R. (1974) Transcendental meditation and productivity. *Academy of Management Journal* **17**, 362–8.

Fuller, U. (1975) *Confessions of a psychic*. Teaneck, NJ: Karl Fulves.

Fuller, U. (1980) *Further confessions of a psychic*. Teaneck, NJ: Karl Fulves.

Galloway, A. (1969) *The Ramsay legend*. Birmingham: Goodliffe Publications.

Gallup, G. and Proctor, W. (1982) *Adventures in immortality: a look beyond the threshold of death*. New York: McGraw-Hill.

Gallup, G.H. and Newport, F. (1991) Belief in paranormal phenomena among adult Americans. *Skeptical Enquirer* **15**, 137–46.

Garde, M.M. and Cowey, A. (2000) 'Deaf hearing': unacknowledged detection of auditory stimuli in a patient with cerebral deafness. *Cortex* **36**, 71–80.

Gauquelin, M. (1955). *L'Influence des astres*. Paris: Editions du Dauphin.

Glover, J. (1999) *Humanity: a moral history of the twentieth century*. London: Jonathan Cape.

Goffman, E. (1974) Frame analysis. Boston, MA: Northeastern University Press.

Gomes, G. (1998) The timing of conscious experience: a critical review and reinterpretation of Libet's research. *Consciousness and Cognition* **7**, 559–95.

Graham, F. K. and Murray, R. (1977) Discordant effects of weak prestimulation on magnitude and latency of the reflex blink. *Physiological Psychology* **5**, 108–14.

Green, C. (1968) *Lucid dreams*. Oxford: Institute of Psychophysical Research.

Green, E.E., Green, A.M. and Walters, E.D. (1970) Voluntary control of internal states. *Journal of Transpersonal Psychology* **2**, 1–25.

Gregory, R.L. (1977) *Eye and brain* 3rd edn. London: Weidenfeld and Nicholson.

Greyson, B. (1983) The near-death experience scale: construction, reliability and validity. *Journal of Nervous and Mental Disease*, **171**, 369–75.

Greyson, B. (1985) A typology of near-death experiences. *American Journal of Psychiatry* **142**, 967–9.

Greyson, B. (1998) The incidence of near-death experiences. *Medicine and Psychiatry* **1**, 92–9.

Greyson, B. (2000) Near-death experiences. In Cardeña, E., Lynn, S.J. and Krippner, S. (eds), *Varieties of anomalous experience: examining the scientific evidence*. Washington, DC: American Psychological Association, 315–52.

Greyson, B. and Stevenson, I. (1980) The phenomenology of near-death experiences. *American Journal of Psychiatry* **137**, 1193–6.

Griffin, J. (1997) *The origin of dreams*. Trowbridge: Redwood Books.

Grof, S. and Halifax, J. (1977) *The human encounter with death*. New York: Dutton.

Grosso, M. (1981) Toward an explanation of near-death phenomena. *Anabiosis: The Journal of Near-Death Studies* **1**, 3–26.

Hahn, R.A. (1997a) The nocebo phenomenon: concept, evidence, and implications for public health. *Preventive Medicine* **26**, 607–11.

Hahn, R.A. (1997b) The nocebo phenomenon: scope and foundations. In Harrington A. (ed.), *The placebo effect: an interdisciplinary exploration*. Cambridge, MA: Harvard University Press, 56–76.

Hansen, G.P. (1990) Deception by subjects in psi research. *Journal of the American Society for Psychical Research* **84**, 25–80.

Haraldsson, E. and Houtkooper, J. (1992) Effects of perceptual defensiveness, personality and belief on extrasensory perception tasks. *Personality and Individual Differences* **13**, 1085–96.

Harrington, A. (1997). Introduction. In Harrington, A. (ed.), *The placebo effect: an interdisciplinary exploration*. Cambridge, MA: Harvard University Press, 1–11.

Harris, B. (1985) *Gellerism revealed*. Calgary: Micky Hades International.

Harris, M. (1986) *Investigating the unexplained*. Buffalo, NY: Prometheus.

Harvey, C. (1984) The stars look down. Meanwhile astrology is looking up. *Guardian* **23 March**, 11.

Harvey, C. and Harvey, S. (1999) *Principles of astrology*. London: Thorson.

Heim, A. v. St. G. (1892) Notizen über den Tod durch absturz. *Schweitzer Alpenclub* **27**, 327–37.

Hewstone, M., Benn, W. and Wilson, A. (1988) Bias in the base rates: racial prejudice in decision-making. *Cognition* **18**, 161–76.

Ho, K.H., Hashish, I., Salmon, P., Freeman, R. and Harvey, W. (1988) Reduction of post-operative swelling by a placebo effect. *Journal of Psychosomatic Research* **32**, 197–205.

Hobson, A. (1988) *The dreaming brain*. New York: Basic Books.

Hobson, A. and McCarely, R. (1977) The brain as a dream state generator: an activation-synthesis hypothesis of the dream process. *American Journal of Psychiatry* **134**, 97–112.

Holden, K. and French, C.C. (2000) *The measurement of paranormal belief. Discussion document*. London: Goldsmiths College, University of London.

Holk, F.H. (1978) Life revisited. *Omega* **9**, 1–11.

Holmes, G. (1918) Disturbances of visual orientation. *British Journal of Opthalmology* **2**, 449–68.

Honorton, C. and Krippner, S. (1969) Hypnosis and ESP: a review of the experimental literature. *Journal of the American Society for Psychical Research* **63**, 214–52.

Honorton, C. and Harper, S. (1974) Psi-mediated imagery and ideation in an experimental procedure for regulating perceptual input. *Journal of the American Society for Psychical Research* **68**, 156–68.

Hopkins, B. (1987) *Intruders: the incredible visitations at Copley Woods*. New York: Random House.

Hopkins, B., Jacobs, D.M. and Westrum, R. (1992) *Unusual personal experiences: an analysis of the data from three national surveys conducted by the Roper Organisation.* Las Vegas, CA: Bigelow Holding Corporation.

Houran, J. and Lange, R. (1998) Modelling precognitive dreams as meaningful coincidences. *Psychological Reports* **83**, 1411–14.

Hufford, D.J. (1982) *The terror that comes in the night.* Philadelphia, PA: University of Pennsylvania Press.

Hunt, H.T. (1989) *The multiplicity of dreams: memory, imagination and consciousness.* New Haven, CT: Yale University Press.

Huntley, J. (2000) *Astrology. An introductory guide to the influence of the stars on your life.* Shaftsbury: Element.

Hyman, R. and Honorton, C. (1986). A joint communiqué: the psi ganzfeld controversy. *Journal of Parapsychology,* **50**, 351–64.

Irwin, H.J. (1986) Perceptual perspective of visual imagery in OBEs, dreams and reminiscence. *Journal of the Society for Psychical Research* **53**, 210–17.

Irwin, H.J. (1991) A study of paranormal belief, psychological adjustment, and fantasy-proneness. *Journal of the American Society for Psychical Research* **85**, 317–31.

Irwin, H.J. (1993) Belief in the paranormal: a review of the empirical literature. *Journal of the American Society for Psychical Research* **87**, 1–39.

Irwin, H.J. (1999) *An introduction to parapsychology.* Jefferson, NC: McFarland.

Jackson, M. and Fiebert, M.S. (1980) Introversion-extraversion and astrology. *Journal of Psychology* **105**, 155–6.

Jacobs, D.M. (1992) *Secret life: first-hand accounts of UFO abductions.* New York: Simon and Schuster.

Jacobs, D.M. (1998) *The threat – the secret agenda: what the aliens really want ... and how they plan to get it.* New York: Simon and Schuster.

Jansen, K.L.R. (1997) The ketamine model of the near-death experience: a central role for the N-methyl-D-aspartate receptor. *Journal of Near-Death Studies* **16**, 5–26.

Jones, W.H. and Russell, D. (1980) The selective processing of belief-disconfirming information. *European Journal of Social Psychology* **10**, 309–12.

Joseph, S. and Masterson, J. (1999) Post-traumatic stress disorder and traumatic brain injury: are they mutually exclusive? *Journal of Traumatic Stress* **12**, 437–53.

Judson, I.R. and Wiltshaw, E. (1983) A near-death experience. *Lancet* **8349**, 561–2.

Jung, C. G. (1959) *Flying saucers: a modern myth of things seen in the skies.* New York: Harcourt Brace.

Kahnemann, D., Slovic, P. and Tversky, A. (eds) (1982) *Judgement under uncertainty: heuristics and biases.* Cambridge: Cambridge University Press.

Kaminer, W. (1999) *Sleeping with extra-terrestrials: the rise of irrationalism and perils of piety.* New York: Pantheon Books.

Kane, N., Curry, S., Butler, S. and Cummins, B. (1993) Electrophysiological indicator of awakening from coma. *Lancet* **341**, 688.

Kellehear, A., Heaven, P. and Gao, J. (1990) Community attitudes towards near-death experiences: a Chinese study. *Journal of Near-Death Studies* **13**, 109–13.

Kelly, G.W. (1955) *The psychology of personal constructs.* New York: W.W. Norton.

Kelly, I.W. (1998) Why astrology doesn't work. *Psychological Reports* **82**, 527–46.

Keri, S., Kelemen, O., Szekeres, G. *et al.* (2000) Schizophrenics know more than they can tell: probabilistic classification learning in schizophrenia. *Psychological Medicine* **30**, 149–55.

Kienle, G.S. and Kiene, H. (1996) Placebo effect and placebo concept: a critical methodological and conceptual analysis of reports on the magnitude of the placebo effect. *Alternative Therapies in Health and Medicine* **2**, 39–54.

Kirsch, I. (1997) Specifying nonspecifics: psychological mechanisms of placebo effects. In Harrington, A. (ed.), *The placebo effect: an interdisciplinary exploration*. Cambridge, MA: Harvard University Press, 166–86.

Klar, Y. and Giladi, E. (1997) No one in my group can be below the group's average: a robust positivity bias in favour of anonymous peers. *Journal of Personality and Social Psychology*, **73**, 885–901.

Klass, P.J. (1983) *UFOs: the public deceived*. Buffalo, NY: Prometheus.

Klass, P.J. (1989) *UFO abductions: a dangerous game*. Buffalo, NY: Prometheus.

Klass, P.J. (1997a) Additional comments about the 'Unusual Personal Experiences Survey'. In Frazier, K., Karr, B. and Nickell, J. (eds), *The UFO invasion: the Roswell incident, alien abductions, and government coverups*. Amherst, NY: Prometheus, 207–9.

Klass, P.J. (1997b) *The real Roswell crashed-saucer cover-up*. Amherst, NY: Prometheus.

Klatzky, R.L. (1980) *Human memory: structures and processes*, 2nd edn. San Francisco, CA: Freeman.

Kletti, R. and Noyes, R. (1981) Mental states in mortal danger. *Essence* **5**, 5–20.

Korff, K.K. (1997) *The Roswell UFO crash: what they don't want you to know*. Amherst, NY: Prometheus.

Kuhn, T. (1962) *The structure of scientific revolutions*. Chicago: University of Chicago Press.

LaBerge, S. and Gackenbach, J. (2000) Lucid dreaming. In Cardeña, E., Lynn, S.J. and Krippner, S. (eds), *Varieties of anomalous experience*. Washington, DC: American Psychological Association, 151–82.

La Fontaine, J.S. (1998). *Speak of the devil: tales of satanic abuse in contemporary England*. Cambridge: Cambridge University Press.

Laing, R.D. and Cooper, D.G. (1964) *Reason and violence*. London: Tavistock.

Laing, R.D. (1967) *The politics of experience and the bird of paradise*. Harmondsworth: Penguin.

Lama Surya Das (1997) *Eight steps to enlightenment: awakening the Buddha within. Tibetan wisdom for the Western world*. New York: Bantam Books.

Lamont, P. and Wiseman, R. (1999) *Magic in theory: an introduction to the theoretical and psychological elements in conjuring*. Hatfield: University of Hertfordshire Press.

Lang, P.J., Bradley, M.M. and Cuthbert, B.N. (1990) Emotion, attention and the startle reflex. *Psychological Review* **97**, 377–95.

Lavey, R.S. and Taylor, C.B. (1985) The nature of relaxation therapy. In Burchfield, S.R. (ed.), *Stress: psychological and physiological interactions*. Washington, DC: Hemisphere.

Lawrence, T., Edwards, C., Barraclough, N., Church, S. and Hetherington, F. (1995) Modelling childhood causes of paranormal belief and experience: childhood trauma and childhood fantasy. *Personality and Individual Differences* **19**, 209–15.

Lawson, A.H. (1984) Perinatal imagery in UFO abduction reports. *Journal of Psychohistory* **12**, 211–39.

Lee, I. and Tyrer, P. (1980) Responses of chronic agoraphobics to subliminal and supraliminal phobic motion pictures. *Journal of Nervous and Mental Disease* **168**, 34–40.

Levine, J.D., Gordon, N.C. and Fields, H.L. (1978) The mechanisms of placebo analgesia. *Lancet* **2**, 654–7.

Levinson, B.W. (1965) States of awareness during general anaesthesia. *British Journal of Anaesthesia* **37**, 544.

Levitan, L. and LaBerge, S. (1993) Day life, night life: how waking and dreaming experiences relate. *NightLight* **5**, 4–6.

Liasis, A., Towell, A. and Boyd, S. (1999) Intracranial auditory detection and discrimination potentials as substrates of echoic memory in children. *Cognitive Brain Research* **7**, 503–6.

Liasis, A., Towell, A. and Boyd, S. (2000) Intracranial evidence for differential encoding of frequency and duration responses. *Ear and Hearing* **21**, 252–6.

Libet, B., Wright, E.W., Feinstein, B. and Pearl, D.K. (1979) Subjective referral of the timing for a conscious sensory experience. A functional role for the somatosensory specific projection system in man. *Brain* **102**, 193–224.

Lindsay, D.S. and Read, J.D. (1995) 'Memory work' and recovered memories of childhood sexual abuse: scientific evidence and public, professional and personal issues. *Psychology, Public Policy and the Law* **1**, 846–908.

Locke, T.P. and Shontz, F.C. (1983) Personality correlates of the near-death experience: a preliminary study. *Journal of the American Society for Psychical Research* **77**, 311–18.

Loftus, E.F. (1993) The reality of repressed memories. *American Psychologist* **48**, 518–37.

Loftus, E.F. and Ketcham, K. (1994) *The myth of repressed memory: false memories and allegations of sexual abuse*. New York: St Martin's Press.

Lynn, S.J. and Rhue, J.W. (1988) Fantasy-proneness: hypnosis, developmental antecedents, and psychopathology. *American Psychologist* **43**, 35–44.

Lynn, S.J. and McConkey, K.M. (eds) (1998) *Truth in memory*. New York: Guilford Press.

Lynn, S.J., Pintar, J. and Rhue, J.W. (1997) Fantasy-proneness, dissociation and narrative construction. In Powers, S.M. and Krippner, S. (eds), *Broken images, broken selves: dissociative narratives in clinical practice*. New York: Brunner, 274–302.

Lyons, G. and Macdonald, R. (1991) Awareness during caesarian section. *Anaesthesia*, **46**, 62–4.

Macaulay, D., Ryan, L. and Eich, E. (1993) Mood dependence in implicit and explicit memory. In Graf, P. and Masson, M.E.J. (eds), *Implicit memory: new directions in cognitive, developmental and neuropsychology*: Hillsdale, NJ: Lawrence Erlbaum Associates.

McGrath, M.J. and Cohen, D.B. (1978) REM sleep facilitation of adaptive waking behaviour: a review of the literature. *Psychological Bulletin* **85**, 24–57.

Macintyre, A. (1992) *M.E. Post viral fatigue syndrome: how to live with it*. London: Thorsons.

Mack, J.E. (1994). *Abduction: human encounters with aliens*. New York: Scribners.

Malcolm, N. (1959) *Dreaming*. Studies in Philosophical Psychology. London: Routledge and Kegan Paul.

Mamelak, A. and Hobson, A. (1989) Dream bizarreness as the cognitive correlate of altered neuronal behaviour in REM sleep. *Journal of Cognitive Neuroscience* **1**, 201–22.

Manktelow, K. (1999) *Reasoning and thinking*. Hove: Psychology Press, Taylor and Francis.

Matheson, T. (1998) *Alien abductions: creating a modern phenomenon*. Amherst, NY: Prometheus.

Matthews, R. and Blackmore, S. (1995). Why are coincidences so impressive? *Perceptual and Motor Skills* **80**, 1121–2.

Maupin, I.W. (1968) Meditations. In Otto, H.A. and Mann, J. (eds), *Ways of growth*. New York: Viking, 189–98.

May, E.C., Spottiswoode, S.J.P. and Faith, L. (2000) The correlation of the gradient of Shannon entropy and anomalous cognition: toward an AC sensory system. *Journal of Scientific Exploration* **14**, 53–72.

Mayo, J. White, O. and Eysenck, H.J. (1978) An empirical study of the relation between astrological factors and personality. *Journal of Social Psychology* **105**, 229–36.

Meijboom, A., Jansen, A., Kampman, M. and Schouten, E. (1999) An experimental test of the relationship between self-esteem and concern about body shape and weight in restrained eaters. *International Journal of Eating Disorders*. **25**, 327–34.

Mills, J. (1979) *Six years with God*. New York: A and W Publishers.

Mills, A. and Lynn, S.J. (2000) Past-life experiences. In Cardeña, E., Lynn, S.J. and Krippner, S. (eds), *Varieties of anomalous experience: examining the scientific evidence*. Washington, DC: American Psychological Association, 283–313.

Milton, J. (1999) Should ganzfeld research continue to be crucial in the search for a replicable psi effect? Part I. Discussion paper and introduction to an electronic-mail discussion. *Journal of Parapsychology* **63**, 309–33.

Milton, J. and Wiseman, R. (1997) *Guidelines for extrasensory perception research*. Hatfield: University of Hertfordshire Press.

Milton, J. and Wiseman, R. (1999) Does psi exist? Lack of replication of an anomalous process of information transfer. *Psychological Bulletin* **125**, 387–91.

Moffitt, A., Kramer, K. and Hoffmann, R. (eds) (1993) *The functions of dreaming*. New York: State University of New York Press.

Montgomery, G.H. and Kirsch, I. (1997) Classical conditioning and the placebo effect. *Pain* **72**, 107–13.

Moody, M. and Perry, P. (1988) *The light beyond*. New York: Bantam Books.

Moody, R.A. (1975) *Life after life*. New York: Bantam Books.

Moorcroft, W.H., (ed.) (1993) *Sleep, dreaming and sleep disorders*. Lanham, MD: University Press of America, Inc.

Morris, R.L. (1986) Minimizing subject fraud in parapsychology laboratories. *European Journal of Parapsychology* **6**, 137–49.

Morris, R.L., Cunningham, S., McAlpine, S. and Taylor, R. (1993) Toward replication and extension of ganzfeld results. In *The Parapsychological Association 36th Annual Convention: Proceedings of Presented Papers*. 177–91. Durham, NC: Parapsychological Association.

Morris, R.L., Dalton, K., Delanoy, D.L. and Watt, C. (1995) Comparison of the sender/no sender condition in the ganzfeld. In *The Parapsychological Association 38th Annual Convention: Proceedings of Presented Papers*. Durham, NC: Parapsychological Association, 244–59.

Morse, M. and Perry, P. (1990) *Closer to the light*. New York: Ivy Books.

Munte, S., Lullwitz, E., Leuwer, M., Mitzlaff, B., Munte, T.F., Hussein, S. and Piepenbrock, S.A. (2000) No implicit memory for stories played during isoflurane/alfentanil/nitrous oxide anesthesia: a reading speed measurement. *Anesthetics and Analgesia* **90**, 733–8.

Naatanen, R. (1995) The mismatch negativity: a powerful tool for cognitive neuro-science. *Ear and Hearing. Special issue: Mismatch Negativity as an Index of Central Auditory Function* **16**, 6–18.

Nash, C.B. (1986) Comparison of subliminal and extrasensory perception. *Journal of the Society for Psychical Research* **53**, 435–55.

Neidhardt, E. and Florin, I. (1999) Memory bias for panic-related material in patients with panic disorder. *Psychopathology* **32**, 260–66.

Newman, L.S. (1997) Intergalactic hostages: people who report abduction by UFOs. *Journal of Social and Clinical Psychology* **16**, 151–77.

Newman, L.S. and Baumeister, R.F. (1996a) Toward an explanation of the UFO abduction phenomenon: hypnotic elaboration, extraterrestrial sadomasochism, and spurious memories. *Psychological Inquiry* **7**, 99–126.

Newman, L.S. and Baumeister, R. F. (1996b) Not just another false memory: further thoughts on the UFO abduction phenomenon. *Psychological Inquiry* **7**, 185–7.

Newman, L.S. and Baumeister, R.F. (1998) Abducted by aliens: spurious memories of interplanetary masochism. In Lynn, S.J. and McConkey, K. M. (eds), *Truth in memory*. New York: Guilford Press, 284–303.

Nickell, J. (1995) *Entities: angels, spirits, demons, and other alien beings*. Amherst, NY: Prometheus.

Nickell, J. (1997) A study of fantasy-proneness in the thirteen cases of alleged encounters in John Mack's abduction. In Frazier, K., Karr, B. and Nickell J. (eds), *The UFO invasion: the Roswell incident, alien abductions, and government coverups*. Amherst, NJ: Prometheus, 207–9.

Norbu, N. (1996) *The self-perfected state*. New York: New Lion Publications.

Noyes, R. (1972) The experience of dying. *Psychiatry*, **35**, 174–84.

Noyes, R. and Kletti, R. (1976) Depersonalisation in the face of life-threatening danger: an interpretation. *Omega* **7**, 103–14.

Noyes, R. and Kletti, R. (1977) Depersonalisation in the face of life-threatening danger. *Comprehensive Psychiatry* **18**, 375–84.

Ofshe, R. and Watters, E. (1995) *Making monsters: false memories, psychotherapy and sexual hysteria*. London: Andre Deutsch.

Orme-Johnson, D. (1973) Autonomic stability and transcendental medication. *Psychosomatic Medicine* **35**, 341–9.

Orwell, G. (1977, first published 1949) *Nineteen Eighty-Four*. Harmondsworth: Penguin.

Osis, K. and Haraldson, E. (1977) *At the hour of death*. New York: Avon.

Owens, J.E., Cook, E.W. and Stevenson, I. (1990) Features of 'near-death experience' in relation to whether or not patients were near death. *Lancet* **336**, 1175–7.

Paley, J. (1997) Satanist abuse and alien abduction: a comparative analysis theorizing temporal lobe activity as a possible connection between anomalous memories. *British Journal of Social Work* **27**, 43–70.

Parnell, J. O. and Sprinkle, R. L. (1990) Personality characteristics of persons who claim UFO experiences. *Journal of UFO Studies* **2**, 45–58.

Pasricha, S. and Stevenson, I. (1986) Near-death experiences in India: a preliminary report. *Journal of Nervous and Mental Disease* **174**, 165–70.

Paulos, J.A. (1988) *Innumeracy*. Harmondsworth: Penguin.

Pendergrast, M. (1996) *Victims of memory: incest accusations and shattered lives*. London: HarperCollins.

Persinger, M.A. (1990) The tectonic strain theory as an explanation for UFO phenomena: a non-technical review of the research, 1970–1990. *Journal of UFO Studies* **2**, 105–37.

Persinger, M.A. and Valliant, P.M. (1985) Temporal lobe signs and reports of subjective paranormal experiences in a normal population. *Perceptual and Motor Skills* **60**, 903–9.

Persinger, M.A., Tiller, S.G. and Koren, S.A. (2000) Experimental simulation of a haunt experience and elicitation of paroxysmal electroencephalographic activity by transcerebral complex magnetic fields: induction of a synthetic 'ghost'? *Perceptual and Motor Skills* **90**, 659–74.

Pirot, M. (1970) The effects of transcendental meditation techniques upon auditory discrimination. In Orme-Johnson, D. and Farrow, J.T. (eds), *Scientific research on the transcendental meditation program: collected papers*. Livingston Manor, NY: Maharishi European Research University Press, 331–4.

Pletcher, G.K. (19987) Coincidence and explanation. In Flew, A. (ed.) *Readings in the philosophical problems of parapsychology*. New York: Prometheus Books, 128–37.

Popper, K. (1972) *Conjectures and refutations*. London: Routledge and Kegan Paul.

Powers, S.M. (1994) Dissociation in alleged extraterrestrial abductees. *Dissociation* **7**, 44–50.

Radin, D. (1996) *The conscious universe: the scientific truth of psychic phenomena*. New York: HarperEdge.

Randi, J. (1982) *Flim-Flam*. Buffalo, NY: Prometheus Books.

Randi, J. (1986) The Project Alpha experiment. Part 1. The first two years. In Frazier, K. (ed.), *Science confronts the paranormal*. Buffalo, NY: Prometheus Books, 158–65.

Randle, K.D., Estes, R. and Cone, W.P. (1999) *The abduction enigma: the truth behind the mass alien abductions of the late twentieth century*. New York: Forge.

Rechtschaffen, A. and Kales, A. (1971) *A manual of standardised terminology, techniques and scoring system for sleep stages of human subjects*. Bethesda, MD: US Department of Health Education and Welfare.

Rhine, L.E. (1969) Case study review. *Journal of Parapsychology* **33**, 228–66.

Ring, K. (1980) *Life after death: a scientific investigation of the near-death experience*. New York: Coward, McCann and Geoghegan.

Ring, K. (1984) *Heading toward omega: in search of the meaning of the near-death experience*. New York: Quill.

Ring, K. and Rosing, C.J. (1990a) The Omega Project: a psychological survey of persons reporting abductions and other UFO encounters. *Journal of UFO Studies* **2**, 59–98.

Ring, K. and Rosing, C.J. (1990b) The Omega Project: an empirical study of the NDE-prone personality. *Journal of Near-Death Studies* **8**, 211–39.

Ring, K. and Lawrence, M. (1993) Further evidence for veridical perception during near-death experiences. *Journal of Near-Death Studies* **11**, 223–9.

Ring, K. and Cooper, S. (1997) Near-death and out-of-body experiences in the blind: a study of apparent eyeless vision. *Journal of Near-Death Studies* **16**, 101–47.

Ring, K. and Cooper, S. (1999) *Mindsight: near-death and out-of-body experiences in the blind*. Palo Alto, CA: William James Center/Institute of Transpersonal Psychology.

Robert-Houdin, J.E. (1878) *The secrets of conjuring and magic* (translated and edited with notes by Professor Hoffmann). London.

Roberts, A.H., Kewman, D.G., Mercier, L. and Hovell, M. (1993) The power of nonspecific effects in healing: implications for psychosocial and biological treatments. *Clinical Psychology Review* **13**, 375–91.

Roberts, G. and Owen, J. (1988) The near-death experience. *British Journal of Psychiatry* **153**, 607–17.

Roberts, R. (1981) Personal Constructs and Dreaming. *New Forum* **7**, 60–62.

Roberts, R. (1988) Recurring themes and images in a series of consecutive REM dreams. Perceptual and Motor Skills **67**, 767–77.

Rodeghier, M., Goodpaster, J. and Blatterbauer, S. (1991) Psychosocial characteristics of abductees: results from the CUFOS abduction project. *Journal of UFO Studies* **3**, 59–90.

Rodin, E.A. (1980) The reality of near-death experiences: a personal perspective. *Journal of Nervous and Mental Disease*, **168**, 259–63.

Roney-Dougal, S. (1986) Subliminal and psi perception: a review of the literature. *Journal of the Society for Psychical Research* **53**, 405–34.

Royce, D. (1985) The near-death experience: a survey of clergy's attitudes and knowledge. *Journal of Pastoral Care* **39**, 31–42.

Russell, B. (1950) *Unpopular essays*. London: Allen and Unwin.

Rycroft, C. (1981) *The innocence of dreams*. London: Oxford University Press.

Sabom, M. (1982) *Recollections of death: a medical investigation*. New York: Harper and Row.

Sabom, M. (1998) *Light and death*. Grand Rapids, MI: Zondervan Publishing House.

Sabom, M. and Kreutziger, S. (1982) Physicians evaluate the near-death experience. In Lundahl, C.R. (ed.), *A collection of near-death research readings*. Chicago: Nelson Hall, 148–59.

Sagan, C. (1979) *Broca's brain: reflections on the romance of science*. New York: Random House.

Sagan, C. (1997). *The demon-haunted world: science as a candle in the dark*. London: Headline Books.

Saklofske, D.H. Kelly, I.W. and McKerracher, D.W. (1981) *Astrology and personality. Yet another failure to replicate*. Unpublished manuscript, University of Saskatchewan, Saskatoon.

Schatzman, M., Worsley, A. and Fenwick, P. (1988) Correspondence during lucid dreams between dreamed and actual events. In Gackenbach, J. and Laberge, S. (eds), *Conscious mind, sleeping brain: perspectives on lucid dreaming*. London: Plenum Press, 155–79.

Schlitz, M.J. and Honorton, C. (1992) Ganzfeld psi performance within an artistically gifted population. *Journal of the American Society for Psychical Research* **86**, 83–98.

Schmeidler, G.R. (1988) *Psychology and parapsychology: matches and mismatches*. Jefferson, NC: McFarland.

Schnabel, J. (1994). *Dark white: aliens, abductions, and the UFO obsession*. London: Hamish Hamilton.

Schorer, C.E. (1985/86) Two native American near-death experiences. *Omega* **16**, 111–13.

Shapiro, A.K. and Shapiro, E. (1997a) *The powerful placebo: from ancient priest to modern physician*. Baltimore, MD: Johns Hopkins University Press.

Shapiro, A.K. and Shapiro, E. (1997b) The placebo: is it much ado about nothing? In Harrington, A. (ed.), *The placebo effect: an interdisciplinary exploration*. Cambridge, MA: Harvard University Press, 12–36.

Shaughnessy, M.F., Neely, R., Manz, A. and Nystul, M. (1990) Effects of birth order, sex, and astrological sign on personality. *Psychological Reports* **66**, 272–4.

Sheaffer, R. (1998) *UFO sightings: the evidence*. Amherst, NY: Prometheus.

Sherwood, S.J., Dalton, K., Steinkamp, F. and Watt, C. (2000) Dream clairvoyance study II using dynamic video-clips: investigation of consensus voting judging procedures and target emotionality. *Dreaming* **10**, in press.

Showalter, E. (1997) Hystories: hysterical epidemics and modern culture. New York: Columbia University Press.

Siegel, R.K. (1980) The psychology of life after death. *American Psychologist* **35**, 911–31.

Silverman, L.H., Frank, S. and Dachinger, P. (1974) A psychoanalytic interpretation of the effectiveness of systematic desensitisation: experimental data bearing on the role of merging fantasies. *Journal of Abnormal Psychology*, **83**, 313–18.

Silverman, L.H., Ross, D.L., Adler, J.N. and Lustig, D.A. (1978) Simple research paradigm for demonstrating subliminal dynamic activation: effects of Oedipal stimuli on dart-throwing accuracy in college males. *Journal of Abnormal Psychology* **87**, 341–57.

Silvers, R.B. (1997) *Hidden histories of science*. London: Granta.

Skrabanek, P. and McCormick, J. (1989) *Follies and fallacies in medicine*. Glasgow: The Tarragon Press.

Smith, C. and Lapp, L. (1986) Prolonged increases in both PS and number of REMs following a shuttle avoidance task. *Physiology and Behaviour* **36**, 1053–7.

Smith, C. and Kelly, G. (1988) Paradoxical sleep deprivation applied two days after the end of training retards learning. *Physiology and Behaviour* **43**, 213–16.

Smith, M.D. (1993) The effect of belief in the paranormal and prior set upon the observation of a 'psychic' demonstration. *European Journal of Parapsychology*, **9**, 24–34.

Smith,M. and Abrahamson, M. (1992) Patterns of selection in six countries. *The Psychologist* **5**, 205–7.

Smithers, A.G. (1984) The zodiac test. *Guardian* 19–23 March.

Smithers, A.G. and Cooper, H.J. (1984) Social class and season of birth. *Journal of Social Psychology* **124**, 79–84.

Snyder, C.R. and Schenkel, R.J. (1975) P.T. Barnum effect. *Psychology Today* **8**, 52–4.

Snyder, T.J. and Gackenbach, J. (1988) Individual differences associated with lucid dreaming. In Gackenbach, J. and LaBerge, S. (eds), *Conscious mind, sleeping brain: perspectives on lucid dreaming*. London: Plenum Press, 221–59.

Sokolov, E.N. (1963) *Perception and the conditioned reflex*. New York: Macmillan.

Spanos, N.P. (1996) *Multiple identities and false memories: a sociocognitive perspective*. Washington, DC: American Psychological Association.

Spanos, N.P., Cross, P.A., Dickson, K. and DuBreuil, S.C. (1993). Close encounters: an examination of UFO experiences. *Journal of Abnormal Psychology* **102**, 624–32.

Spanos, N.P., Burgess, C.A. and Burgess, M.F. (1994) Past-life identities, UFO abductions, and satanic ritual abuse: the social construction of memories. *International Journal of Clinical and Experimental Hypnosis* **42**, 433–46.

Spiegel, H. (1997). Nocebo: the power of suggestibility. *Preventive Medicine* **26**, 616–21.

Stansfeld, S. (1999) Social support and social cohesion. In Marmot, M. and Wilkinson, R.G. (eds), *Social determinants of health*. Oxford: Oxford University Press, 155–78.

Stires, L. (1997) 3.7 million Americans kidnapped by aliens? In Frazier, K., Karr, B. and Nickell, J. (eds), *The UFO invasion: the Roswell incident, alien abductions, and government coverups*. Amherst, NY: Prometheus, 203–6.

Stone-Carmen, J. (1994) A descriptive study of people reporting abduction by unidentified flying objects (UFOs). In Pritchard, A., Pritchard, D.E., Mack, J.E., Kasey, P. and Yapp, C. (eds), *Alien discussions: proceedings of the abduction study conference*. Cambridge, MA: North Cambridge Press, 309–15.

Strassman, R. (1997) Endogenous ketamine-like compounds and the NDE: if so, so what? *Journal of Near-Death Studies* **16**, 27–41.

Strieber, W. (1987) *Communion: a true story*. New York: Morrow.

Swerdlow, N.R., Caine, S.B., Braff, D.L. and Geyer, M.A. (1992) The neural substrates of sensorimotor gating of the startle reflex: a review of recent findings and their implications. *Journal of Psychopharmacology*. **6**, 176–90.

Tamariz, J. (1988) *The magic way*. Madrid: Magic Books.

Targ, E., Schlitz, M. and Irwin, H.J. (2000) Psi-related experiences. In Cardeña, E. Lynn, S.J. and Krippner, S. (eds), *Varieties of anomalous experience*. Washington, DC: American Psychological Association, 219–52.

ter Riet, G., de Craen, A.J.M., de Boer, A. and Kessels, A.J.H. (1998) Is placebo analgesia mediated by endogenous opioids? A systematic review. *Pain* **76**, 273–5.

Thalbourne, M.A. (1982) *A glossary of terms used in parapsychology*. London: Heinemann.

Thomas, K.B. (1987) General practice consultations: is there any point in being positive? *British Medical Journal* **294**, 1200–2.

Tobacyk, J.J. (1988) *A revised paranormal belief scale*. Unpublished manuscript, Louisiana Tech University, Ruston, LA.

Tobacyk, J.J. and Milford, G. (1983) Belief in paranormal phenomena: assessment instrument development and implications for personality functioning. *Journal of Personality and Social Psychology* **44**, 1029–37.

Treisman, A.M. (1988) Features and objects: the fourteenth Bartlett memorial lecture. *Quarterly Journal of Experimental Psychology* **40A**, 201–37.

Tunstall, M. E. (1980) On being aware by request. A mother's unplanned request during the course of a Caesarian section under general anaesthesia. *British Journal of Anaesthesia* **52**, 1049–51.

Tversky, A. and Kahneman, D. (1983) Extensional versus intuitive reasoning: the conjunction fallacy in probability judgement. *Psychological Review* **90**, 293–315.

Twelmlow, S. W. and Gabbard, G. O. (1984) The influence of demographic/psychological factors and pre-existing conditions on the near-death experience. *Omega* **15**, 223–35.

Ullman, M., Krippner, S. and Vaughan, A. (1973) *Dream telepathy*. New York: Macmillan.

Ullman, M., Krippner, S. and Vaughan, A. (1989) *Dream telepathy: experiments in nocturnal ESP*, 2nd edn. London: McFarland and Company.

Utts, J. (1991) Replication and meta-analysis in parapsychology. Statistical Science **6**, 363–403.

Van de Castle, R.L. (1977) Sleep and dreams. In Wolman, B.B. (ed.), *Handbook of parapsychology*. New York: Van Nostrand Reinhold, 473–99.

Van de Castle, R.L. (1989) ESP in dreams: comments on a replication 'failure' by the 'failing' subject. In Ullman, M., Krippner, S. and Vaughan, A. (eds), *Dream telepathy: experiments in nocturnal ESP*, 2nd edn. London: McFarland and Company, 209–16.

Van Hoof, J.C., de Beer, N.A., Brunia, C.H., Cluitmans, P.J. and Korsten, H.H. (1997) Event-related potential measures of information processing during general anaesthesia. *Electroencephalography and Clinical Neurophysiology* **103**, 268–81.

Van Rooj, J.J.F. (1999) Self-concept in terms of astrological sun-sign traits. *Psychological Reports* **84**, 541–6.

Vision, G. (1998) Blindsight and philosophy. *Philosophical Psychology* **11**, 137–59.

Von Grunebaum, G. and Callois, R. (eds) (1966) *The dream and human societies*. Berkeley, CA: University of California Press.

Voudouris, N.J., Peck, C.L. and Coleman, G. (1989) Conditioned response models of placebo phenomena. *Pain* **38**, 109–16.

Voudouris, N.J., Peck, C.L. and Coleman, G. (1990) The role of conditioning and verbal expectancy in the placebo response. *Pain* **43**, 121–8.

Wagner, M.W. and Monnet, M. (1979) Attitudes of college professors toward extra-sensory perception. *Zetetic Scholar* **5**, 7–16.

Walker, S. (1984) *Learning theory and behaviour modification*. London: Methuen.

Wall, P.D. (1999) The placebo and the placebo response. In Wall, P.D. and Melzack, R. (eds), *Textbook of pain*, 4th edn. New York: W.B. Saunders, 1419–30.

Wallace, R.K. (1970) Physiological effects of transcendental meditation. *Science* **167(926)**, 1751–4.

Wason, P.C. (1968) Reasoning about a rule. *Quarterly Journal of Experimental Psychology* **20**, 273–81.

Watt, C.A. and Morris, R.L. (1995) The relationships among performance on a prototype indicator of perceptual defence/vigilance, personality, and extrasensory perception. *Personality and Individual Differences* **19**, 635–48.

Weiskrantz, L. (1986) *Blindsight: a case study and implications*. Oxford: Oxford University Press.

Whinnery, J.E. (1990) Acceleration-induced loss of consciousness: a review of 500 episodes. *Archives of Neurology* **47**, 764–76.

Whinnery, J.E. (1997) Psychophysiologic correlates of unconsciousness and near-death experiences. *Journal of Near-Death Studies* **15**, 231–58.

Wilson, S.C. and Barber, T.X. (1983) The fantasy-prone personality: implications for understanding imagery, hypnosis, and parapsychological phenomena. In Sheikh, A.A. (ed.), *Imagery: current theory, research and application*. New York: John Wiley & Sons, 340–87.

Winget, C. and Kramer, M. (1979) *Dimensions of dreams*. Gainsville, FL: University of Florida.

Winson, J. (1985) *Brain psyche: the biology of the unconscious*. Gardener City, NJ: Anchor Press/Double Day.

Wiseman, R. and Morris, R.L. (1995a) *Guidelines for testing psychic claimants*. Buffalo, NY: Prometheus.

Wiseman, R. and Morris, R.L. (1995b) Recalling pseudo-psychic demonstrations. *British Journal of Psychology* **86**, 113–25.

Wiseman, R., Smith, M. and Wiseman, J. (1995) Eyewitness testimony and the para-normal. *Skeptical Inquirer* **19**, 29–32.

Woodroffe, J. (1972) *The serpent power*, 8th edn. Madras: Ganesh and Company.

Worsley, A. (1988) Personal experiences in lucid dreaming. In Gackenbach, J. and LaBerge, S. (eds), *Conscious mind, sleeping brain: perspectives on lucid dreaming*. London: Plenum Press, 321–41.

Wuthnow, R. (1976) Astrology and marginality. *Journal for the Scientific Study of Religion* **15**, 157–68.

Wynder, E.L. (1997) Introduction: the American Health Foundation's Nocebo Conference. *Preventive Medicine* **26**, 605–6.

Index